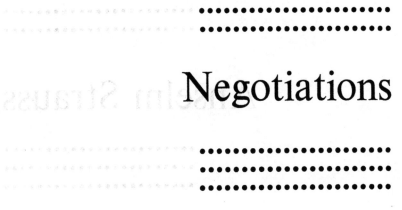

Negotiations

*Varieties, Contexts,
Processes, and
Social Order*

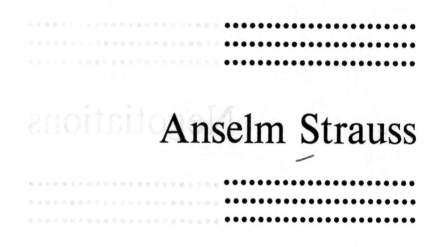

Anselm Strauss

Negotiations

Varieties, Contexts, Processes, and Social Order

Jossey-Bass Publishers
San Francisco • Washington • London • 1978

NEGOTIATIONS
Varieties, Contexts, Processes, and Social Order
        by Anselm Strauss

Copyright © 1978 by: Jossey-Bass, Inc., Publishers
                    433 California Street
                    San Francisco, California 94104
                                    &
                    Jossey-Bass Limited
                    28 Banner Street
                    London EC1Y 8QE

Library of Congress Catalogue Card Number LC 78-1156

International Standard Book Number ISBN 0-87589-369-4

Manufactured in the United States of America

JACKET DESIGN BY WILLI BAUM

FIRST EDITION

Code 7812

*The Jossey-Bass Social and
Behavioral Science Series*

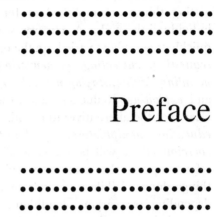

Preface

*T*his book is about negotiation in relation to social orders. A social order—even the most repressive—without some forms of negotiation would be inconceivable. Even dictators find it impossible and inexpedient simply and always to order, command, demand, threaten, manipulate, or use force; about some issues and activities they must persuade and negotiate. So we do not agree with Zartman that ours is "an age of Negotiation" simply because old rules and roles are breaking down and new ones are arising through negotiation (Zartman, 1976, p. 2). Rules and roles are always breaking down—and when they do not, they do not miraculously remain intact without some effort, including negotiation effort, to maintain them. What we can assent to is that when individuals or groups or organizations of any size work together "to get things done" then agreement is required about such matters as what, how, when, where, and how much. Continued agreement itself may be something to be worked at. Even enemies may have to negotiate, to work together to arrive at their quite discrepant ends. Putting the matter thus suggests that negotiations pertain to the ordering and articulation of an enormous variety of activities.

However, negotiation certainly is not the only means for getting things accomplished or for working toward collective or individualistic ends. A cursory scanning of the dictionary will quickly suggest how varied are the options: *stealing, cheating, lying, requesting, entreating, maneuvering, pressuring, threatening, demanding, killing, staying neutral, arguing by the rules, monitoring,* and *exploiting.* Reducing these to a few overarching rubrics, it is clear that the alternatives to negotiating include at least *persuading, educating, manipulating, appealing to the rules or to authority,* and *coercion* (these will be the generalized terms used in this book to refer to options that actors may review when considering how to get things done). While one mode or another may be given priority, depending on varying conditions, this mode may be preceded, succeeded, or supplemented by alternative modes or combined with them. Particular organizations will perhaps tend to give certain modes (such as education or persuasion) very high priority; other societies (for example, slave societies) may seem to rest primarily on coercion. Inevitably, however, when we scrutinize those societies or organizations we find mixes of negotiation, coercion, education, and other processes. If one is interested especially in negotiation, as I am, a basic question then concerns under what conditions it is given priority over other modes—and placed in conjunction with what other modes—and what consequences it has for various interested parties, whether they are persons, groups, organizations, or societies.

Viewing negotiation in those terms leads to a different approach from the prevalent ones. A conventional assumption is that negotiation is important only to certain kinds of activity or in certain kinds of areas, especially business arrangements, labor relations, and international relations. Most of the research about negotiation and negotiations has taken place in those substantive areas. That is altogether too narrow a focus, although lately the range of areas has been enlarged. Yet when negotiation is taken as a relatively universal phenomenon ("Negotiation is . . . one of the basic processes of decision making"—Zartman, 1976, p. 7), other assumptions are made that confine negotiation to rationalistic, efficiency-based perspectives. Thus a central question about negotiation will be "What caused a particular outcome?" (Zartman, 1976). In general, I believe that issues pertaining to how to negotiate are related to other modes of action and to varying kinds of social order. This means that larger structural considerations need to be linked *explicitly* with a more microscopic analysis of negotiation processes.

Moreover, if negotiations are indeed relatively universal, then social scientists ought to develop conceptualizations that deal with the whole range of the phenomena—or, less ambitiously, at least with a very great variety of negotiation situations and their structural contexts. In this book, I offer such a conceptualization. It falls far short of constituting a theory of negotiation; rather, it is presented in the form of a theoretical paradigm with applications to a variety of negotiations and in a form that other researchers can qualify, amend, add to, and work over in such a fashion that eventually we may actually have a theory of negotiation. In any event, the paradigm should be immediately useful to those who are interested in negotiations. It should also direct attention to the necessity for analyzing social orders in relationship to implicated negotiation processes. Indeed, one of the central arguments of this book is that social orders are always in some sense also negotiated orders—in what sense, this book attempts both to illustrate and to clarify.

Negotiations is therefore addressed not only to people who are directly concerned with negotiation itself but also to those who work with an eye on the larger issues of organizational and societal order. To those matters, my basic stance is what is today called "the negotiated order approach or perspective." In the opening chapter, some origins of that position are discussed and its implications sketched. In the concluding chapter, I return to the more basic issues involved in the current debate over this perspective.

Acknowledgments

A number of colleagues cast eyes on drafts of this book and, although their counsel was not always followed, gave the critical feedback that every author needs but does not always get. My thanks, first of all, to Berenice Fisher, School of Education, New York University, for her penetrating critiques, which forced me to face issues I would never have thought of confronting. I have also a special indebtedness to Elihu Gerson and Barney Glaser (affiliated, respectively, with Pragmatica Systems, San Francisco, and the Department of Social and Behavioral Sciences, University of California, San Francisco), each of whom has carried on continuous discussion with me about many of the issues raised in this book. My thanks also to Rue Bucher, Department of Sociology, University of Illinois, Chicago; Jean Claud Chamboredon, Centre de Sociologie Européenne, Ecole Pratique des Hautes Études, Paris; Fred Davis and Joseph Gusfield, Department of Sociology, University of California, San Diego; Norman Denzin, Department of Sociology, University of Illinois, Urbana; Orrin Klapp, Department of Sociology, University of Western Ontario, London, Ontario; Alexandre Métraux, Department of Psychology, University of Heidelberg; Leonard Schatzman, Department of Behavioral and Social Sciences, University of California, San Francisco; Charlotte Schwartz, Department of Psychiatry, Massachusetts Institute of Technology; Tomatsu Shibutani, Department of Sociology, University of California, Santa Barbara; and William E. Henry, Committee on Human Development, University of Chicago. The roots of this book, however, go back to collaborative work, from 1958–1963, at the Institute for Psychosomatic and Psychiatric Research, Michael Reese Hospital, Chicago—two of my collaborators (Bucher and Schatzman) have already been mentioned; the others were Danuta Ehrlich and Melvin Sabshin. And some years ago certain early ideas of mine about negotiation were given a stimulating reception by colleagues in an evening seminar at Cambridge University: Among these colleagues were Ray Abrahams, Michael Mulkay, Peter Sheldrake, and Cyril Sofer. Last, but certainly not the least, my thanks again to Elaine McLarin, who shepherded the book through its innumerable drafts.

San Francisco   ANSELM STRAUSS
January 1978

Contents

The Author

ANSELM STRAUSS is professor of sociology at the University of California, San Francisco, where he chairs the Department of Social and Behavioral Sciences and is also a faculty member of the Graduate Program in Sociology.

Strauss was born in New York City in 1916; he was awarded the B.A. degree in sociology from the University of Virginia (1939) and the M.A. and Ph.D. degrees in sociology from the University of Chicago (1942, 1945). His first teaching position was at Lawrence College (1944–1946), followed by positions at Indiana University (1946–1952) and the University of Chicago (1952–1958). He has been a guest professor at the University of Frankfort, Cambridge University, Manchester University, the University of Paris, and the University of Constance.

Among the books that he has authored or coauthored are *Social Psychology* (with A. Lindesmith and N. Denzin, first edition 1949, fourth edition 1975); *Mirrors and Masks* (1958, reprinted 1969); *Images of the American City* (1961, reprinted 1976); *Psychiatric Ideologies and Institutions* (with R. Bucher, L. Schatzman, D. Ehrlich, and M. Sabshin, 1964); *Awareness of Dying* (with B. Glaser, 1965); *The Discovery of Grounded Theory* (with B. Glaser, 1967); and *Time for Dying* (with B. Glaser, 1968). Another research monograph, *The Politics of Pain Management* (with S. Fagerhaugh) has recently been published (1977); Strauss is now engaged in a study that developed from research on the latter project, pertaining to the impact of medical machinery on hospital organization, staff work, and patient care. Two other current areas of interest are the phenomena known as "social worlds" and "intellectual traditions." The second interest is leading him, with B. Fisher, to examine and write about the Chicago sociological tradition.

Strauss lives with his wife, Frances, in downtown San Francisco. His chief hobby, besides traveling and visiting museums, is practicing the piano.

To Lindy, in remembrance of times past

Negotiations

*Varieties, Contexts,
Processes, and
Social Order*

Negotiate—*bargain,* contract, arrange
Bargain—negotiate, *contract*
Contract—*agreement,* bargain, arrangement
Agreement—accord, reconcilement, understanding, contract, *compact*
Compact—contract, settlement, bargain, negotiation, arrangement, *understanding*
Understanding—compact, agreement, *adjustment*
Adjustment—*reconcile,* settle, arrange
Reconcile—adjust, *settle*
Settle—reconcile, fix, stabilize (see *arrangement*)
Arrangement—settle, organize, *coordinate,* orderliness
Coordinate—adjust, *organize*
Organize—arrange, coordinate, *systematize*
Systematize—arrange, organize, coordinate
Order—arrangement, systematization

—*Roget's International Thesaurus*

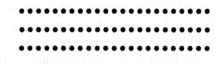

General Considerations: An Introduction

Negotiation goes by many names, is referred to by many synonyms: *bargaining, wheeling and dealing, compromising, making deals, reaching agreements after disagreement, making arrangements, getting tacit understandings, mediating, power brokering, trading off, exchanging,* and *engaging in collusion.* As those referents suggest, negotiations appear in many forms, appearing in every and all areas of life. They appear not only in industrial societies, where both clashing and cooperating groups find negotiation frequently necessary, but also in the most seemingly stable societies studied by the anthropologists. Negotiation certainly seems generic to human relationships and arrangements.

Two dictionary definitions of negotiation are: "to treat for, obtain, or arrange by bargain, conference, or agreement" and "to deal or bargain with another or others . . . to confer with another so as to arrive at the settlement of some matter." Those definitions give no clear guidance for making distinctions between negotiation and agreements arrived at without negotiation, nor between negotiation and other modes of attaining desired ends—such as persuasion,

1

education, appeal to authority, or the use of coercion or coercive threat. Those dictionary definitions do not necessarily yield a directive, either, for studying negotiations in relation to the social settings within which they occur: as we shall see, theorists of negotiation can quite easily ignore those settings or take them for granted, reducing negotiation to a kind of bargaining between persons (often studied under laboratory conditions). Also, the dictionary definitions are so general that they allow students of negotiation the dubious privilege of taking specific areas of negotiation, such as diplomatic bargaining, as adequately representing all types of negotiation. A working definition of negotiation surely would need to take into account all those distinctions or issues. In this book, negotiation generally will stand for one of the possible means of "getting things accomplished" when parties need to deal with each other to get those things done. The choice of negotiation as a means is neither fortuitous nor divorced from the social conditions under which it is made.

Currently, the topic of negotiation verges on becoming fashionable. It is "in the air." The technical literature is increasing rapidly, and students of negotiation, such as William Zartman (1976, p. 4), a political scientist, quote with approval such sociologists as Herbert Gans, who remarked that "traditional values now have to be negotiated, and in many ways America has become a negotiating society." That view of history is altogether too "gemeinschaft-to-gesellschaft"—negotiation, it suggests, is characteristic only or primarily of a nowadays continuously changing world—but we can agree that the following kinds of situations might lead scholars to an increased focus on negotiation: "the family as a negotiating situation, hostage and holdup bargaining, the drafting of a resolution in committee, patterns of market haggling . . . colonial independence negotiations, commodity agreements" (Zartman, 1976, p. 7), not to speak of long drawn-out disarmament negotiations, detente itself, and even what, with more microscopic vision, some social psychologists and sociologists are now referring to as "identity negotiations."

Perhaps the explanation for the interest in negotiation is less its increased presence than its increased visibility because of trends internal to social science itself. The past decade has seen much dissatisfaction on the part of some social scientists with rationalistic models for explaining human behavior. Conflict among and inside organizations has been increasingly noted and studied. Actors are increasingly regarded as active shapers of their own destinies, so that the stricter determinisms (economic, technological, social, biological) appear of dubious validity. Perhaps there is also a tendency to play down the role of force, despite the world's obvious violence, and to emphasize the counterbalancing role of agreement making. One cannot be sure those are the actual reasons for the focus on negotiation as a researchable and theoretical topic, but I offer as a suggestive case study, next, what currently is happening within the area of organizational studies.

For some years, the literature on organizations has included descriptions of bargaining and other types of negotiation interaction. However, researchers have not really analyzed the negotiations, and certainly they do not often make them central to their analysis. An instructive example can be seen in Warren, Rose, and Bergunder (1974). The authors present a study of what they term an "interorganizational field"—essentially, a structural context within which operate several community agencies. This field demonstrably affects the major actions and perceived options of those agencies with respect to each other, as well as of those agencies newly evolving in each of the cities studied by the authors. The analysis does not deal directly with negotiation, but negotiation processes lie at the heart of the phenomena studied. Thus the central concept of interorganizational field pertains to the fact that the community agencies "have reached more or less routinized and mutually agreed-upon notions of their respective *domains* . . . norms have developed which govern the range of acceptable behavior . . . in their interaction with each other and with other actors. . . . These norms in turn are supported by an underlying norm of 'live and let live' " (Warren, Rose, and Bergunder, 1974, p. 19). In short, a number of tacit agreements have previously been worked out (possibly quite explicitly talked about) that now affect the kinds of issues that can be fought over, negotiated explicitly, and that are related to coalition formation in the face of threats from new organizations that may challenge the existing implicit agreements. This innovative treatment of interorganizational relations by the researchers could have been given, I would hazard, even greater power by a negotiation analysis. However, the researchers neither draw on the literature of negotiation nor develop their own analysis of negotiations in relation to the structure of organizational relationships that they have discovered.

Meanwhile, in the writings about organizations, long dominated by rationalistic and functionalist perspectives, there are now beginning to appear occasional statements that suggest the possible relevance and even crucial importance of negotiation. The following two examples give some of the flavor of this contemporary commentary. Paul Goodman and Johannes Pennings (1977, pp. 168–169) suggest that "The establishment of constraints, goals, and referents in the focal organization follows from the bargaining process between the constituencies or their representatives in the dominant coalition. Constituencies are likely to bring different preferences to the bargaining process, and conflict is likely to occur. . . . Bargaining between constituencies has two main effects. First, it focuses attention on a specific set of constraints, outcomes, and referents. . . . The second effect . . . is that it requires the dominant coalition to assess alternative combinations of constraints, goals, and referents as they bear on the organization's ratio of inducements to contributions." That quote reflects the fact that some social scientists no longer regard organizations as relatively homogeneous or as free of conflicting views held by their members about the goals, policies, and means of an organization. Larry L. Cummings (Goodman, Pennings, and Associates, 1977, p. 61), taking that perspective, remarks about negotiation, "Increasingly, scholars from varying disciplines and orientations are depicting organizations as arenas within which actors play out their own agendas or as performances without script or program. That is, organizations are seen as being enacted in process. These perspectives imply that the criterion of effectiveness and its assessment are multidimensional, time-bound, and dynamic, subject to negotiation, and organizationally, or even unit, specific."

In the late 1950s, quite by accident, my coresearchers and I stumbled on that very notion of arena, of flexibly acted-out organizational scripts without firm rules, and on the crucial importance of negotiation to social order (see Strauss and others, 1963, 1964).

The problem forced itself on our attention, as we observed personnel and patients in two psychiatric hospitals, for everyone seemed to be negotiating about something. So central did this negotiation seem to the events being studied that when writing up the conclusions we made negotiation a key concept, along with several others, and coined the term *negotiated order*. Although sticking closely to assertions about psychiatric personnel and their hospitals, rather than writing about organizations in general, we did suggest that the usual structural and organizational approaches quite underplayed the important phenomenon called *negotiation*. The idea of negotiated order has achieved some currency since and has stimulated some attention to negotiation (see Maines, 1977), although later studies have focused mainly on substantive concerns or on attacking overly deterministic perspectives. Some studies, however, have rightly emphasized the political, power, and further structural aspects of negotiation. (I shall discuss this literature in the concluding section of this book.)

In the presentation of a decade ago, several main points were underlined. I will briefly review them because I wish to bring out what is especially needed in contemporary study of negotiations.

1. We stated that social order was negotiated order: In the organizations studied, apparently there could be no organizational relationships without accompanying negotiations.

2. Specific negotiations seemed contingent on specific structural conditions: who negotiated with whom, when, and about what. So the negotiations were patterned, not accidental. They could be studied in terms of their conditions, character, and consequences for persons and organizations.

3. The products of negotiation (contracts, understandings, agreements, "rules," and so forth) all had temporal limits, for eventually they would be reviewed, reevaluated, revised, revoked, or renewed.

4. Negotiated order had to be worked at, and the bases of concerted action needed to be continually reconstituted. Not only were negotiations continually terminated, but new ones were also made daily.

5. The negotiated order on any given day could be conceived

of as the sum total of the organization's rules and policies, along with whatever agreements, understandings, pacts, contracts, and other working arrangements currently obtained. These include agreements at every level of the organization, of every clique and coalition, and include covert as well as overt agreements.

6. Any changes impinging on the negotiated order—whether something ordinary, such as a new staff member, a disrupting event, or a betrayed contract, or whether more unusual, such as the introduction of a new technological element or a new ideology—called for renegotiation or reappraisal. This meant consequent changes in the negotiated order.

7. We went on to suggest that the reconstitution of social or organizational order (which was our central concern) might be fruitfully conceived of in terms of a complex relationship between the daily negotiation process and a periodic appraisal process. The form not only allowed the daily work to get done but also reacted on the more formalized and permanent organizational rules, policies, and established conventions and understandings. In turn, the latter served to set the limits and some directions of negotiation.

8. We suggested, finally, that future studies of the complex relationships that exist between the more stable elements of organizational order and the more fleeting working arrangements might profit by examining the former as if they were sometimes a background, against which the latter were being evolved in the foreground, and sometimes as if the reverse obtained. What was needed was both a concentrated focus on and the development of a terminology adequate to handle this kind of background-foreground metaphor. But, whether that metaphor or another, the central question was "How do negotiation and appraisal play into each other and into the rules, policies and other 'more stable' elements of social order?"

What was omitted by this treatment of negotiation I shall attempt here, in some part, to rectify. Thus, in the earlier book there was no mention of a very important phenomenon: *actors' theories of negotiation*. There was no detailing of negotiation *subprocesses*. Hence there was no explicit specifying of *conditions* and *consequences* associated with those subprocesses. There was talk about patterning of negotiation, but no working out of a paradigmatic analysis in terms of *structural contexts* and *negotiation contexts,* such as will be developed in Part Two of this book. There was virtually no reference to the *options* for alternatives to negotiation: coercion, persuasion, manipulation of contingencies, and so on. Issues relating to rules, norms, and the like were handled explicitly, but others, relating to *power, coalition, politics,* and the like, were touched on only implicitly. The duration of negotiations was dwelt on, but not such other *temporal features* as their timing or their sequencing. The linkage among multiple negotiations was only implicit in our previous discussion. So was the obvious phenomenon of interorganizational negotiations, since that was not then researched. However, there was clear recognition that most of the time people negotiated as *representatives* (including as representatives within an organization) of outside groupings such as professions or professional "segments" (Bucher and Strauss, 1961). Also, in the earlier study, there was no presentation of *negotiation dimensions,* that most important topic that constitutes the core of the paradigm presented and applied in Part Two of this volume.

In Part Two, I shall be interested in varieties of social order, which means *varieties of negotiations* rather than the *negotiation process;* for the latter term involves the assumption that, to paraphrase Gertrude Stein, a negotiation is a negotiation is a negotiation. Some students of those negotiation phenomena have committed that error. It is time now to turn to them and to others who have written about negotiations.

The Literature on Negotiation

As noted earlier, there are several traditional areas around which the literature tends to cluster, among them labor bargaining, diplomatic negotiations, arms control negotiation, "conflict resolution," and market bargaining. For such topics, there are many publications, in the form of narratives about particular negotiations, memoirs by the participants, and general discussion of negotiation types. There are relatively few theoretical analyses that pertain to such substantive negotiation areas. Examples of the analytic writing include Fred Ikle's work (1964) on negotiation and Thomas

Schelling's book (1960) on considerations to be taken into account in the arms race between powerful nations, as well as a number of publications in the well-worked field of bargaining between labor unions and employers (see Chamberlain, 1951). Recently, a number of economists and political scientists have extended these few restricted topical interests to a more general attack on salient features of negotiation as such (Zartman, 1976; Coddington, 1968, 1972; Cross, 1969; Young, 1976; Harsanyi, 1962). Their materials are still noticeably drawn from traditional areas of negotiation (see the bibliography in Zartman, 1976).

In a review of approaches to the study of negotiation, Zartman (1976, pp. 20–32) suggested a classification of "seven schools, each explaining outcomes in terms of a different variable and each with something to tell the observer and the practitioner, although it must be said that the line between any two schools is not always very sharp." The seven schools focus on particular interests:

1. *Pure historical description of particular negotiations.*
2. *Contextual study of the contents of negotiations.* Particular outcomes are seen as determined by a particular phaseological interpretation either of the history of the negotiation itself, or of the larger phase of history into which the negotiation fits.
3. *Structural.* Explanation of outcomes is found in the patterns of relationships between parties or their goals.
4. *Strategic.* Focus is on the element of choice, as determined by the structure of the values at stake and also by the other parties' pattern of selection.
5. *Developing personality types in order to explain negotiation outcomes.*
6. *Behavioral skills as explanations of the outcomes.*
7. *Process.* Negotiation is viewed as a challenge-and-response encounter in which the moves are the inputs and negotiating is a learning process. Parties use their bids both to respond to the previous counteroffer and to influence the next. The offers themselves become an exercise in power.

It is significant that Zartman believes those attempts to explain "the negotiation process" are inadequate. Equally significant is that, even when writing on particular types of negotiation, social scientists seem not especially to utilize much, if any, of this literature on negotiation (for example, see Roth, 1963; Martin, 1976; Scheff, 1968). One difficulty is that the literature on negotiation is primarily topical in focus: Even such stimulating writing as that by Ikle or Schelling—although general in scope—would seem of restricted use to people interested, for example, in organizations, social movements, families, or communes. Also, the more general negotiation analyses and analytic models handle only limited substantive phenomena and incorporate only a limited number of variables, and, again, those writings seem of no particular interest to, for example, sociologists interested in organizations or work, where negotiations do have some visibility to the researchers. (On the other hand, exchange theory, an approach that seems close to bargaining and that has enjoyed some popularity both among sociologists and political scientists, is so focused on particular theoretical concerns that it must, to judge by absence of reference to it there, be of little guidance to anyone engaged in studies of negotiation.)

There are additional, perhaps related, reasons why the more general literature on negotiations is not utilized very much by nonspecialists in negotiation. First, the theorists may offer a relatively structureless analysis that in fact presumes a type of social order: game theory, for instance, with its rationalistic assumptions (and its relatively impersonal "suppose that A wishes to" kind of terminology). Even when a clear-headed theorist such as Schelling, who is quite aware of social order premises, offers a model for negotiation analysis, it appears deficient when applied to situations unlike those he himself studied—and these are many and varied. Thus Baldwin (in Zartman, 1976, pp. 421–422), who has studied the phenomenon of bargaining with hijackers, has found Schelling's work not altogether useful because "there are some very significant differences between the usual assumptions of bargaining theory and the reality of hijacking situations. . . . In the first place, there are almost no outcomes or bargains that both participants would regard as legitimate. In the second place, it is very difficult for either participant to make a binding promise to the other. In the third place, the government's desire to deter potential future hijackers severely hinders its ability to strike a bargain with an actual hijacker. And, in the fourth place, the value system and rationality of the hijacker are likely to be in doubt during most of the negotiations. . . . Traditional bargaining theory assumes that participants are rational . . . and that each participant is aware of the other participants' value systems." The assumptions about the type of social order being studied that underlie such analyses as bargaining theory doubtless are related to their seeming inapplicability for the work of those who are not centrally interested in negotiation itself but who are still cognizant of negotiations in their own data.

The writings of prominent contributors to bargaining theory or to other kinds of negotiation theory yield rather less for understanding the great variety of negotiations in the real world than for how they might function as a springboard for effective "theoretical sampling" (see Glaser and Strauss, 1967); that is, for theory-oriented sampling of a multitude of contrasting situations. The very abstractness of most of the conceptions, with either little awareness of or implicit assumptions about the structural conditions under which imagined or illustrative bargainings occur, as in Schelling's work, raises interesting questions about the actual variety of sets of such structural conditions for varying kinds of negotiations. Also (as in Schelling), the predominant focus on strategies and tactics—along with such associated concepts as commitment, promises, and threats—raises immediately pertinent questions about the conditions that must obtain for those particular tactics and strategies to appear and, of course, questions about what other kinds of tactics and strategies would appear under other conditions. An important inquiry then is "Where would one expect to find these particular strategies and tactics—in what kinds of data?" In effect, then, the scrutiny of such writings as those by Ikle or Schelling could allow the drawing out of their theoretical conceptions and frameworks for theoretical sampling purposes (see Strauss, 1970). A careful reader could discover differences and similarities between the negotiations that appear in their substantive data and in his own and could capitalize on that discovery.

A second and related point: Sometimes the general analyses of negotiation are not very closely linked with the larger "macroscopic" or social setting considerations, except to take them (for example, market conditions or international relations) for granted or to utilize them as a general background. When specific considerations are taken into account, macroanalysis of the setting is often excellent, but the negotiation analysis drops down to a descriptive or even narrative level.

A third point is that some negotiation analysts focus on prediction or outcomes because they are concerned, presumably, with efficiency, effectiveness, or some other measure of "Under what conditions are these negotiations more or less successful or unsuccessful?" We can view the efficiency focus either as very narrow or as practical; in any event, it is probably not a central focus for most social scientists who just happen on negotiations in the course of their studies and so might wonder what to do with those data.

All three points, along with my previous remarks about negotiated order, add up to several directives. First, theorists of negotiation need to look at a much *fuller range* of negotiations. Second, they need to relate the negotiations to what *other modes* of action are available to actors who are considering whether to negotiate. Third, they need to look at the negotiations in close relationship to the *larger structural contexts* within which they take place. Fourth, they need to consider the matter of the actors' views or *theories of negotiation* as these enter and affect the negotiations themselves. In writing this book, I have endeavored to follow those directives.

Social Theorists, Social Order, and Negotiation

Having touched on some weaknesses of the literature on negotiation, I turn next to some weaknesses of theory and research about social order that can, at least in part, be viewed as flowing from inadequate considerations of the place of negotiation *in* social order. One place to begin that discussion is with the question "What is the point of negotiation?" Negotiation is, as noted earlier, one of the possible means for "getting things accomplished." It is used to get done the things that an actor (person, group, organization, nation, and so on) wishes to get done. This includes "making things work" or making them "continue to work." Necessarily, other actors are involved in such enterprises. Indeed, I would draw a crucial distinction between agreement and negotiation (which always implies some tension between parties, else they would not be nego-

tiating). People can agree about or to something without negotiating
("Here's $10 for your goods: Take it or leave it"). Having an
agreement allows room for negotiation, of course, if the agreement
begins to break down.

Since working together and the implied negotiation (or
alternate means to negotiation, such as coercion) take place within
some structural context, that leads, or so it seems to me, to the wider
issue, "What is the nature of the particular social order 'within
which' actors are choosing to negotiate?" I use the term *social order*
in the very loose sense, as referring to the larger lineaments of groups,
organizations, nations, societies, and international orders that yield
the structural conditions under which negotiations of particular kinds
are or are not initiated by or forced on actors. Negotiations of "particular kinds," of course, include by whom, with whom, over what
issues, with what involved stakes, and with what implied negotiation
subprocesses. In some social orders (for example, the pre-Civil War
American South), the structural conditions are such that certain
kinds of negotiations are impossible or improbable, while others are
probable and frequent. The structural conditions also affect how
actors see social order and what they believe is, for themselves and
others, possible or impossible, problematic or probable.

Like all members of various social orders (plantation owners
and slaves, or prison guards and inmates), social scientists, too, may
have explicit or implicit conceptions about particular social orders.
In any case, the conceptions involve judgments about the limits of
the possible and the probable, the options open and closed to those
who actually live (or have lived) in those social orders. If theorists
engage in social planning or in counseling others, then various
options, including negotiations, are seen as relatively impossible,
problematic, possible, or probable. If they merely write theory, they
will still be stating something about those options, and those statements will relate to their assumptions about social order. (The
statements will also relate to their conceptions of social change and
of history, matters I shall discuss directly hereafter, as well as in
Part One of this book.)

Now, one of the intriguing questions about social theorists is
why they virtually all have neglected to single out negotiation as one
of the major phenomena of human life. We have only to think of our

favorite theorists and their vocabularies of explanation in order to see where their respective emphases lie: on class, exploitation, force, conflict, accommodation, cooperation, alienation, values, pattern variables, functions, generalized others, routine grounds of action, or development. Any consequent prescriptions for affecting desirable change then turn logically on various activities: for example, counseling the elites, educating the public or particular publics, building an appropriate technology, working with incipient entrepreneurs, raising the class consciousness of the workers. Even such social theorists as Hobbes and Rousseau, who postulate some variety of initial social contract, simply assume that particular form of negotiation to get the social order underway; thereafter, the important processes and events may rest on that basic contract but are themselves altogether something else than the contract. Interestingly enough, even in the writings of a "consensus" theorist, such as Dewey, the focus is on such matters as public discussion, participatory democracy, and the sharing of symbols. Negotiation processes as essential to the building of consensus are simply assumed, not analyzed, as a glance at the indexes to Dewey's writings will quickly show.

It is easy to see that certain types of theory cannot readily accommodate the idea that negotiation is very important. I have in mind the various forms of determinism. For instance, any variety of biological determinism will entail causal explanations attributing major power to biological bases, such as bodily drives, instincts, genes, or DNA. Similarly, extreme forms of cultural determinism place the basic causes back into culture or cultural elements, disposing of other theorists' causal elements (biological, psychological, or social) as derivative or secondary. In either form of determinism, is it conceivable that negotiation could play anything but a peripheral explanatory role, if indeed the determinist happens to notice negotiation as something more than a practical activity—practical action being entirely secondary for the theorist? Structural determinists, of course, locate causal elements in various kinds of structures (class, values, organizations, economic variables); again, negotiation is unlikely to be seen as anything but a consequence of the structural variables. Modern structuralist determinists, including many sociologists, are no more likely to notice negotiation than, say, Herbert Spencer a century ago. Need I argue that all these, as well

as the positions mentioned earlier, embody at least an implicit theory
of negotiation, to the extent that they give it very little place in their
theory of human behavior and/or society? (I shall say more about
this hereafter.)

One of the intellectual traditions that would logically seem
more hospitable to considering negotiations as among the central
processes is that known as "interactionism" or "Chicago sociology."
It will be useful to make a brief examination of how the early
figures (William I. Thomas, Robert Park, and George Mead)
viewed the processes that they conceived as essential to social order.
Such an examination provides some illumination on how even
theorists disposed to think nondeterministically can "miss" negotiation processes.

Among the emphases deep in the interactionist tradition are
those on social processes and on freedom in relation to constraint
(Fisher and Strauss, in press). Thus the interactionists have been
much interested in social processes, the reason being that they have
been so impressed with the immensity as well as the potentialities of
social change. At the same time, they have assumed that human
beings are active creatures, shaping their environments and their
futures but also facing the constraints bearing on their actions. Interactionists take an intermediate position between a world of no
constraints whatever—one depending entirely on human beings'
wills—and a structurally deterministic world. In developing views
of the mechanics of social change, each interactionist has tended
to discover and discuss certain processes that are central to his
formulated theory. Thus, Thomas (1966) held an evolutionary
view, which ranged all societies along a developmental ladder. At
each level, there was the possibility that benevolently motivated
higher groups would reach down to groups immediately below and
educate them to progress upward: in Poland, the reform-minded
aristocracy and the peasants; in the United States, the reformers
and the immigrant groups "in need of guidance." Besides this educational interactive process, Thomas also emphasized—and his
view deeply influenced Chicago sociology thereafter—processes
involving the disorganization of group organization and then the
building up through reorganization (to higher evolutionary levels of

organization). Understandably, he never mentioned negotiation as a special topic. For Thomas, there was implicit room for negotiation wherever there was disagreement between the groups, but he deemphasized disagreement and tension between them.

Even more influential were the teachings and writings of Robert Park (1967), which introduced into the interactionist tradition a set of linked processes; namely, conflict, accommodation, and assimilation. Those were directly related to Park's worldwide view of groups in motion, migrating across space and meeting in contacts that resulted in the previously mentioned processes. Park also enduringly introduced into interactionist thought the importance of collective behavior, his chief process here being that of institutionalization: the movement from inchoate crowd or initial stages of a social movement, through a development career or natural history, toward routine organization and institutionalization. Other processes that the interactionists inherited from Park were associated with his spatial conflict ideas. These processes were termed "ecological," and chief among them were invasion and succession. Although Park's actors actively shape some of their own conditions of life, seeking solutions to their essential problems, Park is not especially interested in how they do that other than in terms of his key processual concepts. So he never particularly noted negotiation processes.

George Mead, the third scholar generally credited with influencing Chicago sociology, was not a sociologist himself but a professional philosopher. In the course of working out his philosophic positions, he (1934) developed the social psychology that still influences sociologists, coining such concepts as "the generalized other" and "taking the role of the other." His views of social change and social progress were largely couched in terms of the movement from primitive, biologically rooted origins toward an increasingly complex and broad-gauged civilization (Fisher and Strauss, 1977). For Mead, in contrast with Thomas' and Park's emphasis on group conflict, the emergence of mechanisms by which the species could direct its progress represented crucial steps by which all mankind moved forward. The basic problem was to keep the civilizational march moving; for, although the march was inevitable, wherever and whenever it stalled human suffering was increased. Chief among the means for reducing suffering was the reflective intelligence of self-aware actors, who had learned to take the roles of others. Mead's approach to social change and social order further emphasized two processes (universalizing and concretizing)', themselves fostered by two central institutions (religion and economic exchange), through which people learned to see each other as human—through which they learned to take each other's roles. Mead, of course, refers to bargaining and other economic exchanges when discussing economic transactions, but he never focuses on negotiation as such: Given his perspective, he had no need to do so.

Mead, Thomas, and Park were antideterministic, in the sense that they sought a balance between completely free-willed actors and actors whose actions were fairly strictly determined— that is, constrained. Interactionists are essentially antideterministic, but, as the preceding thumbnail intellectual sketches suggest, they have addressed the freedom-constraint issue in a variety of ways, which need not include any emphasis on negotiation. Recently, interactionists are beginning to write explicitly about negotiation and to build on the concept of "negotiated order" I discussed earlier (Bucher, 1970; Bucher and Stelling, 1969; Stelling and Bucher, 1972; Morgan, 1975; Martin, 1976; Gerson, 1976; Maines and Denzin, in press; Denzin, in press). Why this should occur now is explainable largely in terms of the heightened search by some interactionists for a joining of social structural and social interactional considerations but with the antideterministic stance still intact: "Social structure, interaction, form, and process are tightly interwoven, and . . . bear little resemblance to the older functionalist view of an impersonal social structure" (Maines, 1977, p. 256; see also Benson and Day, 1976; Day and Day, 1977).

I should add that my own theoretical position is a variant of the interactionist approach. The final chapter of this book takes up in some detail some of my elaboration of and divergence from certain aspects of the interactionist tradition. That is done in terms both of the topic of negotiation and of the more important topics of social structure and social order. Involved in each is really another question: "What degree of freedom versus constraint is implied in one's theories of social order and negotiation?" Of course, that is not just an interactionist's question.

Returning now to social theorists in general: What is additionally interesting about their relationships to negotiation is that whenever one of them engages in concerted social action—whether in reform or revolution—in accordance with his prescriptive vocabulary, then he will be found engaging, willy-nilly, in negotiation activities. How does a revolutionary elite rule after seizing governmental power—let alone line up alliances beforehand, let alone build an elitist core ready to seize power—without engaging in varieties of negotiation? Or, if the reformist theorist engages in political theory (as does Charles Merriam), in public education (as do Richard Ely and John Kenneth Galbraith), or in persuading agency professionals to one's views (as do W. I. Thomas and E. W. Burgess), how can he avoid, especially at critical junctures, combining those modes of action with negotiation? None of those theorists would deny that they did so. But they do not alter their theories so as to build negotiation into their vocabularies of explanation. Pragmatics is not theoretics!

Yet I shall argue again that they do have implicit theories of negotiation ("of little importance") embedded in their general theories of human action or society. In contrast, when they act they hold other theories of negotiation in closer accord with their practical actions. There is a *gap* between those two sets of theories. If the theorists actually acted in accordance with their more "theoretical" formulations and later altered them in accordance with how well or badly those theories worked in practice, then there would be a reciprocity and closer correspondence between the two sets of theories. In the next section, we look at that kind of theorist-in-action. His intellectual biography also strikingly illustrates how negotiation theories have developmental careers: As practical contingencies change, they have their counterpart in the qualifying or abandoning of guiding theories of negotiation—when the theories seem not to fit "reality" entirely or at all. Perhaps the account will strike some readers as a digression, but I believe it is exactly this kind of glimpse behind the scenes of how perspectives on social order and negotiation are formed, formulated, and changed that

will help to release us from narrow or vitiating conceptions of negotiation and social order.

Li Ta-Chao's Options: Joining Theory with Action

What happens when someone consciously joins theory *with*
action—scarcely distinguishing between the two? People who do
so, of course, are found prominently in revolutionary movements
where "correct" theory is deemed essential to effective action but
ought not merely to be theory. Incorrect theory is out of touch with
reality, and action without theory leads equally to disaster. Genuine
theory and effective action are simply considered two sides of the
same coin.

My illustrative case of a theorist-in-action is meant specifically
to underscore several points that, taken together, are not much
dwelt on either by students of negotiation or by social theorists generally. First, theories of social order and change (and history) are
crucially relevant to how actors see the options, including negotiation, open to themselves—what modes of action are possible and in
what combinations. (That implies they have theories of negotiation.) Second, the social scientist can properly understand the
choice of modes and their specific combinations only by recognizing
those underlying theories of social order and change. Third, it is not
sufficient to pay attention to actors' perceptions of the potential
efficacy of chosen modes (including negotiation); they require
analysis in terms of those more embracing conceptions of society.
Fourth, insofar as conceptions change over time, actors' perceptions
and utilizations of options change. Negotiation analysis requires that
the social scientist focus on the changing context for negotiations
vis-à-vis coercion, persuasion, education, and the other alternatives
to negotiation.

The following case materials are taken from Maurice
Meisner's *Li Ta-Chao and the Origins of Chinese Marxism*
(1967). Li, a teacher of Mao himself, was "China's first Marxist."
Born in 1888, he was killed in 1929. The most relevant part of his
biography for us relates to the years between 1919 and 1929, when
Li was faced with fateful political choices.

The major lines of his intellectual development were as follows. Very early, he became suspicious of corrupt governmental officials and politicians. And from "the very beginning of his mature intellectual life his basic loyalties had been to China as a nation and a people rather than to the particular values and beliefs of the past" (Meisner, 1967, p. 5). His antiforeign stance "merged with and reinforced his modern nationalist commitment to the survival and power of the Chinese nation in a world of contending nation-states" (p. 23). His relatively early discovery of Bergson and Emerson seemed to have been consequential: From Bergson he drew lessons about a voluntaristic approach to solving China's problem, while from Emerson's writings about rebirth he drew support for his own ideas about the possibilities of a new China that nevertheless would retain organic linkages with the old China. Throughout his life, voluntarism and the possibilities of a revitalized nation remained central to his thought.

Previous to the October Revolution in Russia, Li believed socialist theories to be of little relevance to China. That revolution and World War I convinced him that the future belonged to the newly emerging nations, especially China. National backwardness was a positive advantage, containing the seeds of youth and progress. He began to conceive of world revolution as soon to sweep the globe. Shortly after, he discovered the prerevolutionary Russian populists, who had spread the principles of humanism and socialism. He also began to contrast urban vice with village purity. Conceiving that the Chinese revolutionary movement was still in its populist stage, Li "implicitly recognized" that socialism might be further away than he had anticipated. In any case, by 1919 he was almost ready to accept the more activist, voluntary aspects of Marxism but was critical of the "deterministic aspects" that encouraged passivity or implied a long period of economic development before revolutionary political change was possible. Meisner argues that although Lenin's thought influenced Li's own Li never accepted Lenin's essential reliance on discipline and organizational restraint. Generally Li hewed to the "original populist conception wherein the relationship between the 'consciousness' of the intelligentsia and the 'spontaneous' energies and ideas of 'the people' remained undefined" (p. 209).

After 1921, much of Li's energy was devoted to organizing

urban workers. This activity, Meisner suggests, was governed by both the demands of Marxist theory and the "advice" that the Comintern had given to the newly formed Chinese Party. During this period, the Third International became interested in alliances with "bourgeois nationalist" forces within China, meaning almost any group that would cooperate with the Chinese Communist Party. Li played a central role in negotiating a loose accord with an important northern warlord and assumed the primary responsibility for the maintenance of that accord. What Li thought of this alliance is not known, but it did greatly facilitate "the organizational work" in which he was engaged. (That is, a negotiated relationship fed into and supported his organizational efforts to affect potentially crucial political events.) His establishment of a railroad workers' union was made possible by the agreement, but shortly thereafter the workers went on strike and were brutally suppressed by the warlord's troops. "For all practical purposes, the proletarian base of the Communist Party in the north had been abruptly and, as it proved, irreparably destroyed" (p. 212). (Thus the negotiated agreement was coercively terminated; the consequences were of major importance.) This course of events also destroyed whatever hopes Li may have had that the urban working class would lead the Chinese revolution.

Meanwhile, events caused the Soviet government to attempt a normalization of diplomatic relations with the West. This meant looking to alliances in Asia with "bourgeois nationalists," so the Chinese Communists were told that the Chinese revolution was still in its bourgeois democratic phase. The main vehicle of that revolution in China was to be the Kuomintang, with whom the party members were to join in a common front against imperialism. The Chinese Communists who had believed a socialist revolution was imminent were deeply disappointed: They were now supposed to join in the revolution only as individuals, not as party members. Li became the principal Chinese Communist advocate of the alliance with the Kuomintang, eventually succeeding in persuading most of his fellow Communists in Peking. (In short, persuasion plus negotiation were then his principal operating modes.) He reassured the Kuomintang that the Communists would not form a party within a party.

How did Li view the alliance and the national revolution that "he so fervently promoted"? He had begun to conceive that international capitalism—rather than Chinese capitalism—was the main enemy; so the revolutionary struggle should include virtually all social classes, since almost everybody suffered under imperialism. In Moscow, they held quite a different view of the alliance: In Stalin's later phraseology, the Kuomintang was to be "utilized to the end, squeezed out like a lemon, and then flung away" (p. 223). Li's contrary conception was that the national revolution was not merely a stage in the larger social and political evolution, nor was the alliance simply tactical. He thought of both "as logical expressions of the particular nature of the Chinese revolution . . . fundamentally a mass uprising of the entire Chinese nation against the forces of world imperialism" (p. 224). The Chinese revolution would increasingly flow into the world proletarian revolution, with the Chinese playing a very special and creative role in the universal transformation of humanity. As long as he could believe all that, he would remain a firm supporter of the alliance, working in its behalf, organizing, persuading, mediating, and so on.

What happened thereafter was crucial to other developments in his thought and action. Li's Communists in North China were only able to form an alliance with a minority left-wing faction of a predominantly antagonistic Kuomintang. During 1925, Li's activities reflected the Communists' lack of strength in the North. He was a member of the Kuomintang central executive committee and was concerned with reunifying China through the convocation of a national assembly. He mediated between the Communists and whatever left-wing Kuomintang segments remained in Peking and also mediated between the Soviet envoy to the Peking government and the government itself. (These types of negotiation were deemed appropriate to the times, as he saw them.) However, Meisner notes that the "contrast between Li's radical theory and his rather benign practice did not last for long" (p. 236). The Communist position in the north became increasingly precarious, tending to become more and more confined to the students and ex-students of Peking University. Li's response to this dangerous isolation was to "move toward a linking up with the potentially explosive force of the peasant revolution, thus closing the yawning gap between intellect-

uals and the people" (p. 238). He was now thinking in terms of
agrarian revolution strengthening the national government and its
completion of the national revolution.

Now Li was emphasizing a number of means to getting, in
his words (p. 239), "the great peasant masses to organize together
and participate in the national revolution." Communists were to
work in the peasant movement and assist in organizing the spon-
taneously arising, or arisen, peasant organization, including the
peasants' "self-protection" armies. (Li was essentially urging a
combination of education and persuasion.) At first, Li was alone in
this view of the peasants' revolutionary potential, but by 1926 after
a "largely spontaneous revolutionary upsurge" throughout much of
rural China, the peasant question became the center of a sharp
debate within the Communist Party. Previously, Comintern representatives and the party's central committee had been concerned
with preventing the peasant movement from becoming too radical
and perhaps undermining the united front, for the committee had
promoted a united front of all rural people of whatever class.

Li's conceptions of history and the peasants' role in it
proved to be quite different. By now, Li perceived that any revolutionary hopes for China had to be based entirely on the "possibility
of an elemental mass uprising of the peasantry through the most
militant of the existing peasant groups in the northern provinces—
the armed peasant secret societies" (p. 248). The peasantry itself
was capable of carrying out the revolution. In Li's words (pp. 248–
249): "The Chinese peasants have already become awakened and
know that they can rely only upon their own combined strength to
liberate themselves from the disorders . . . that have been created
by imperialism and militarism." (Education, persuasion, and
coercion were now his major options.)

The Communists, Li taught, should appeal to the class
loyalties of the peasants who were serving in his armies of the war-
lords. They had to be loosened from authority. He (p. 250) suggested a battle cry for the peasants:

There has never been a savior.
Neither the gods nor the emperors.
Who can liberate us if not ourselves?
We can only depend upon ourselves to save ourselves.

It was the party members, however, who were to make the peasants fully conscious of that possibility. Communists had to make them aware of their massive power. The peasants were also to be persuaded away from their antiforeign animus and taught about revolutionary nationalism—they have, Li said, to understand imperialism "which is oppressing and exploiting" them; that is, their "narrow racial views" had to be broadened. Thus the peasants had to be educated and persuaded into an awareness of themselves. Meisner suggests that in Li's conception of the peasant revolution "there was that characteristically populist contradiction between a passionate faith in the spontaneous energies of the people and a conviction that the revolutionary intellectuals must bring enlightenment and leadership to the mass movement" (p. 251), including the formation of a centralized organization to further the revolution. Or, to quote Li's passionate directive, "Comrades, several hundred million peasants are waiting to be released from the deep waters of the sea and the hot fires of hell . . . They longingly wait for you to lead them out of this vile pit onto the road of brightness" (p. 252). In those last words, of course, Li joins social theory and social action indissolubly. Theory functions in the service of action—it has no other purpose—but effective (and moral) action is possible only through theory that apprehends the true nature of reality.

Reading this historical account, we quickly become cognizant that the meaning of negotiation processes (such as the forming of alliances or mediating between groups) cannot be grasped unless they are seen within the larger context of Chinese relations and events. That context is necessarily a changing one. Furthermore, negotiation takes place in specific relationships with other modes of action, in accordance with how the actors perceive current situations. But what modes are judged as possible, impossible, probable, improbable, are linked not only with their perceived efficacy but also with the actors' views of how change can be effected, given what they believe is the nature of history and society and of negotiation. One additional point: Like any social theorist, or social researcher for that matter, who directs or counsels others or himself into action, Li was advising on the limits of the possible. Negotiation may or may not be—or be seen as—possible. Perhaps later. Perhaps later in combination with threats of coercion? With the manipulating of certain contingencies? In short, Li was address-

ing—and, understandably, giving different answers over time to—
the issue of constraint (limits) versus freedom (options).

Social Researchers, Social Orders, and Negotiations

Social theorists who write about social order are paralleled
by social researchers who study a plurality of social orders. Faced
with understanding a particular group, organization, institution,
nation, or society, the researcher generally either must ask "What is
this all about? What is its structure of relations?" or perhaps will
simply assume—explicitly or implicitly—an answer to that question
and then will proceed to study whatever is central to his or her
interests. The very different approaches to social order versus
social orders have, indeed, been argued by Stephen Mennel (1974,
pp. 116–117):

> We are frequently told that the central question
> of sociological theory is why there is order in society
> . . . the question posed by Thomas Hobbes (1651):
> Why do men cooperate with each other in society? Why
> is there not a continual "war of everyone against every-
> one," as each individual pursues his own self-interest by
> whatever means, including force, that are at hand? . . .
> How, in other words, is a degree of *harmony* in society
> achieved? In the past, sociologists have tended to
> espouse one or other of the contradictory answers pro-
> posed by political philosophers. Social order is the result
> of some people being able to coerce others into obedi-
> ence; or it rests on general agreement among the
> members of society; or it stems from their striking bar-
> gains with each other which are to everyone's individual
> advantage as well as the collective advantage. But it is
> unhelpful to see these viewpoints as mutually exclusive.
> For the sociologist, social order must be a matter for
> empirical investigation. It is obvious that each of the
> old philosophical views has a grain of truth in it, for
> each comes near to describing what is observed in some
> societies, or parts of societies, of different types, at differ-
> ent periods of history, in particular circumstances.

Alas, that easily made dichotomy between older philosophers and modern social scientists masks its supportive rhetorical function for the more "science"-oriented of the social scientists. It also blurs the possibility that researchers may import assumptions about social order and negotiation into their studies of particular social orders. And indeed they do. Perhaps that is not so startling, nor is it even unexpected that they usually do so quite unwittingly. For our purposes, it is more important to recognize that their conceptions lead them either to overlook or misconstrue their data on negotiations. Close examination of those data raises, in turn, some sharply critical questions about the researchers' conceptions of social order and, not incidentally, about some of their research conclusions. A focus on negotiation, in other words, can lead to questioning some contemporary perspectives on social order and social change. Since those perspectives also carry directives for action and carry implications about the perceived efficacy of particular modes of action as well as the perceived limits to action, our focus on negotiation can also speak to those practical concerns.

In Part One of this book, some of those issues will be addressed through a critical scrutiny of research done by well-known people. This material is presented early in the book because I wish to direct attention to the primary issue concerning negotiation (including theories of negotiation); namely, its linkages with social order. In Part Two, the analysis of negotiations is the main topic. Actual cases of negotiation, covering a very considerable range of types, are analyzed by utilizing the negotiation paradigm mentioned earlier. That paradigm continually forces us to think about negotiation interactions in terms of the larger social setting, with its implied structural conditions that bear on those interactions. The range of settings reminds us, too, that negotiations take place not only in the most intimate of settings but also in the largest and across maximum geographic spaces; they also may be of the briefest duration or take place over long periods of time, and, of course, they may be "over" the merest trifles or the most momentous of issues.

Any paradigm for analyzing negotiations necessarily will have to cover that entire range. It must also answer to the kinds of criticisms nowadays being raised against the presumed importance of negotiation (and negotiated order), such as that some things are

"nonnegotiable," that there are "limits to negotiation," that negotiation analysis only looks at relatively microscopic interaction, and
that it ignores the vital role of social structure. Those criticisms—
which I believe are erroneous—will be discussed in the last pages
of the concluding chapter.

Part One

• • • • • • • • • • • • • • • • • • • •
• •
• •

SOCIAL
RESEARCHERS
AND
SOCIAL ORDERS

• •
• •
• •

*I*n investigating particular groups, organizations, institutions, or social movements, researchers may or may not be aware of some of their theoretical presuppositions, including those about social change, social order, and negotiation. The presuppositions usually include little emphasis on negotiation processes as central to the construction, maintenance, and change of those objects under study. The questions, then, are "What are the consequences of this underemphasis of negotiation for those particular researches—which are, after all, supposed to flow back and affect the researchers' 'larger' theories? Or do the studies only exemplify the theories? Or do they affect the immediate substantive

theories addressed or formulated by the researchers, but not the
undergirding theories (or metatheories)?"

Further questions, specifically concerning negotiation, are,
"Can indeed the research affect the larger theory if the researcher
does not see negotiation theoretically—that is, in *terms* of theory?
What happens if the researcher sees negotiation 'in the data' but
does not build theoretically on those particular data? What kinds of
description or what kinds of substantive theory do we then get? Or,
blinded by theoretical preconceptions, do researchers actually overlook the negotiations that are represented in the collected data?
Finally, what would happen if researchers (or we) found negotiations in their data and took them seriously: How would that affect
what was offered by way of descriptions, substantive theories, and
theoretical conceptions?"

To answer those questions, probably it is better to examine
"classic" (that is, recognized) research writings by persons who also
have considerable reputations as general theorists. Examining such
writings is the main agenda of Part One of this book. It involves
looking closely at the stances, concepts, and treatments of negotiation that are associated with the research of several well-known
sociologists and political scientists. I have included work in which
theory or conceptual frameworks are supported by—or at least associated with—reported data, except in one instance (James Coleman). I have stayed close to the materials themselves and have not
attacked, as such, the more general positions that the authors represent (interactionism, functionalism, political pluralism, game theory,
and mass society theory). My critiques are, however, entirely
pertinent to the issue of how adequate are the conceptions of social
order that are utilized in the particular versions of the more general
positions under review.

Part One begins with my critique of a paper by Erving
Goffman, a paper that focuses on the holding back of individual
commitment to (coercive) institutions. Then there follow critiques
of two books, by Peter Blau and Alvin Gouldner, respectively, that
represent functionalist inquiries into bureaucratic structures as they
develop or change. The next two studies treated are by political
scientists; one, Edward Banfield, was writing about political influence, and the second, William Riker, was applying game theory to

coalition formation. Each research volume represents a different variety of American pluralistic theory. Next is a critique of a paper by James Coleman, addressed to the lack of power of individual shareholders in corporations: His conception of corporate (and societal) order is perhaps a variety of alienation or mass society theory. A final paper, by Edward Morse, about the "bargaining structure" of NATO is discussed as a contrasting case. My commentary on each work is designed to bring out the researcher's implicit theory of negotiation (more explicit, in the instances of Banfield and Morse) and its impact on the researcher's interpretation of his data. It would have been possible to analyze each case in accordance with the paradigm and procedures used in Part Two, but the emphasis in Part One is quite different, so this was not done.

Perhaps it ought to be added that none of these researchers is interested solely in narrow substantive topics. They were writing about some of the larger aspects of contemporary life and central theoretical issues in their respective fields. The publications are rightfully regarded either as classics or at least as very important, and most are surely worth rereading and discussing today. I do not mean to fault their authors for failing to pay attention to what I allege to be important, in contrast to what they thought—sometimes several years ago—was important. I do mean, however, to claim that future effective work on social orders of every kind must have a proper focus on negotiation and on such associated or alternative processes as manipulation, persuasion, and coercion. For the sake of substantiating my claim, I shall comment on each publication as if it had been published recently: If the commentary sometimes seems overly severe, considering the durable readability of some of these writings, that can be counterbalanced by regarding my commentary as a device employed against past excellent work in order to emphasize the necessity of negotiation analysis so as to accomplish better work in the future.

Chapter One

●●●●●●●●●●●●●●●●●●●●●
●●●●●●●●●●●●●●●●●●●●●●
●●●●●●●●●●●●●●●●●●●●●●●

Erving Goffman:
Coercive Institutions
and Individual Commitment

●●●●●●●●●●●●●●●●●●●●●●●
●●●●●●●●●●●●●●●●●●●●●●●
●●●●●●●●●●●●●●●●●●●●●●●

*E*rving Goffman's reputation as an influential social theorist was launched early in his career, with publications that included his "On the Characteristics of Total Institutions" (1961a, pp. 1–124, but originally delivered as a speech in 1957). The thrust of argument and analysis in this widely cited paper is that there exists a class of institutions (among them, prisons, concentration camps, and—to the consternation of many psychiatrists—mental hospitals) that share certain important features; notably, relationships within them are structured primarily along coercive lines because of the very nature of the institutions. (The adjective *coercive* is mine: Goffman makes no technical use of the term, although he uses a host of synonyms or equivalent phrases, such as "enforced," "imposed from above," "all treated alike and required to do the same thing together.") The principal actors in the total institution drama are the inmates and the personnel, whom Goffman portrays respectively as the coerced and coercing. He carefully and exhaustively examines what there is about the nature of these institutions that throws those categories of persons generally into those respective roles. He gives a social structural analysis of why persons of differing status act as they do.

In another paper (1961b, pp. 171–320), apparently written during the same year, Goffman turned to what he conceived of as an associated theoretical problem: How do the inmates manage to avoid being completely controlled (coerced) by the institutions and their managers? Control here means not merely something mechanical or external but also includes internal controls in the form of personal commitments to the institution. Goffman phrases this issue in terms of individual commitment to an organization. An individual commits himself to an organization but only commits just so much of himself and no more, even in total institutions.

Although he does not say so, Goffman is addressing the classical issue of constraint versus freedom: How much, if any, freedom of human action is possible in this world? In these research papers, Goffman is well within the tradition of Chicago interactionism, whose practitioners have been centrally concerned with the interplay of social constraints and individual action (see Fisher and Strauss, in press). Interactionists will accept no form of strict determinism that makes human behavior merely, or even mainly, an outcome of biological, psychological, or social variables. Like others in this intellectual tradition, Goffman is especially concerned with countering the position of social structuralists, whether sociologists or anthropologists.

His own version of Chicago sociology, as every reader of Goffman will recognize, emphasizes the importance in interaction of rules, often implicit, that profoundly affect the interaction but do not altogether govern it. Individuals manage their own and others' interactional behavior, but always with respect to those rules. Goffman regards social order as very fragile, as capable of being shattered relatively easily in actual interaction, and as requiring social mechanisms for getting it back again into undisrupted running order. Although interaction itself is not strictly determined by social structure, for Goffman the selves of individuals are related nonetheless to the framework of social structure.

Returning now to his interpretation of total institutions, but moving somewhat ahead of my story line, I shall note that Goffman is well aware of the relations between coercion and inmates' attempts to manipulate situations, events, persons, and even their selves, but he is little cognizant of potential relationships between negotiation and coercion or manipulation. Also, I shall recognize that Goffman's argument is indeed directed explicitly and forcefully against too strict a structural determinism, such as ironically has often been the construction laid on his own analysis of total institutions. Related to his argument with structural determinism is the depiction of total institutions as coercive organizations that are relieved, not incidentally, by a degree of human detachment, a lack of commitment—that is, individual freedom—on the part of inmates who are by no means totally coerced by these organizations.

A key to Goffman's stance on these matters is his paraphrasing of a statement by Durkheim, which leaves ambiguous whether "participants" in an organization should be read as individuals or as something more than mere individuals: "As Durkheim has taught us, behind each contract there are noncontractual assumptions about the character of the participants" (1961b, p. 174). Goffman misses the ambiguity in his paraphrase because, as we shall see, he is focused on the "individual's" problem of commitment vis-à-vis organizations. To Durkheim's contractual statement, he wishes to add considerations of self: "If every bond creates a broad conception of the person tied to it, then we should go on to ask how the individual handles this defining of himself" (p. 175).

In brief, his argument is that every organization has "official expectations as to what the participant owes" it. But participants always "decline in some way to accept" the official view "of what they should be putting into and getting out of the organization" (p. 304)—and that amounts to a declining of the organization's view "of what sort of self and world they are to accept for themselves" (1961b, p. 175). They fall short of making a total commitment to the organization. In practice, "the individual . . . holds himself off from fully embracing all the self-implications of his affiliation, allowing some of this dissatisfaction to be seen even while expressing his major obligations" (p. 175). This theme of balancing commitment and detachment, of status and self, Goffman calls "expressed distance."

For instruction on how the individual manages this, Goffman turns to an examination of "the underlife" of a mental hospital—a total institution in which the individual's resources are at a minimum. "When existence is cut to the bone, we can learn what people do to flesh out their lives" (p. 189). Life in such an institution can underline for us the kinds of "secondary adjustments" that are made in any organization. Secondary adjustments are "any habitual arrangement by which a member of an organization employs unauthorized means, or obtains unauthorized ends, or both, thus getting around the organization's assumptions as to what he should do and get and hence what he should be" (p. 189). Goffman's account is mainly a lengthy description and discussion of how those secondary adjustments are carried out—and they are primarily and characteristically manipulative, although Goffman does not use that term.

Then, in a last section, Goffman discusses a classification of tactics that pertain to "fitting another's efforts into" one's "own designs." Thus "the individual can greatly increase the range and scope of his secondary adjustments" (1961b, p. 263). This use of another person is very important. It includes private coercion, economic exchange involving a sale or a trade, "social exchanges" (including those associated with courting, clique relations, and having buddies), and patron relationships between hospital employees and inmates. However, to "ensure that the individual can incorporate into his own plan of action the efforts of others," there need to be certain "social arrangements, . . . some form of social control . . . to keep people in line, to make them live up to their bargains and their obligation to perform favors and ceremonies for the others" (p. 299). These forms of social control "constitute secondary adjustments" of a very special class—"a class of adjustments" that "underlie and stabilize a vast complex of unofficial, undercover practices"; "these controls will have to be exerted over both inmates and staff" (p. 299).

That last set of sentences begins to suggest the implicit premises of Goffman's approach. If these social arrangements are so important, why does he devote only 3 pages to them (his paper is 146 pages long)? Of course, there are numerous examples, sprinkled throughout his paper, of deals, bargains, trade-offs, agreements, cooperative arrangements, and so on. Sometimes these are glimpsed by the reader as data; sometimes Goffman explicitly discusses them when presenting the topics of economic exchange, social exchange, and the patron relationships. Goffman would hardly deny that a tremendous amount of negotiation goes on among inmates and some even between them and the hospital's employees, but he is so concerned with showing how secondary adjustments are made and with their significance for the individual's holdback of commitment from the organization that he does not ask what all that negotiation signifies.

One can appreciate the extent of Goffman's analytic blindness by viewing some of his footnotes, in which he gives illustrations of manipulative secondary adjustments but which might just as well be used to illustrate various forms of negotiated agreements. Here are two from an account of life in a concentration camp (many of the examples in the footnotes are taken from such coercive organizations as concentration camps and prisons). First, "When an inmate had died in the tents, the fact was concealed, and the dead man was dragged or carried by one or two men to the bread issue point, where the ration was issued to the 'helpers.' The body was then simply dumped anywhere in the roll-call area." Second, "In every concentration camp where the political prisoners attained any degree of ascendancy, they turned the prisoner hospital, scene of fearful SS horrors that it was, into a rescue station for countless prisoners. Not only were patients actually cured wherever possible; healthy prisoners, in danger of being killed or shipped to a death camp, were smuggled on the sick list to put them beyond the clutches of the SS. In special cases, where there was no other way out, men in danger were nominally permitted to 'die' living under the names of prisoners who had actually died." (The quotes are from Kogan, no date, pp. 180 and 137, in Goffman, 1961b, pp. 222, 212, and 215.)

What becomes clear, both from Goffman's scattered bits of data and from his discussion of negotiation behavior, is that the individual cannot gain his purely personal ends (of withholding full commitment from the organization) *without negotiating* with other participants. This means that he becomes part of social circles—transitory or more permanent—and draws on their resources, not simply his own, for keeping his organizational commitment minimal. To do so, he necessarily sacrifices some of his independence from others—that is, he yields commitment to some other or others, even to cliques, in order to gain some independence from the organization at large. A perfect loner would not last long. In a prison or concentration camp, he might even get killed by other inmates. That does not mean that he may not "use" the others or even betray them at crucial junctures—but he had better choose those junctures very carefully. If we add to this assertion Goffman's explicit but really unexplored statement about the sustaining social arrangements necessary to keep people in line, then we see that his basic theoretical problem (commitment) cannot be handled without a more forthright examination of the negotiations occurring throughout the entire organization and of their relations with coercion, manipulation, persuasion, and so on. All this is really involved in translating "the individual" into a genuine "participant."

The primary reason for Goffman's swinging back and forth from *individual* to *participant,* in terminology as well as in meaning and in ways apparently unnoticed by him, is suggested by the antideterministic argument in his closing pages. There, he repudiates two possible explanations for the development of secondary adjustments. One is biological or psychological: "the individual possesses an array of needs, native or cultivated, and . . . when lodged in a milieu that denied those needs the individual simply responds by developing makeshift means of satisfaction" (1961b, pp. 318–319). The second is sociological—more specifically what I would term *social* or *structurally deterministic:* "Sociologists have always had a vested interest in pointing to how the individual is formed by groups, identifies with groups, and wilts away unless he obtains emotional support from the group" (p. 319). But the individual always uses "methods to keep some distance, some elbow room, between himself and that with which others assume he should be identified" (p. 319). Goffman's message here is that the participant "erects defenses against his social bondedness." When pressed, the sociologist will grant qualifiers in his usual view—the self may not yet be formed or may exhibit conflicting dedications—but perhaps "we should further complicate" that usual sociological view "by elevating those qualifiers to a central place." Initially defining the individual, for sociological purposes, as a "stance-taking entity" who is balancing somewhere "between identification with an organization and opposition to it," Goffman ends by noting that, therefore, it is *"against something* that the self can emerge" (pp. 319–320). No, he does not quite end there: He closes his long paper by giving his solution to the issue of constraint versus freedom, phrasing it, not unexpectedly, in terms of the group versus the individual and status versus self. Our sense of being a person can come from being drawn into a wider social unit; our sense of selfhood can arise through the little ways in which we resist the pull. Our status is backed by the solid buildings of the world, while "our sense of personal identity often resides in the cracks" (1961b, p. 320).

That solution to the constraint-freedom issue is his answer to too strict a structural determinism. In effect, he turns the tables on any literal reading of his own total institutions paper by arguing that specific kinds of social structures provide the material for the evolution of specific kinds of selves. Yet those structures do not totally determine the individual's actions, and they certainly do not totally determine his evolving self.

Goffman's argument with structural determinism leaves him locked in its embrace, so the best he can manage is a conception of a social order that is not merely determinative (in the instance of a total institution, not merely coercive) but that does permit a fair amount of manipulation of various kinds. His conception also admits a fair amount of negotiation, but notably between individuals. Negotiation seems subsidiary, however, to manipulative action by each individual as he withholds his total commitment to the organization. Negotiation is not, at least in coercive organizations, a central feature of the social order.

Of course, we need to recognize that Goffman is writing here only about one type of organization or social order, so perhaps he is writing in a very special vein. It may be that careful examination of his other publications would show another conception, or other conceptions, of social order—more or less socially deterministic, or with more emphasis on negotiation, persuasion, or some other mode of activity. (However, in his latest book, *Frame Analysis*, 1974, he attempts to give a perspective on and analysis of the organization of individual experience. This, again, can be read largely as a reasoned attack on structural determinism while also keeping the individual a highly socialized creature.)

As I noted earlier, Goffman's social order is extremely fragile, its rules subject to disobedience or unwitting breakage, its interaction continually subject to potential or actual disruption. Manipulation of events, of self, of other's situations, of props, and so on, is a constant feature of that interaction. At most, negotiation serves mainly to maintain that fragile order in some sort of uneasy equilibrium or to reinstate it after its disruption—certainly not to change the features of that order, to develop it into something new. Goffman, for the most part, seems relatively uninterested in social change. Neither social change nor negotiation is central to his thought.

But to return again to Goffman's substantive account of total institutions: In his analysis, the personnel are mainly acting, most of the time, to maintain the coercive order, and the inmates are either playing by the rules, both explicit and implicit, or acting around the margins of those rules. Their actions may or may not disrupt the ongoing order of events, but certainly they do not, ultimately, shape anew the nature of social order of the total institution itself. Of course, we must readily agree that inmates must come to terms with institutional coercion—so must the coercive personnel, in their own way—but we may disagree with Goffman about how they come to terms. We may wonder, too, whether they necessarily develop selves primarily in reaction against the coercive elements of the institution.

Chapter Two

••••••••••••••••••••
••••••••••••••••••••••
•••••••••••••••••••••••

Peter Blau:
Bureaucracy,
Unofficial Norms,
and Functionalism

•••••••••••••••••••••
•••••••••••••••••••••••
•••••••••••••••••••••••

*I*n the mid 1950s, Peter Blau published the first of many writings that would be rooted in an avowed functionalist position. Blau had studied with Merton and from him had derived both a version of functionalism and an interest in Weber's conception of bureaucracy. What Blau attempted to do in his monograph *The Dynamics of Bureaucracy* (1955) was to extend and qualify Weber's views of bureaucracy by attacking— through research—aspects that had either been overlooked or left analytically blurred by the great German sociologist. Blau's research involved a modified Mertonian functionalist analysis. From our own standpoint, Blau's study is extremely useful: It illustrates clearly how a functionalist might go about answering the question "Just what is bureaucracy, anyhow?" If Weber had not entirely grasped the nature of its order, then what was it? Blau's answer is relatively preordained, in all but its details, by his perspective. Furthermore, his handling of negotiation—which he sometimes sees as data but does *not* build into his theory—underlines some consequences of approaching social order questions with a functionalist solution, including his view of the limits of individual action possible within the bureaucratic order studied here. An additional way to read this case is to regard Blau as addressing the process whereby persons are coerced by others via enforcement of or appeal to rules, whether legal or organizational.

Blau's point of departure is Weber's focus on official regulations and requirements and their significance for administrative efficiency. Blau noted that Weber was not actually concerned with how operations are carried out within the bureaucratic organization. "Consequently, his analysis ignored the fact that, in the course of operations, new elements arise in the structure which influence subsequent operations" (Blau, 1955, p. 2). Recent research, however, had shown the importance of "emergent factors, such as informal relationships or unofficial norms" (p. 2). Blau calls attention particularly to the *emergent* aspect of organizations and notes that his own study is concerned with analyzing "these processes of organizational development" (p. 2). He does this by examining the daily operations and the interpersonal relationships of government officials in two agencies. Thus we should watch for how he handles processes, development within organizations, and the appearance of new informal relationships and "unofficial norms."

How Blau handled these phenomena is related to his particular version of functionalism. "Conceptions of functional analysis are used to organize the data of this study. . . . The basic tenet of this theoretical orientation is that the social consequences of phenomena . . . must be taken into account in sociological inquiry" (Blau, 1955, p. 6). He goes on to say that "specifically, their contribution to and interference with adjustment or function in the social structure" (p. 6) must be examined. Then he detailed four considerations about functional analysis. First, the concept of function "directs the researcher to ascertain the consequences of a given phenomenon and to evaluate their significance for the structure" (p. 6). That is, instead of focusing merely on origins of phenomena, one searches intensively for their consequences for the particular "structure" that one is studying. Second, one looks for the "mechanisms or processes through which a contribution is effected" (p. 7). Third, one looks for the "latent functions," the unanticipated consequences that "contribute to structural adjustment." This puts a new twist, Blau notes, on the study of contributory mechanisms. It especially forces one to look closely at the unofficial practices within an organization that might otherwise appear "irrational and irrelevant to operations" (p. 8). And, fourth, since consequences may also be negative, "attention must also be paid to 'dysfunctions, those observed consequences which lessen the adaptation or adjustment of the system'" (p. 8; he is quoting Merton). The dysfunctions are particularly important because "they frequently are indicators of potential modifications of the structure" (p. 8)—the aspect of bureaucracy that is of most concern to Blau. In fact, dysfunctions often give rise to structural change.

Blau is arguing against versions of functionalism and conceptions of bureaucracy that posit "rigid equilibrium" and neglect "processes of social development." In short, he has a conception of bureaucracies "as organizations in flux," whose "analysis . . . is facilitated by the conceptions of functionalism" (p. 9). In our terminology, he is assuming that the social order of any bureaucratic structure is far from static. The problem, then, is how to characterize those changing social orders called *bureaucratic* and their possibilities and limitations for action. One key to Blau's answer is how he handles negotiation.

In one part of his monograph, Chapter 10 on unofficial norms, Blau refers directly and frequently to negotiations, so perhaps this is the best place to see how negotiation looks to him. (Elsewhere, either negotiation is implicit, as in the chapter on consultation, or one would have to read it into his discussion of data.) In Department Y of the agency, the agents hardly competed with each other at all—it was a rather "cohesive situation," which engendered "the development of social norms to check the rivalry for outstanding performance that superiors encouraged" (Blau, 1955, p. 146). A set of unofficial norms developed that functioned not so much to restrict productivity as to freeze the established differentials in the agents' performance. Thus, working overtime without compensation, which officials sometimes required when in difficulties with meeting the production quota, was generally disapproved of by the agents. Blau gives evidence of this disapproval and of their criticism of occasional breaches of that unofficial norm.

Moving along, now, to the section of his chapter that most concerns us, we read about the taboo on reporting offers of bribes by clients. First, a word about the work of the agents. Part of that work was to be a law enforcer. "The duties of investigating business establishments and/or ordering violators to cease illegal practices in the future required a detached approach to employers that was polite but firm" (p. 148). The operative law did not empower them to force violators to make retroactive adjustments, but the organization expected the agents to convince the violators to do so voluntarily. So success in the task involved both "complex investigations and negotiations," as well as a "pseudopersonal and adaptive approach." He had to handle the client "with the harsh firmness of the law enforcement officials at some times and with the amicable persuasiveness of the salesman at others. The skillful negotiator . . . learned to adapt his approach to the shifting demands of the situation" (p. 148). (Blau is not drawing distinctions among negotiation, manipulation, and persuasion, but only between all of them and the coercion of the law.) One such situation arises when a client offers a bribe after the agent has uncovered violations of the law. The client typically begins with a "feeler"—for instance, "Mr. Smith asked in a low voice if they could talk about this informally." Typically, too, the agent rejects the feeler or bribe itself. There is an unequivocal rule: Offers of bribes must be reported to higher levels for possible prosecution. But there is an unofficial norm among the agents that they will not report such bribe offers. Although clients recurrently offered bribes and some offers were very direct, "all agents were strongly opposed to reporting such offers for prosecution, regardless of their attitudes toward clients" (p. 148). They "considered it *wrong*" to report the bribes. In fact, this taboo on reporting attempted bribes, Blau asserts, was the strongest unofficial norm of the group. Questioned about this by him, they "defended the righteousness of the norm in emotional language," saying, for example, that they did not like squealers. Indeed, Blau equates this unofficial norm—perhaps loosely, but nonetheless clearly—with being as strong a sanction as the mores: "Strong mores are rarely violated. Just two cases of bribes had been reported and prosecuted in the entire agency in recent years" (p. 149). Only one agent had violated the unofficial norm, possibly because he was no longer a member of the agent group, as he had been promoted to another assignment. The second violator now questioned his own wisdom in having reported an attempted bribery; he had only reported it because of the repeated and insistent offer and because it had been made in the presence of third persons—and he said he would not do so again because, in fact, he had been ostracized thereafter by other agents. (It is worth noting that the other agents felt their colleague had really acted as an agent provocateur, egging on and then trapping the client. They were wrong but did not know it.) Agents generally felt that it was not, as one of them said, "right to punish a businessman because he does something that every businessman has to do in order to stay in business. . . . It's the fault of our system. . . . So I don't think he should be punished. . . . I feel very strongly about [bribes], but I don't think it's fair to punish an employer; he has to do this" (p. 150).

Now, this agency administered quite complex legal regulations, which an honest businessman, agents felt, could quite inadvertently violate. The agent's job was to help them correct their mistakes. Violators sometimes were ordered to stop their illegal practices, but only a minor proportion of them, "typically willful repeated offenders, were brought into court to be penalized for having broken the law" (p. 151). So this tolerant attitude was reflected in the agent's views of bribes and in his conciliatory approach toward the client. If he had treated them as culprits, "he would have invited their refusal to cooperate." But his "major weapon in negotiations," Blau adds, "was the disadvantaged position of the employer who had violated the law and was confronted by an official representative of the government. . . . The skillful agent . . . could exploit his discomfort to obtain voluntary agreements in many cases" (p. 151).

And, in fact, if the agent were offered a bribe, this gave him a special tactical advantage: The client had compounded his guilt by violating still another law. "Agents exploited this situation to strengthen their position in negotiations"—rather openly coercive ones, we might add. By "putting the briber in his place," rejecting his offer firmly, and telling him what he really had to do, the agent was more easily able to get the client to make the necessary retroactive adjustment in his business practices.

This facilitation of the agent's work (receiving but not reporting offers of bribes) "can only explain why this [reporting] was rarely done, but not why there was a social norm prohibiting it" (p. 152). Blau suggests that the norm's existence meant that reporting the bribe offer would have a disadvantage for the whole group, while not reporting it had an advantage for the group. The second point has to do with the tendency in hierarchical organizations of the peer group to react negatively to "excessive compliance" of subordinates to superiors. So the "first social function" of the norm was to stop overeager colleagues from getting out of line that way— "the protection of the reputations and promotion changes that agents had established in the course of performing their regular duties" (p. 152). A second function of the unofficial norm was "that it inhibited behavior in investigations that was detrimental to future operations." Blau cites one case of detrimental investigation, noting that an agent had reported a bribe offer, evidently "not to improve his record of successful negotiations, but to impress his superiors in a different way" (p. 153). Hence the client's hostility did not stop him. In the future, however, when any other agent is assigned to this client, the agent is in for trouble: He will not easily induce the client "to make *voluntary* adjustments." So, argues Blau, if attempted bribes were frequently prosecuted, it would be difficult, if not impossible, to get these important voluntary concessions. So, Blau concludes that the taboo, "although contrary to an official rule, not only facilitated the task of agents but also contributed to the achievement of the goals of this agency" (p. 153). God *does* watch over this functioning functional world!

Blau's functionalist position is, of course, open to most of the many standard attacks on that general position. My purpose, however, is not to criticize functionalism, but rather (1) to note how Blau handles negotiation behavior and (2) to explore a few implications of his functionalist approach to bureaucratic order. We can begin by noting that he focuses analytically on the negotiations between agents and client, but he touches on negotiation among agents only descriptively, and spottily at that, throughout his book. Let us look first at the latter consideration, since the kinds of agreements among agents will surely affect their negotiation dealings with clients.

A simple way to get at agent negotiations is to convert Blau's discussion (in another chapter, pp. 99–116) of consultation among the agents of Department Y into the language of negotiation. Blau reports that each agent needed a considerable level of knowledge and competence to carry out his tasks, while failure at them was counted heavily against his record. Evaluation rested on results rather than on his specific operations. That "put a premium on the ability to make decisions independently" (p. 103). Faced with difficult cases, the agent—by organizational "rule"—was required to go to his supervisor; actually, agents were "reluctant to reveal their inability to solve a problem . . . for fear that their ratings would be adversely affected" (p. 105). The consequence was that the agents averaged five contacts per hour with colleagues, although in fact they worked independently on their assigned cases. Aside from genuinely private conversations, many collegial contacts involved talk about work. These varied from simple requests for information to consultations about complex problems. In the latter instances, certain patterns of consultation showed up. Thus, most agents had one or two regular partners with whom they discussed problems. Although one partnership involved a more competent agent generally advising the less competent, each member of a pair habitually consulted with the other. There were four agents without partners, and three of them were very popular consultants—they participated so widely in "the exchange of advice" (p. 108) that they spent relatively little time with any given colleague.

Blau remarks that a consultation can be conceived of as "an exchange of values," since both gain and lose something by the transaction. The man who asks for advice gets it without revealing his difficulties to a supervisor; at the same time, "he implicitly pays his respect to the superior proficiency of his colleague" (p. 108). The consultant gains prestige but pays the price of taking time from his work and some disruption of his work. The really popular consultants also gained considerable peer-group status from their consultants. But those who asked excessively for consultations too often ran the risk of being turned down. There were also partnerships involving mutual consultation, which "virtually eliminated the danger of rejections as well as the status threat implicit in asking for help" (p. 109). Mutual consultation partnerships also enabled an agent to save his most difficult cases for the most respected consultants, thus reducing the chances of his request for advice being turned down. There were also consultations in disguise; for instance, the conversation at lunch during which information and opinions were exchanged.

Blau concludes that consultation had the "functions" (that is, consequences) of making effective law enforcement possible, since it improved the quality of agents' decisions, as well as making an aggregate of agents into a cohesive group. If we amend the latter conclusion to "contributing to" a generally more cooperative, less competitive group, then doubtless he is correct in his conclusions. He can be viewed also as having given us evidence that a network of agreements had developed among particular agents based on a history of implicit (known, but not openly discussed as such) negotiations. In fact, Blau suggests that a basic reorganization had rather recently taken place in the agency, and so the fact that consultations were tolerated by the supervisors "suggests that their unofficial character was incidental to their relative newness" (p. 116). His data (and that is all we have to go on) also suggest that supervisors knew about the practice—and perhaps about particular consultation partnerships—hence, some sort of implicit negotiation had also transpired between supervisors and their subordinates. The data also suggest a history of initiated negotiations and accepted or rejected negotiations, with shifts of negotiation relationships over time. But the important point for us is that complex negotiated agreements had evolved among the agents.

Now, why Blau does not refer to the generally agreed-on propriety of consultation as an unofficial norm is unclear. But in what way would it be different from the unofficial norm against reporting bribe offers by clients? And why just assume that there is a norm—why not think about a general negotiated agreement among agents (arrived at over time) not to report those offers of bribes? What Blau has done is to posit a norm, then to arrange his data so as to show its existence, and then to posit two social functions for the norm. For the first function (to stop overeager colleagues from getting out of line in complying with supervisors), he offers no evidence whatever. For the second (inhibiting behavior detrimental to future dealings with a client), we need not necessarily assume "a social function." Alternatively, we can regard this behavior as inhibited by a standing agreement, based on past experiences, that reporting offers of bribes makes matters unnecessarily difficult—usually for another agent.

That perspective leaves the way open for—indeed, leads directly to—asking research questions about the standing agreement: How did it develop? What is its processual history? Blau gives no history; he merely refers to the norm's existence. He makes no queries about its evolution. Then there is the question, "How does the agreement keep alive and not break down?" Blau does not ask that question, perhaps for three reasons: First, he is focused on the norm's functions. Second, although he is interested in organizational development, his general approach is neither historical nor evolutionary, so apparently it does not much direct his interview questions backward in time. And, third, he looks for enforcement of group norms to a conglomerate collection of mechanisms—acceptance by all members of the group, endeavors to conceal violations, myths that develop about the advantages of conforming, and ostracism, which is the penalty for violations of the most basic norms.

Aside from the evolution and maintenance of such an important general agreement, we ought to ask questions about what amendments or transformations would appear in such an agreement; for surely it will not live forever. If we do not have enough time to pursue that inquiry, at least the question should be raised analytically. Blau does trace some consequences of the rare, past cases of violation of the bribery norm, but what he misses entirely, of course, are the processes by which newcomers are initiated into a standing agreement (an agreement not made by them but to which they are expected to adhere). Said another way, those processes pertain to the maintenance of the agreement.

Also we should not be surprised that violations of the norm do not seem to lead to significant changes either in departmental relations or the larger organization. This is all the more surprising since Blau's main aim is to pinpoint and explain organizational change. He does somewhat better in that regard elsewhere in his book; but the emphasis on norms and on such allied concepts as cohesion and authority tends to hobble his developmental focus and, in fact, makes him especially attentive to the structural conditions for things being what they *are* and to the immediate consequences of their being what they *are*. In the end, a norm such as the "no reporting of attempted bribery" is analyzed largely in terms of its contribution to organizational efficiency and group cohesiveness—an analysis not appreciably different from any number of studies of informal organization that preceded his and that he faults for not going deeply enough into organizational development.

That said, it seems rather unnecessary now to analyze closely what actually is reported as going on in the negotiations between the agents and their clients. Perhaps all that is necessary is to indicate that various negotiation dimensions (in relation to relevant social structural conditions as discussed in Part Two) can handle those transactions. Among the salient dimensions are the matter of boundaries within which negotiations can legitimately occur; the fact that these are repeated negotiations with possibly differentially experienced negotiators and often a changing agent representative; the balance of power, which usually is very strongly in favor of the agent, because of his potential recourse to the option of a court trial; and some ambiguity about the agent's dual representativeness in the transaction—acting for the agency at large, but, at least in the matter of "no reporting of attempted bribes," acting as a representative of his collegial group. Also, the stakes respectively seem to be—in a trade-off—a success for the agent's record, plus a promissory note for future cooperation from the client, as contrasted with the latter's escaping legal punishment or possibly even a court trial.

Having noted all this, it seems pointless to insist that following through on such an analysis would lead to a number of specific questions, pertaining not merely to the mechanics of the negotiations themselves but also to the richly complex network of negotiations among the agents. Imagine only how the consultations might relate to the agent-client negotiations and vice versa, let alone how the punishment of an occasional "violator" agent affects negotiated agreements about him, his behavior in numerous future situations, and, of course, the behavior of other agents. It might be added that the analysis raises questions about the conditions under which an agent breaks the general agreement, rather than merely about the fact that we regard such a transgression as rather accidental.

Finally, a theoretical focus on negotiation raises the issue, what kind of phenomenon, anyhow, is bureaucratic development and change? One specific criticism usually directed against Blau's kind of functionalism is that he puts an organizational structure "out there" and poses it against an individual who is rather passive. It is true that Blau's agents are active people, enforcing and breaking the norms, including informal ones that they are busily either keeping secret from or maintaining a mutual pretense about with their superiors. Yet they seem not to be very actively shaping the organization's development.

In short, the limits to action are relatively preordained or at least drastically narrowed by Blau's functionalist approach. He cannot even ask to what extent clients maneuver around the rules and so possibly shape some of the organization's features, if only indirectly. With this theoretical perspective, one also cannot really ask (or at least would be unlikely to do so) about relationships that might obtain among the various principal options facing the actors—or about the combinations of options (such as coercive negotiation or negotiation in conjunction with coercion)—in an organization where the "bureaucratic order" seems to reflect much enforcement of and appeal to organizational and legal rules.

Chapter Three

• • • • • • • • • • • • • • • • • • • •
• •
• •

Alvin Gouldner: Two Types of Bureaucratic Order

• • • • • • • • • • • • • • • • • • • •
• •
• •

*L*ike Blau, Alvin Gouldner was also interested, throughout his *Industrial Bureaucracy* (1954a), in qualifying Max Weber's account of bureaucracy and in looking at organizational change. (He, like Blau, had studied with Merton.) Gouldner singles out two aspects of Weber's writings on bureaucracy for specific qualification. First, Weber rather cavalierly had bracketed two kinds of rules—imposed and agreed-on rules. Gouldner, however, anticipates that how rules are initiated will affect an organization's characteristics, including its effectiveness. Weber apparently thought of bureaucracy "as a Janus-faced organization, looking two ways at once"—administration based on expertise and administration based on discipline. Thus Weber really described two types rather than a single type of bureaucracy. In Gouldner's words (1954a, p. 24), "One of these may be termed the 'representative' form of bureaucracy, based on rules established by agreement, rules which are technically justified and administered by specially qualified personnel and to which consent is given voluntarily." The second form is "the 'punishment-centered bureaucracy'" (that is, coercive) based on the "imposition of rules and on obedience for its own sake."

A second, related qualification of Weber is necessary because of Weber's tendency to assume that "the ends of different strata within a bureaucracy" were identical, or at least highly similar; thus he did not distinguish between them. But it is necessary to specify the ends of different strata—to ask, "To *whom* did the rules have to be useful, if bureaucratic authority was to be useful?" and "In terms of *whose* goals were the rules a rational device? Whose end did they have to realize if the bureaucracy was to operate *effectively?*" In short, "Do the bureaucratic rules prove equally *efficient* for realizing the ends of all strata in an organization?" Those are Gouldner's specific queries (p. 20). His larger aim is to clarify some of the "social processes leading to different degrees of bureaucracy"—that is, the issue of organizational change.

I have singled out this research of Gouldner's, although it represents another functionalist approach to social order, precisely because of his two explicitly expressed interests in bureaucracy. First, he is concerned with the relationship of coercion ("punishment centered") to negotiation ("established by agreement"). Second, he is concerned with that relationship as, in turn, it relates to differential intraorganizational interests—which surely present the respective parties with a multiplicity of options for acting. In addition, Gouldner really depicts an organization in the process of change, with data ample enough to allow good guesses as to the consequence of choices of action modes by those respective parties.

What Gouldner gives in his monograph is a description and analysis of what happened in an industrial plant when a new manager succeeded another, who had died. The latter had been a local man; the new manager was imported from outside the locality. Top management instructed the new one to tighten up the running of the plant and to improve production. Working conditions under the preceding manager are characterized by Gouldner as adding up to "The Indulgency Pattern." Subheadings in a chapter thus titled show

Gouldner's conception of life under the old manager: " 'They Ain't Very Strict,' " "Rational Discipline," "The Second Chance," "Job Shift" (relatively easy), "Government Jobs" (leniency in personal use of material and machinery), "Flexible Application of Rules," and "Management Responsiveness" (to the worker). In sum, bureaucratic rules were comparatively few in number and not strictly enforced. The indulgency pattern is, then, "a connected set of concrete judgments and underlying sentiments" disposing workers to react favorably both to the plant and to their supervisors. It is an important source of job satisfaction for them.

After the new manager arrived, there was a great increase of organizational complexity. How could this be explained? Gouldner explains that the manager was to play the role of a successor. He was on trial himself—he had to get production increased—he had to make good. He had been promoted from a smaller plant and was both grateful to higher executives for his promotion and accepted their expectations that he would quickly improve production at his new job. Unhampered by commitments to the informal understandings established in the plant, the successor arrived with a disposition toward "rational, efficiency-oriented action." He needed to control or eliminate the resistance by "the old lieutenants" to his plan and to handle the resistance that his first steps toward increasing efficiency had developed among the workers.

According to Gouldner, the manager had two principal options: to act on and through the informal system of relations or to utilize the formal system of organization in the plant. The first option was difficult to implement because his very program "violated the workers' informal sentiments." Besides, "successful manipulation of the informal network requires a knowledge of the intimate events and sentiments" (p. 85), which the successor could not have. So he began to flit about the plant, using a tactic of close supervision. He also made strategic replacements in the supervisory ranks but was somewhat limited in doing this by a variety of contingencies. Also, since there was a breakdown in communication upward to him, he understandably moved toward the elaboration of a system of paper reports to keep on top of things. And he began to emphasize adherence to rules, for he could not rely on using the informal system of controls. In other words, succession tends to lead to "a surge of bureaucratic development, particularly in the direction of bureaucratic rules" (p. 85).

That is pretty much Gouldner's descriptive-analytic story. Also important for us is a chapter titled "A Provisional Analysis of Bureaucratic Types," in which he distinguishes among several kinds of rules. First, there are mock bureaucratic rules; for instance, the state rule about not smoking on the job. Everybody, from top to bottom in the plant, seemed to regard that rule as a dead letter. Ordinarily, nobody attempted to enforce it. In fact, "their joint violation . . . and their cooperative effort to outwit the 'outsider,' the insurance company, allied them as fellow 'conspirators' " (p. 183). Second, there were rules that characterize a representative bureaucracy; for instance, the safety rules. The safety operations involved work that was more bureaucratically organized than any other in the plant. The rules were more numerous and complex than those governing other activities, and a "complex system of 'paperwork' and 'reports' . . . was centered on the safety program" (p. 187). These were rules of "representative bureaucracy," because the workers participated daily in their administration; also, management attempted to elicit such participation but appeared not to be deliberately manipulative. Weber's efficiency explanation of the growth of bureaucratic rules, Gouldner remarks, manifestly makes no sense in the instance of these safety rules. Rather, Gouldner hypothesizes that the growth developed because management pushed to bureaucratize this area (since the managers believe workers are careless or ignorant of safety requirements), combined with the low degree of worker resistance—amended by Gouldner's emphasis that this explanation is "obviously a simplification . . . *workers also* initiated a bureaucratic organization of safety work, because they believed that management sometimes failed in its safety obligations" (p. 206). In other words, both sides found those rules made sense.

A third type of rule arises "where responses to deviations take the form of *punishments.*" Two subtypes are distinguishable, "depending on *who* exercises the punishment and who receives it" (1954a, p. 207). If management utilizes punishments, that is the "disciplinary pattern." If the workers subject management to punishments when a rule is broken, that is the "grievance pattern." At this particular plant, the workers and their union held strongly to a bidding system for the posting of job vacancies and new jobs. Management responded to this with considerable resistance, withholding full support and sometimes deliberately evading the rules; but these rules were strongly supported by most workers, and there was grievance machinery for achieving conformity to these rules. An example of management's disciplinary rules was that there should be no absenteeism. Notably, both of these subtypes of punishment-centered bureaucratic rules were attended by considerable conflict and tension between management and the workers.

What can we say about Gouldner's attempt to account for the increasing degree of bureaucracy at this industrial plant? Our commentary, as usual, will be related to the handling or ignoring of negotiation aspects of data. The first—if relatively minor—point that can be made is that, in his effort to contrast the presuccession with the postsuccession period, Gouldner probably tends to underestimate the bureaucratic aspects of the former period. After all, the heavily bureaucratic safety program and the workers' bidding system existed before succession, as did the managerial insistence on no absenteeism and other managerial rules. To Gouldner, as well as to the participants, some of these bureaucratic features may not have *felt* bureaucratic, because so much agreement was involved— notably, on the mock and representative bureaucratic rules.

Thus, on the no-smoking rule, management actually forewarned workers before the fire inspector's occasional visits, in return for which they were supposed temporarily to stop smoking. The implicit trade-off: "friendly and cooperative attitudes toward management were evoked insofar as management *withheld* enforcement" (p. 186) of the rule. Again, concerning the representative rules concerning safety, formal as well as informal agreements existed: The formal was embedded in a union-management contract clause that "The company agrees to all such safety devices." The differential stakes in more informal negotiations are sensed in Gouldner's summarization that "In brief, management tended to support safety work when this aided production and thereby garnered status gains for themselves. They resisted safety efforts when these were seen as increasing status losses" (p. 196). (An instance of the former: A special exam was supposed to be given to job applicants before they entered the mining part of the plant, but the exam consumed time, and workers were badly needed, so the manager decided "you have to relax the rules sometimes.")

Let us, however, assume that Gouldner is correct and that bureaucratic rules increased very appreciably because of the succession. Gouldner sees the new manager as having had two possible options: to act through the informal system of relations or to act through the formal system of organization. But really, says Gouldner, the first option was closed, in effect, partly because Gouldner equates it with "drawing on his resources as a 'person.' " (Personal resources are exemplified by such tactics as be-a-good-fellow appeals and proffers of friendship to the workers.) For a sociologist, that is an extremely psychological conception of why the successor could make little or no headway against the existing informal relationships (even though Gouldner explicitly eschews psychological explanations) and so was limited to the second option. We need not assume that the manager could only have taken the first option if—given the other limiting contingencies—he was more skilled at "personal touches." Change any number of structural contingencies, and the potential equation will change. We know that the pressure was on Peele, the new manager, to act quickly and that he was on trial as a manager. Suppose he could have acted much more slowly? Suppose, besides more time, he had been given other resources to reach his goal, such as additional men or better equipment? Suppose he had had no pressure on him to increase production? Suppose he had had other kinds of resources on which to draw, such as a very friendly lieutenant who could have mediated between him and the workers? Or if he had had a close kinsman or two among the workers? Or— a very important qualification—if he had had considerable previous experience in a very similar kind of managerial post? And finally, suppose the preceding manager had been demoted rather than died?—presumably then the workers' resistance would have been even greater. Or what if in this plant there had not been "a widespread conception of the proper line of succession to the position of plant manager" by way of "the supervisor of the 'board building' "—so that Peele had not been viewed as an illegitimate successor? Or if, nonetheless, he wisely had followed through on his predecessor's negotiations with subordinates and promoted those who had been promised promotions? "When Doug was here, he asked me [about becoming foreman], and I said I would like it very much and would appreciate it. . . . He asked me, but then he died and we got this new man, Mr. Peele" (1954a, p. 74).

Each of the foregoing structural considerations (and more) bears on this particular successor's difficulties in perceiving that his goals must be reached through formal and often coercive rules. Each affects the negotiations initiated by others he will reject or how he will handle them if acceptable. In not noting this, Gouldner overlooks—except descriptively and in his interview quotes—the relevance of an undoubtedly rich texture of agreements, understandings, and arrangements, on which Peele could have drawn for resources and which he ignored to his peril. (As Elihu Gerson has put it, "Resources are dependent on the state of prior negotiation arrangements"—private communication.) Peele challenged a negotiated order and ran afoul of it—two years later, it brought about his demotion, when he got involved in a stalemate with the union over a wage dispute (we learn of this demotion in another book by Gouldner, *The Wildcat Strike*, 1954b).

Do I need to reiterate that Gouldner's data suggest the great extent of expectable and ongoing negotiation at the plant? " 'If the foreman doesn't work well with us, we don't give him as good work as we can. . . . I just don't care, I let things slide' " (p. 160). " 'Well, if that's the way he wants it, that's the way he wants it. But I'll be damned if I put in any overtime when things get rough and they'd like us to' " (p. 175). Or, Gouldner's own statement that, paradoxically, the formal rules give supervisors something "with which they could 'bargain' " in order to secure informal cooperation from the workers. Punishment might be withheld, the rules not enforced, providing the workers were cooperative. But such negotiations are far out on the fringes of Gouldner's attention. Consequently, he does not integrate those negotiation phenomena into his analyses. The closest he gets is in recognizing that agreements are reached about mock and representative rules, but he thinks of the agreement as a product that supports violation of or adherence to a bureaucratic rule; he does not think of negotiation as a process. For him, the primary phenomena are the violating or adhering—not the negotiating about whether *to* violate or support the rules. And, of course, he is assuming that these rule adherences and violations have consequences—that is, "functions"—for the organization, although, unlike Blau, he is not explicitly concerned with rule functions.

However, to return to the manager's increasing imposition of bureaucratic rules: In my view, the real issue is that he did not know how to negotiate successfully in order to increase the plant's production. Therefore, what he did was either to use certain tactics in place of negotiating or to utilize negotiations that involved explicit or implicit threats of punishment. The result was a cycle of events that only his removal as manager could break. Presumably this cycle involved an elaboration of covert negotiated arrangements among the workers in order to circumvent Peele's imposed rules— I say "presumably," because Gouldner offers no data on that particular set of consequences.

Finally, I would suggest that an alternative to talking merely or primarily about rules (whether imposed or agreed-on—a perfectly good distinction) is to talk of the behavior of the manager and the workers: Some of that behavior is more bureaucratic, as well as coercive, and some less. The manager's rules were not "out there" but are something that he *chose* to attempt to impose and enforce because of the conditions noted earlier. If we took such a perspective, then we would actually be able to research how those increasing number of bureaucratic rules did indeed increase—from the moment that others of Peele's tactics seemed to him to fail until his final reliance on bureaucratic tactics (coercive, appealing to authority, and so on) in some situations (but on abeyance in others)—as well as how he was able to negotiate with, or meet the negotiations of, his subordinates along more informal or at least less bureaucratic lines.

Also, we could ask questions about the relationships of negotiation to the manipulation of events, to attempts at persuading opponents and allies, and so on. Not only would we get a better purchase on the processes whereby bureaucratic behavior increased, but eventually we would get quite a different picture of what this organization was like in its pre-Peele and post-Peele days. One would also be directed to explore the implications of the difference between bureaucratic rules and behavior qua coercion ("imposed," "enforced") and qua noninformal but official (written directives).

That is not to say that everything in such an organization is negotiated! But even things laid down, imposed, are negotiable; after all, each person at Gouldner's factory has choices (can even quit the place), since it is a voluntary organization and not completely a "total institution."

In sum, Gouldner's version of functionalism has led him both to depict the bureaucratic order and its change as he did as well as to foreclose on interpreting data that raise questions about his functionalist assumptions.

Chapter Four

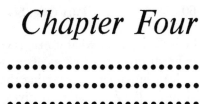

Edward Banfield: Pluralistic Theory, Urban Politics, and Political Influence

One variety of political theory—
theory about the nature of political order—is pluralism. Social
scientists who study American politics are very frequently adherents
of pluralistic premises, carrying them explicitly—but perhaps more
often implicitly—into their interpretations and studies of American
society. Frequently their attention is drawn to political bargains,
deals, and other types of negotiation among the many interest
groups maneuvering toward their differing goals through political
activity.

Among the pluralists is Edward Banfield, whose well-known
version of pluralistic theory is carefully developed in a book (1962)
on "political influence" and the way it "works in a large American
city." His interpretation of how influences work in Chicago should

59

be instructive for what it may reveal about pluralistic conceptions of political order, as well as about where those conceptions are likely to lead in studies interpreting that order. I use the term *order* advisedly: Banfield aims to give an understanding of how things work in a presumed pluralistic society, since, after all, how things work is not at all self-evident. In Banfield's version of pluralism, negotiations are necessary because a multiplicity of interest groups must deal with one another, accepting as they do the framework provided by commonly shared American values. But how Banfield actually integrates negotiation as such into his substantive theory of influence and how he relates negotiation to other modes of action can be severely questioned. So, perhaps, can his pluralistic assumptions.

By *influence,* Banfield means the "ability to get others to act, think, or feel as one intends" (1962, p. 3). This definition is followed by three examples, of which the latter two are instances of what one would generally term *negotiation:* Thus, a mayor persuades voters to approve a bond issue; a businessman's promises of support induce a mayor to take action; a precinct captain controls votes by doing favors. "Any cooperative activity—and so any organization, formal or informal, ephemeral or lasting—may be viewed as a system of influence." Such organizations include government. Thus, to study patterns of influence "whereby action is concerted in public matters" is to study government.

Banfield approaches his analysis of political influence through six case studies, each portraying a major controversial issue fought out by Chicagoans. Since all the events evolved during the course of Banfield's research, he was able to gather good interview data from the principals, supplemented by relevant documents. We shall look at his case approach later; first, we need to know what Banfield has made of the cases. For our purposes, his key chapter is "The Process of Influence" (pp. 263–285), which appears after the presented cases and is meant to interpret certain of their features.

According to Banfield, civic controversies arise not because politicians try to get votes, nor because of differences between group interests nor of ideology, nor because of hidden maneuvers by a power elite; the controversies usually arise because the heads of organizations perceive an advantage to be gained by changing some situation. So they propose changes that other organizational heads see as threatening and hence oppose. That is how most controversies seem to get generated, and Banfield's cases, he notes, fit that picture very well. The organizations that play leading roles in these civic controversies are profit-making enterprises (department stores, newspapers), public agencies that give free service (the welfare agencies), and public or semi-public agencies that sell services (hospitals, universities). The heads of such organizations tend to be important figures, and in many of the cases studied by Banfield they are career civil servants.

When those controversial issues arise, the chief executive of the affected organization does not go directly to the appropriate political official or head to obtain satisfaction. Rather, he uses intermediaries who present the organization's position to the politician, to the newspapers, the civic associations, and to the small but "important body of citizens" who are concerned with civic affairs. The intermediaries are prestigious citizens (what the press terms "civic leaders"), whose links with the organization give weight and legitimacy to their demands. Sometimes these civic leaders merely have lent their names to the organization; sometimes as "co-opted leaders," they have at least nominal control over the organizations, although a paid staff member often does the work and develops most or much of the policy. Sometimes, when special skills are needed during the public controversy, important outsiders are coopted "on an *ad hoc* basis." And sometimes the intermediary may be a civic association, such as the NAACP or the League of Women Voters; civic associations may pass resolutions, issue press releases, testify at hearings, and make direct representations to politicians pro and con proposals advanced by the affected organizations. And sometimes, since a civic organization may not act because of fear of alienating some of its supporters, *ad hoc* bodies are created to do the work of the civic bodies.

When a controversial issue arises, the civic leaders who approach the relevant political head do not find him eager to make a decision. He knows that the aims of any organization are apt to be opposed by another; so he waits to see what kinds of coalitions will form, the positions they will formulate, the strengths they can muster. "The longer the evil hour of decision can be postponed, the better he likes it; he has nothing to lose as long as the argument continues and any settlement he imposes will make him enemies" (p. 270). He is further supported in his delay by the general "Chicago view" of politics, namely that any given policy should be formulated by the interests involved, rather than by the political head or his staff. So the involved parties should work out for themselves the "best" solution (usually a compromise). The proper role of the political head is to see that all the major affected interests are represented, that residual interests (that is, "the general public") are not entirely disregarded, and that "no interest suffers unduly." Hence, Banfield asserts, the political head will ratify almost any proposal already agreed to by the main contending parties. If there is no such agreement, he will continue to delay. Therefore, the major contenders tend to settle out of court. Consequently, the principal civic leaders are "constantly engaged in negotiations with each other, and skill in negotiation is an important base of influence among them" (p. 272).

Out-of-court settlements are not always reached, so eventually the political head is forced to make a decision. In imposing a settlement, he deals "only with those aspects of the issue which cannot be put off." He avoids settling general principles or larger issues, confining himself to the particular, concrete problem in focus. And his decision rests neither on the intrinsic merits of a position nor on his own personal beliefs, but on the principle that all parties should get something "and no one should be hurt very much." He is satisfied, in other words, to patch things up temporarily—so the basic controversy usually continues, "renewing itself in a slightly different form."

In offering negotiated settlements (and Banfield sees them as such) to the political head or in presenting one side of the issue still under dispute, the organizational representatives usually attempt to claim that they represent a broad section of the community, since generally, in making a settlement, the political head will favor widely representative interests. He judges the representative interests and the representativeness of a position partly by the number and character of civic associations supporting it. In the end, he "sees before him a particular configuration of support and opposition, finding in it clues by which to form an estimate of how the matter is received by the public at large" (p. 276).

Banfield closes his discussion of the decision-making process by a fairly lengthy discussion of the political head's tactics for getting approval for his settlement from various civic leaders, including his using certain friendly civic leaders who function as intermediaries, negotiators, publicists of policy, and even as a kind of cover who give him the requisite privacy for doing "his work."

With regard to the big controversial issues, Banfield clearly regards the head's work as a kind of above-the-battle, last-minute ratification or making of settlements. Of course, the politician may take public credit for the settlement, but in a sense its terms are made through the multitude of complex negotiations—negotiations that are both cooperative (among allies) and antagonistic (between opponents). Banfield's analysis implies that Chicago and its metropolitan region is a decentralized, pluralistic order—no central figure or power elite makes the important policy decisions. (Indeed, in his next chapter, "The Mythology of Influence," he argues just that point.) Banfield also implies that those who win the controversial battles probably deserve to win them, in the sense that those with the most resources—including political and negotiational skills and civic influence—will come out best. Those with less resources will not win (unless joined in a winning coalition), but they will get something that approximates what they deserve by virtue of their particular resources. We might characterize this general view of pluralistic "influence" (or power?) as a *moving equilibrium*: *equilibrium* because things are more or less in balance and *moving* because the balance is continually changing. A powerful political leader, such as Daley (and even lesser figures, who nevertheless have considerable power in their own bailiwicks), functions—in this metaphor—as a kind of gyroscope, who by his delaying tactics, shrewd reading of cues of adversary strengths, and decisive "settlement" action at the appropriate moment (and not too many mistakes of settlement or timing) keeps the whole, complex metropolitan game in dynamic equilibrium.

Some readers may sense that this view is supportive of the status quo, taking what "is" or "must be" as the best of all possible worlds because it is the way the real world works. More important to our own inquiry is whether Banfield's "process of influence" is genuinely in line with his own data. When we scrutinize the case studies, we see that his general picture of complex negotiation among organizations and their representatives (including the civic leaders) is accurate enough; also that no central agent or agency does or can impose a quick settlement. We also see that Banfield oversimplifies the various processes of influence and far overgeneralizes his view of the political head's above-the-battle role. A genuine analysis of negotiations would, I suggest, have prevented both oversimplification and overgeneralization.

A close look at a single case study will help to show the shortcomings of Banfield's interpretation of influence. In his narrative about the controversy over the Chicago Transit Authority (CTA), Banfield first notes that after a decade of operation, "something had to be done about the CTA"—it was in financial trouble, and that was widely known. Banfield lines up a general list of adversaries for and against a financial subsidy for the CTA and then gets his story moving. It contains much explicit, descriptive material about negotiations—but it is a rather different story from that told in his analytic chapter on the process of influence. In fact, we would all recognize the descriptive story as a not unusual kind of civic battle, decided on, at least in its last phases, through the state legislative process.

The CTA's resources came almost wholly from fares, and the number of passengers actually was dropping. The mayor of Chicago, Daley, was very eager to avert a fare increase. In a strictly legal sense, Daley had no responsibility for the CTA, but Chicagoans naturally linked him with it—he'd take some blame for a fare increase. Also, Daley believed the future of Chicago depended somewhat on mass transportation—if people shifted to autos, that would make for more congestion, and he'd get blamed some for that, too. Moreover, more auto traffic meant less business for Chicago and more for the suburbs. In favor generally of a state subsidy for the CTA, Banfield notes, were a variety of business interests in central Chicago, as well as the daily newspapers. A fare increase to support a state subsidy would not, however, be favored by many of the passengers, and certainly no subsidy itself would be favored by auto drivers, by industries that heavily utilized the highways, by suburban citizens and businesses, and by downstate citizens.

The big controversy got underway essentially when Gunlock, chairman of the CTA board (and its dominant member), a career civil servant, sounded Daley out on CTA's plan for expansion. That was early in 1956. The mayor requested estimates, to be submitted in the autumn. That done, in October he asked for plans about financing, and a month later a brief policy statement was given to him, to the governor, and to others. The statement suggested that the subsidy money was to come largely from highway funds and possibly from a property tax. Adverse reaction from a pro-CTA newspaper and from the mayor caused the board quickly to drop the property tax idea. It recommended instead a tax of one cent per gallon of gas.

Early in January—and two days before the state legislature convened—the governor, mayor, Gunlock and others met in the first of several conferences on metropolitan mass transportation. The meeting was focused on the suggestion of citizens from two Republican suburban counties. They wanted the CA & E, a private railroad line, to make a deal with Cook County: to give one half mile of its right of way to the county for allowing construction of an expressway to Chicago's downtown. Unless the railroad and county came to terms, condemnation procedures on the railroad would be necessary, while work on the expressway would be delayed. (The railroad had for some time tried to drop its passenger service.) The governor already had proposed publicly that the state buy the CA & E with highway funds and turn it over to the CTA. In the next two months, three more meetings took place; finally Gunlock presented a plan for operation of the railroad by the CTA, and the governor agreed that the CTA be subsidized. Although the mayor was in favor of a gas tax, to raise the subsidy funds, the governor said, "I don't believe I could sell that downstate. I just wouldn't have a chance" (p. 104). But Gunlock felt the governor would support the subsidy if only a means could be found that would not start a major fight. Not long after, the governor, the mayor, and Gunlock announced an agreement that amounted not to a state subsidy but only to the plan that each county of over 100,000 people be allowed to impose a gas tax of not more than one cent a gallon. As Banfield remarks (p. 105), "The governor had not yielded much. . . . If the people of Cook County wanted to tax themselves for the system's support, they were at liberty to do so. . . . Mayor Daley, however, could claim some advantage from the plan. It might avoid a fare increase."

The announcement drew reactions from various interested parties—and precipitated much lobbying activity and behind-the-scenes negotiating. For instance, the National Highway Users Conference pulled two lobbyists from Washington and sent them to Springfield. One surprising event (to the governor) was that the commuters of the CA & E, although desiring to keep the railroad alive, were much opposed to the gas tax. The subsidy, they told the governor, was the responsibility of the state. Meanwhile it developed that the Central Area Committee (of businessmen) were split on the issue—somewhat to Daley's surprise, for he thought he had understood, from their representative, that they were for the tax; indeed, they now seemed to favor postponement of all plans for at least two years and had nothing at all to say about the source of a subsidy. Their statement to the mayor actually was a delicate compromise managed by a skilled negotiator member. The Chicago Association of Commerce and Industry also split on the issue.

Meanwhile, down at the state legislature some curious events were transpiring. The majority leaders essentially came out against the draft bills on the CTA. As Banfield says, this was a remarkable development because they were in close touch with and loyal to the governor. Actually, he "had made plain to them that he did not regard the CTA bills as 'must' legislation. He thought they were sound and should be passed. He hoped they would see fit to support them. But he was not going to insist on them" (p. 117). He had known the legislative leaders were against the subsidy yet "had not brought them into negotiation . . . thus ensuring that the operation would have their support."

To make a long story short, there was much maneuvering in the legislative corridors. Gunlock himself took to lobbying. Then the Democratic leader supported a Republican-initiated move to create a legislative commission on metropolitan mass transportation. The governor appointed a Republican as legislative chairman, an auto salesman who earlier had helped pilot CTA legislation through the house. This chairman now acted vigorously to bring out compromise bills—to release CTA from city and state taxes but to delay pushing for a direct subsidy in the current legislative session. The Democrats on the commission had eventually to agree to this compromise. Suddenly, however, an event occurred that seemed to change the situation altogether. An administration bill favoring an increase of state police was introduced; just before the actual vote, the Democratic leader of the house received a call from Daley—and the Cook County Democrats caucused and voted for the governor's bill. "That Daley had . . . engineered the sudden shift of the Democratic votes was obvious. That he would not have done so except for something in return was equally obvious" (p. 121). But it did not follow that the trade had to do with the CTA. At about this time, some watered-down bills concerning the CTA were to be introduced—stronger ones had been killed in committees earlier—but the house majority leader said it was one of the worst set of bills he had ever seen. The majority whip also was against them. The Democrats began then to talk about a filibuster, but Daley and his principal legislative leader decided the public "would not stand for one" on that issue. The commission head asked, on nearly the last day of the legislature, for recognition. The speaker instead asked him to the rostrum and displayed dismay at his intention to call up his bill. "To do so," the speaker said, "would create havoc with the timetable." Several representatives from suburban Chicago had followed the commission head to the rostrum—they were very opposed to any subsidy to be footed by the metropolitan area. They would filibuster if the bill were called up. The commission head finally looked to the Democratic leader, from whom earlier he had gotten a promise of help, but the man had temporarily vanished. Banfield concludes his resume of the controversy: "The case was hopeless, and [the commission head] returned to his seat" (p. 125).

If this story seems fairly standard for some legislative fights—especially those involving downstate versus metropolitan areas (or governor versus mayor) and varied perhaps only by the strong intracity cleavages—we should not be surprised; we should only be surprised that the story does not much correspond with Banfield's analytic outlining of the general process of influence. Of course, there are some correspondences: One organization did initiate the interorganizational controversy, and the governor did seem to delay taking a position, in the beginning phases at least. Yet Banfield seems to be telling two rather different stories. As contrasted to the analytic story, the CTA narrative involves two political heads, of whom at least one (the mayor) has a very considerable stake in the outcome of the negotiated controversy and who is deeply engaged in the web of negotiations; the governor also is not really above the battle, although perhaps his stakes in the many negotiations in which he engages are less vital to him. Certainly the final settlement is affected by the governor's covert negotiations, but he neither imposes nor ratifies the settlement. And there is no great compromise in which even the losers get a little something!

What Banfield has given us is a narrative that involves an incredibly complex sequence of mainly covert negotiations—most of which are only hinted at in the case narrative. (In four of the remaining case studies, the political heads are involved, deeply or at least considerably, as negotiating parties; they are not above the battle: see especially pp. 15–16, 69–70, 132, 135, 146, 193–194.) It is my belief that, if Banfield, as an analyst of political influence, had managed to unearth the most important of those negotiations (admittedly an immensely difficult task) and then analyzed their sequence and linkages, he would have arrived at a very different analysis from that which he had outlined as "the process of influence."

My criticism of Banfield's misreading of the involvement of the political heads is entirely secondary to the point that he has analytically oversimplified the negotiation processes reflected in his case studies. A quick summary of one other case will underline this point. There was another civic controversy that lasted a full decade. An extraordinarily successful urban developer had conceived a bold plan to redevelop a sizable area ("The Fort Dearborn Project") near the downtown area of Chicago. Banfield's model of various associations lining up, pro and con, with the building of alliances, covert negotiations, and so on, fits the case; but his general analysis scarcely begins to handle its complexity. Perhaps it is sufficient just to note that over the years some negotiating parties pulled out of the negotiations entirely (including the originator of the project), while whole sets of new ones entered and left. Among the new negotiators was the new mayor, whose stakes in the redevelopment also shifted over the years from enthusiasm to final disapproval. A number of changing contingencies also affected the alliances pro and con the project—over a decade, much can happen to business, land values, markets, and careers. Understandably, some of the negotiation issues and stakes also shifted—holding actions instead of the aggressive lining up of allies, for instance; possibly also final negotiations to kill off, finally, the whole long sequence of negotiations themselves. As of the time that Banfield wrote up this case, the process had been dealt a probably fatal blow via an adverse report, by the City Planning Department, through its recommendation of an alternative long-range plan. This recommendation, Banfield surmises, was probably linked with some compromises made among divergent business interests brought about by a skilled businessman negotiator, between whom and the mayor, Banfield thinks, some sort of agreement had presumably been reached. These final negotiations were so covert and probably so complex that Banfield, understandably, was not able precisely to pin them down through his interviews. At any rate, when Banfield wrote up the case, negotiations were still going on: "Whether all major business interests would be able to agree upon the Central Area Plan, or any plan at all, remained to be seen" (p. 158). If the plan "could be taken seriously, this proposal was the beginning of a new round" of negotiations.

Confronted by the discrepancies between Banfield's analysis of a generalized influence process and his actual case materials, we are forced to conclude that probably he preconceived his analysis, grounding it less in his data than on his adherence to a benign pluralistic position. Doubtless the analysis was also affected by his rhetorical, pluralistic focus on combating the unreality of centralized decision making. Whatever the reasons for the discrepancy, it leads to some grave questions about his concept of influence and his notions about how influence works in metropolitan politics. Perhaps the most charitable, and at the same time most constructive, comment that can be made about his substantive analysis and theory is that they might yield a relatively accurate (if oversimplified) "fit" with data providing that the analyst carefully specified the social structural conditions under which the influence process sometimes obtained—and located it in comparison with other conditions and their associated processes. These might be partly like the original ones but partly—and specifiably—different. If he had done that, of course, the general lineaments of the political and social order that he has depicted probably would look quite different. So would his analytic depiction of options, open and closed, probable and improbable: the mayor's, for instance, or those of successive negotiation parties in the case just described.

Chapter Five

●●●●●●●●●●●●●●●●●●●
●●●●●●●●●●●●●●●●●●●●●
●●●●●●●●●●●●●●●●●●●●●●

William Riker: Pluralism, Game Theory, and Coalition Formation

●●●●●●●●●●●●●●●●●●●●
●●●●●●●●●●●●●●●●●●●●
●●●●●●●●●●●●●●●●●●●●

The next target for scrutiny is an analysis by another political scientist, William Riker (1962), who provides us with an instructive lesson on what happens when a different variant of pluralism—game theory—is used in order to understand and predict the formation of political coalitions through negotiations. Behind Riker's analysis of the coalition-forming process is a set of pluralistic premises about the nature of American social (or at least political) order. Since he does not make his premises explicit, we are required to guess at them. In general, he assumes, as does Banfield, the existence of a multiplicity of groups with differing interests, of some of which interests (their own and others') they are very cognizant. These interests may bring the groups into conflict within the arena of politics. In acting to reach their ends, they make rational decisions as to their options—their choices of requisite means. One such means may involve the forming of political coalitions with other groups. Another of Riker's premises about social order is that, for the analyst, historical considerations ("considerations of sentiment or passion") are not of major importance except as they can be analytically or related to ongoing current events. We shall see that Riker has a tendency to underplay those considerations.

Probably those kinds of premises are shared by most game theorists. When applied to the study of a society, game theory can surely be viewed as one type of pluralistic social theory. One of its virtues is that it does focus attention *directly* on negotiations and on such related modes of activity as coercing, persuading, and manipulating; but it just as surely preconceives the nature of the social orders that game theorists study and interpret, as well as the possibilities for action within the interpreted orders. Riker's monograph is especially revealing for what a game theorist pluralist may take for granted about the kinds of structural conditions alluded to in our previous discussion of Banfield.

The specific purpose of Riker's analysis is "to construct, with the help of an existing general theory of coalitions (the theory of *n*-person games), a theory of coalitions that will be useful in studying politics" (p. vii). But his deeper rhetorical intent is to begin to handle what he sees as "a failure of political scientists to live up to the promise in the name of political *science*" (p. viii). One way out of that failure, perhaps, is "to create specifically *political* theories of behavior to serve as a base for future *political* science" (p. ix). Riker hopes that his theory will "serve as an example of the possibilities of genuine political science" (p. ix). The theory may turn out to be false or unusable, he adds, but if true will inspire others to join in the "work of creating a new political theory for a new political science."

From the work of men such as Thomas Schelling, who have made Von Neumann and Morgenstern's work on game theory applicable to social behavior, Riker derives various notions concerning coalitions—especially their size. He deduces the following statement (a major one for his theory) from their work: "In social situations similar to *n*-person, zero-sum games with side payments, participants create coalitions just as large as they believe will ensure winning and no larger" (pp. 32–33). (He calls this "the size principle.") Side payments include the threat of reprisal, payments of objects the value of which can be reckoned in money, promises on policy, promises about subsequent decisions, and payments of an emotional kind—in short, some of the familiar descriptive language used by students of negotiation.

We shall leave out of consideration Riker's use of mathematical symbols, which, he remarks, are not actually mathematical but involve reasoning about curves "in a geometrical model, somewhat [as] economists reason about supply and demand curves" (1962, p. 147). The part of Riker's analysis, an essential part, that we shall focus on is suggested by the following summary statement. There are "abstract considerations of strategy in the growth" of potential coalitions (which Riker terms "protocoalitions"). Action in earlier stages of the formation process "might be affected by anticipations about the necessary strategy in the penultimate stage" (p. 147). Hence, Riker looks closely at "the relative positions in the end play . . . to discover differences in the situations of protocoalitions (distinguished by their relative weights)" (p. 147). Riker's main tool of discovery is his size principle. And his analysis "did reveal differences of position in the end play, differences that might affect strategy at earlier stages"; these differences of position consisted of "some sort of advantage possessed uniquely by one protocoalition or by one prospective coalition" (p. 147). And the "most startling" advantage was that generally the smaller protocoalitions frequently had more advantageous positions than did the larger ones.

Because that analysis of "the strategic possibilities of end play in the model may have seemed to many readers rather arid and lifeless" (p. 149)—that is, to readers less resolutely on the trail of a new political science—Riker devotes his next chapter to applying his analysis to a specific historical event in American politics. It is this application that is of most interest to us. Riker describes the so-called corrupt bargain of 1825, a bargain that involved "realpolitik in at least some of its participants"; moreover, "it occurred in the end play of a process that had been going on for about five years" (p. 149) so the potential coalitions had been reduced to four in number. "And since the weight of each participant was fixed by the Constitution (of the U.S.) at each of the final stages in the process, we can speak rather confidently of the weights, at least in the end play" (pp. 149–150). In brief, there was a dissolving of the Republican Party into numerous factions after Monroe's 1820 election; by 1824, the major factions centered around the candidacies of John Quincy Adams, William Crawford, John Calhoun, Andrew Jackson, and Henry Clay. Initially, perhaps Crawford had the most strength, but in 1823 he suffered a stroke that essentially put him out of the running. Also, Calhoun settled for the vice-presidency. Adams had the advantage of being secretary of state, at that time thought of as a preparation for the presidential office. Jackson and Clay both had popular appeal, although Jackson was better known. There were a few die-hard supporters of Crawford. The result was that no candidate could obtain the absolute majority necessary for election in the electoral college. The standings were as follows:

States in Which Candidate Held a Majority

Jackson	11
Adams	7
Crawford	3
Clay	3

The election then went to the House where, according to the Twelfth Amendment, only three candidates could be allowed: Clay therefore had to transfer his votes. In the House, voting was by states, each having one vote cast as decided by a plurality of its representatives. According to Riker's model, Adams, Crawford, and Clay are "members of a uniquely preferred winning coalition," and Jackson is strategically weak. Hence it is appropriate for some of Jackson's supporters to defect, "especially if time is available for extensive bargaining." That is what happened: Jackson's support dissolved. "It might not have dissolved so easily had electors and representatives been the same persons (they could not be by law), but dissolve it did" (p. 152), despite intensive pressure from Jacksonians. Riker names which electors switched to whom. As the session opened, then

Adams	9
Jackson	7
Crawford	4
Clay	4

Again, no protocoalition has a unique advantage, but where either Adams in combination with Crawford or Adams in combination with Clay is a minimal coalition. Hence one can expect desperate bargaining, with Clay and Adams as natural allies. "Note that it is Clay and Adams, rather than Crawford and Adams, not only because Clay was formally excluded but also because, a principal in Washington rather than in a Georgian sickbed, he was able to maneuver more effectively" (p. 153). Moreover, as Missouri gradually went to Adams from Clay, "whether by his own design, or by a small-scale 'corrupt bargain' between Adams' managers and the representatives from Missouri, the situation hardened" (p. 153).

Thus the scene shifts again:

Adams	10
Jackson	7
Crawford	4
Clay	3

Now Adams and Clay have become "members of a uniquely preferred winning coalition. The alliance of Adams and Clay is the only possible minimal winning coalition." And that is what happened. The Kentucky legislature had instructed its representatives to vote for Jackson after Clay was out of the running, but the congressmen "proved to be far more loyal to Clay in Washington than to a legislature in Kentucky, which, moreover, had no authoritative control over them anyhow" (1962, p. 153). If Clay had followed the Kentucky legislature's instructions, then Adams and Jackson would have been tied at ten to ten, and so Crawford's supporters would have been able to drive a very hard bargain. Or, if Clay had joined Crawford, he would have gained no advantage—even if Adams had negotiated with both, the gains would have had to be split three ways.

So rationally, Riker concludes, Clay had to go into alliance with Adams. This was the "corrupt bargain" (Clay to become secretary of state). "Adams apparently had no hesitation in paying it" (p. 154). After Clay's decision, great pressure was put by Crawford's men on several of Adams' men, trying to get enough votes to give them a winning Jackson-Crawford coalition (thirteen votes versus eleven for Adams-Clay). "But this was a last-minute maneuver with little hope of success. Why should men break up a minimal winning coalition in order to form a protocoalition which is at best a member of a uniquely preferred winning coalition?" (p. 154). However, Riker notes, if the Crawford people had had two months more, "they might well have shaken up the winning coalition"— but they did not. So at the last moment before the March 4th vote, the following situation obtained:

Adams	12
Jackson	7
Crawford	4
(New York)	1

(New York had to go with Adams anyway, since he had an absolute majority.)

Summing up, Riker claims that, first, "just as the theory from the model dictates, Jackson lost support" (p. 155). It is true, he adds, that electors and representatives were not the same people—"nevertheless the loss occurred despite great political pressures." Second, again, in accordance with the theory, Clay allied with Adams. "Again it is true that the corrupt bargain was facilitated by Clay's not being eligible—nevertheless, the bargain was struck with Adams and not Jackson" (p. 154). Third, the "*minimal* winning coalition of Adams and Clay suffered no desertions," once formed. Riker goes on to say that in all of the crucial decisions, local institutional or personalistic reasons are available "to explain the adoption of a rational strategy," yet in each the rational strategy was adopted. "And this fact leads me to believe that it was not so much custom or prayer [in the instance of one elector] that determined conduct as it was the intuitive perception of the abstractly 'best' strategy here calculated from the model" (p. 157). Historians' usual explanations of the corrupt bargain are in personalistic terms; or they deny the corrupt bargain, arguing that Adams really chose the best man; or cynically justify the bargain as a typical feature of democracy. But none interpret the bargain as "a rationally best choice" by those who deserted Jackson, followed Clay, or resisted the seductions of Crawford's men.

What can we say about this illustration or application of the model at work? The rationality of choice certainly seems plausible—if one accepts all the provisos entered *sotto voce* into the account: if Clay had been eligible by law; if the electors and representatives had not been different people; if the Kentucky representatives had not lived in Washington and been available to Clay's persuasions, rather than to Crawford sick in bed in Georgia, or if the legislature had had more control over their representatives; if the Crawford men had had two months in which to persuade others away from a winning coalition; and so on. These are very substantial provisos. They amount to specifiable conditions: Change any one and the processes of coalition formation might look very different—perhaps with just as rational a set of strategies operative, but at least different ones—including possibly the workings of Riker's size principle itself.

We also sense that other conditions might actually have been operative but were left unexplored by Riker since he is so focused on his size principle and on choices in terms of rational self-interest. Thus, the one example given of extreme hesitation by an elector concerned someone who hated Adams' father, yet whose self-interest dictated that he vote for Adams. Only at the very last instant did he make his decision for Adams—through prayer, but, as Riker remarks, in accordance with the advice of most friends, with the general principles of his political ideology, "and, most of all, the dictates of realpolitik." Either there were other such cases or built into the situation are men who have especially strong pragmatic stances. What if this vote for the presidency had represented a considerable ideological struggle? What if Adams could not have provided Clay with the office of secretary of state or if Clay had felt he could trust Adams somewhat less than he could Jackson? In short, Riker's application of his theory (or model) hardly takes much cognizance of structural conditions—of time, place, and institutional and social relations—it notes them in passing but does not consider them seriously. They are merely descriptive asides to the presumed business at hand.

Also, what looks like a usefully parsimonious aspect of the theory model is actually a crippling limitation. The formation of coalitions, ending in the corrupt bargain, is handled with clarity, good logic, and considerable dispatch—in an effort to get beyond the merely personalistic (or ideological) explanations offered by historians and political scientists who have dealt with this particular set of events. Weighed against clarity, logic, and dispatch is everything that has been omitted. We are told little, either descriptively or analytically, about the actual negotiations. Who spoke to whom, in what ways, in what sequences, and with what responses and results? What range of negotiation processes occurred? What alternatives and options—negotiation and others—were considered? And how might all this be related to the major properties of this particular negotiation context? Against this criticism, it might be argued that all this was not Riker's aim or task. Admitted! But I argue that his theoretical model gives a spuriously simplistic explanation (or interpretation) of events that led up to the corrupt bargain voting. In Riker's interpretation, things actually are sneaked in by the back door, implicit contextual items such as the small number of possible coalitions (that is, major negotiating parties); the institutional provision (that is, "agreed on") for the elimination of one party after the first round of voting; the relatively fixed and universally recognized amount of time before the final vote; the possibility for each party genuinely to negotiate for alliance with each other; and the settlement of the main issue (winning the vote) through negotiation itself. Riker's size principle may work—but under what specific social structural and negotiation conditions? At best, Riker's model does not speak to the maintenance and dissolution of coalitions and to the reemergence of new ones. That last point is related to an additional query: What kinds of coalitions is Riker really writing about, at least in his historical example? Presumably, agreements are being reached between each national political leader and the state legislative leaders—some of those agreements being related to previous agreements reached on other issues—who in turn have made agreements with other legislators and powerful nonlegislators from their own states. And what are the coalitions all about? Presumably they are not just to get a winning candidate, but to share some of the rewards of victory. But who is to share, and what is the nature of the rewards? And have the members (and which ones) of the winning coalition agreed to stay in business after the victory or only long enough to distribute the rewards?

In short, this application of game theory, elegant as it might be and neat as it might look with its use of mathematical symbols, is based on what some readers might regard as a very messy or at least questionable set of assumptions about what was happening in this particular historical context. Among Riker's major assumptions are those mentioned earlier about the nature of American pluralism. Basically, I believe, those assumptions led him to find game theory useful for his argument against the nonscientist population of his discipline. His pluralistic premises also foreclose on inquiry, as well as prefigure the nature of the political order that he depicts for his readers. Even his view of history turns out to be amazingly static— he uses long-transpired events as a slice of history to be treated, in game theory terms, as though they were a set of contemporary events: Ford versus Carter, Adams versus Jackson—no matter!

Chapter Six

••••••••••••••••••••••
••••••••••••••••••••••
••••••••••••••••••••••

James Coleman:
Corporate Structure
and Internal Power

••••••••••••••••••••••
••••••••••••••••••••••
••••••••••••••••••••••

*R*iker, Banfield, Gouldner, and Blau all focus our attention on negotiation; but James Coleman (1973), in his recent treatment of power, like Goffman, illustrates what happens in a conception of social order when negotiation either is ignored or left quite implicit. (I shall specify what his conception is at the close of this section.) Coleman's main problem in his paper "Loss of Power" pertains to the balance of power. "How is power in society divided between these two types of actor? . . . How much power is divided between these two sides? How much control over events of consequence does each side have? And how has that balance shifted over time?" (p. 2).

Coleman remarks that a person yields direct control over his resources (money, agent rights, time, and effort) to a corporate actor by joining it or investing resources in it. The individual gives up his "usage rights" but receives "benefit rights" (the right to benefit from the use of the corporation's resources). "The right to use resources is what is ordinarily meant by power, while the right to benefit is the right to gain from the exercise of power" (p. 3).

Coleman turns to such topics as the probability of an individual preventing corporate action. In yielding his usage rights, "Just what in the corporate actor does he control?" Clearly, "an individual's power declines sharply as he joins with others to form corporate actors"—but he does this to get the potential benefits of membership. Another issue concerns how much power an individual has in a world of corporate actors (since he belongs to many— that is, in taking up residence in a state, he yields control over many activities). We "can assess the amount of control he retains over his actions [if] we know the size of the corporate actor to which he has yielded control" (p. 3). Another issue is coalition formation: A coalition within a corporation will "have greater power in the corporate body than one would himself." But, generally speaking, the larger and more powerful the coalition becomes, the more an individual's power declines. Each person in the coalition expects to have a say in its action. "As the coalition gains power by increasing in size, the individual loses power within it" (1973, p. 9). Yet the frequency of coalitions "in social life, constructing coalitions to fight internal battles in corporate bodies" suggests that individual power may sometimes be increased. For example, consider a coalition with a bare majority of one. Then what is the best coalition size for the individual? More than a bare majority? No—for he wants "a coalition of such size that the product of the probability of his controlling the coalition and the probability of the coalition controlling the corporate actor is maximum" (p. 9). Nevertheless, when all is said and done, coalitions are not a very "satisfactory means for the individual to recover power lost in the corporate world."

There is one further option available to the individual: He can withdraw or threaten to withdraw his investment from the corporate body. "However, this threat is powerful only insofar as such a withdrawal will not result in a person's loss of benefits" (p. 12). Examples are withdrawing investment from a business corporation; moving from a country; withdrawal from a marriage. Some of those cases suggest it would be costly for someone to withdraw—as in moving from one community to another. "In such situations, the right of withdrawal is not an important means of control"; in fact, then, "the corporate actor can divert the benefit from usage to itself, bringing about its own growth without benefit to members" (p. 12). Thus the individual can maximize his withdrawal power by investing in highly competitive markets—if he can find them.

A final issue: Why have individuals given up control? In fact, there has been "a continual loss of power to corporate actors," including, of course, to the nation. Coleman's answer is "I think two central processes bring this about. One [is] the desire to augment our power vis-à-vis even larger bodies by creating others, a process which is called the creation of 'countervailing power.' " The second is that "Men sometimes yield their usage rights . . . in hopes of a greater gain" (p. 13), whether money; or satisfaction, as from a marriage; or glory, as in sports. Having been led by his analysis to quite "psychological processes"—"giving gratification or distress through a corporate actor's success or failure" (p. 13)— Coleman disavows competence in the psychological area; besides, it is beyond the scope of his inquiry. He closes, however, by making a few observations about these psychological processes—rather commonsense observations, I might add. The paper closes with the statement that "We cannot live without these artificial persons, corporate bodies, within our midst. But we have yet to discover how we can live with them" (p. 14).

Let us see how Coleman's focal concerns can be located. Aside from some confusion about what kinds of corporate bodies he is addressing himself to (what does it mean to say that we cannot live without corporate bodies such as marriages or families?), it seems fair to say that Coleman really takes the business corporation and the individual investor as his principal image of the corporate body and its member. (He borrows usage and benefit rights from the Berle and Means, 1940, study of business corporations.) To continue this locational game: Coleman is talking about voluntary associations and the voluntary yielding of power (despite reference to nation and citizenship). He addresses himself specifically to the central issue of balance of power between individual and voluntary association and to inferred conditions for such matters as the yielding of personal resources to and the decision to withdraw resources from a voluntary association. Coleman's focus is all from the individual's side—we do not see the matter from the perspective either of the corporation at large or of its executives. We are given no analysis or even description of corporate options and strategies vis-à-vis the corporation's members. Nor is there any discussion of the interplay among the individual's memberships in multiple corporate bodies: The focus, in short, is restricted to one membership at a time—or rather in isolation, since sequence as well as simultaneity of membership is ignored. Nor is there any mention of an individual's strategies of control through allies external to the corporate body—only "internal coalitions" are noted. And internal coalitions are left abstract or at least are treated from the member's viewpoint, rather than in terms of internal alliances of executives. Presumably these would, for Coleman, form anyhow and be turned to use against member (investor) coalitions. Furthermore, Coleman assumes a "one man, one vote" rule of procedure, a rather limiting assumption even for investors in business corporations. Apparently he also tends to assume—or at least does not follow through the implications of the obverse—that the resources contributed by each individual are equal both in kind and amount: "One man, one vote" is a specific case.

Turning more specifically to questions about negotiation: It is clear that Coleman is assuming a negotiation process—for instance, coalition formation—but, because his focus is so exclusively on the individual (strange for a sociologist) and on individual "motivations," he tends not to note how negotiations may be involved in decisions to enter, stay with, or withdraw from voluntary associations—even investors in business corporations. ("OK, investment counselor, I'll buy 100 shares of GE and stay with it for six months, but if it doesn't move, let's agree to shift to something else. . . . And you're on trial for your recommendation too.") Coleman's "individual" somehow is not a very sociological person; he is not embedded in a texture of social relationships that would affect and be affected by his decision to give over his usage rights to a voluntary association. So Coleman cannot have a very accurate view of the options and limitations of action pertaining to what he has under analytical focus.

More specifically, as far as negotiation dimensions are concerned Coleman really only considers systematically the impact of one dimension (the number of negotiators) on the balance of power, while secondarily some others are touched on in passing, such as options to avoid agreement (that is, joining or withdrawing). He does not consider any of the range of negotiation dimensions discussed later in this book (legitimation, routine-novel, experience, covert-overt), any of which may have a crucial impact on the matter that he considers central in his paper.

To summarize: first, one cannot talk sensibly about (political) power without a serious consideration of negotiation processes. "Power" then would look different from the way it does in Coleman's analysis. When those processes are taken analytically and seriously into account, one gets a depiction of corporate structure— that is, the social order that constitutes both the corporation and the social context in which it is embedded—more in line with the qualifications offered earlier. Coleman's premises, which apparently include notions of aggregate membership and the effective power of corporate structures, lead him to interpret as he does both corporate power and social order in general.

Coleman's book *Power and the Structure of Society* (1974) reveals more clearly what is only dimly apparent in his paper; namely, that his conception of social order is a variant of the "alienation" or "mass society" perspective, as expressed by a relatively optimistic reformer. Coleman perceives that individuals have a sense of powerlessness in the face of today's large corporate structures. Yet the latter cannot be dispensed with, he says: They are the very agents of our progress; they must be lived with. So "How can persons in society regain a sense of control and over the sense of powerlessness that large corporate actors induce" (1974, pp. 104–105)? In the "stable egalitarian communities" of the past, characterized by face-to-face transactions between persons, ethical norms functioned well. There was "proper functioning of the social order," in accordance, essentially, with Kant's categorical imperative. In modern society, corporate actors have changed all that. A "portion of the rational basis for a moral system is cut away where persons and corporate actors must coexist" (1974, p. 98), so the big problem is "What can replace it?" As part and parcel of that problem, how are we to transform a society that functions less than fully in the interests of the persons who make it up? An essential part of the answer is that the social scientist, as well as others, should examine those processes through which the loss of power to persons takes place. Despite this critical juncture in mankind's history, "persons can regain a sense of control" (1974, p. 106). In those words, which close his book, Coleman merges person and society in his own struggle with the knotty problem of freedom versus constraint. Understanding that, we can understand better how his particular conception of social order and social change affects his substantive theory of corporate power and organization.

Chapter Seven

•••••••••••••••••••
••••••••••••••••••••••
••••••••••••••••••••••

Edward Morse:
The Bargaining
Structure of NATO

•••••••••••••••••••••
••••••••••••••••••••••
•••••••••••••••••••••

*E*ach researcher discussed thus far has asked social order questions; that is, "What is going on here, what is 'it' that I am studying?" Yet none chose to focus analytically on negotiations, asking how negotiations functioned in the specific social order under review. Against the background of the previous discussion, I wish to present another instance of research that will answer the following questions: "What if a researcher were struck by the central importance of negotiations for (or 'in') a given social order *but* was not certain of the precise nature of that order? Suppose, then, he examined the negotiation data to get a purchase on the social order rather than merely to understand the negotiation as such? Would he not also be making his theory of negotiation fairly explicit and grounding it fairly directly on his data?"

My colleagues and I confronted that situation (described earlier) in studying psychiatric hospitals, arriving at the concept and formulation of "negotiated order." But an additional case will afford a sharp contrast to those researches in which negotiation is neglected or handled descriptively and at the same time will build a bridge to the materials discussed in Part Two of this book. So next we shall look at a paper by Edward Morse (1976). His writing can help direct our attention to the principal issues that I believe are involved in the study of negotiations. (As noted earlier, often in studies of negotiations themselves, the researchers are either too absorbed with the details of the negotiations or are focused on their descriptive aspects rather than the analytic; and often they omit or mute social order questions.)

The subtitle of Morse's paper, "Multi-Issue Negotiations in an Interdependent World," suggests its focus. The paper is not really about bargaining as such but about the structural conditions that affect negotiation among the members of the North Atlantic Treaty Organization (NATO). More precisely, the author is confronting the fascinating puzzle of exactly what NATO is. What is its nature? What are we to make of it? As he says, his paper represents an effort to define "the general structure of relations" among NATO members.

Morse is contesting a conceptualization termed *coalition theory*, derived from pre-NATO days when the world was populated by truly autonomous national governments, which in pursuing their goals frequently formed alliances with other governments. Morse argues that this conception no longer fits relationships among nations in the Western world. What conceptualization, then, can substitute? Morse offers a version of contemporary theory known as "core-periphery relations." The United States and its political and economic system is viewed as the core area and Europe as its periphery. He remarks that this distinction is now commonplace in both neo-Marxist and ultra-Keynesian analysis. It evolved, of course, from studies of the relationships between more- and less-developed nations, with core areas seen as tending "to attract all factors of production (technology, capital, and labor) due to higher expectation and lower risks that they provide," and eventually "real losses at the periphery, where governments' abilities to achieve their political and economic goals decline" (p. 73). Therefore, inevitable tension develops between core and periphery areas. Morse gives a qualified application of this "model" to the NATO situation, noting that,

while somewhat misleading as a description of the relationships between the United States and western Europe, it nevertheless is a
very useful conception.

Morse employs this conceptualization in conjunction with
the interesting concept of "bargaining context," which refers to
what I would call the more general, structural conditions that bear
on the whole texture of continuous bargaining among NATO
members. Bargaining, Morse notes, transpires within a very "complex environment" that includes not only defense and security issues
but also economic, financial, and political ones. NATO relationships are simply too complex to confine analysis of them merely to
military and security issues. Under the rubric of bargaining context,
Morse considers such matters as the diverse areas within which
bargaining occurs (political, economic, and so on), the considerable
(nine) number of nations involved; their relative power, which
may shift on various issues (the United States is paramount in
defense); their "urge" for autonomy—but the relative lack of it
because of their interdependence; and the distinction between the
United States as core and other nations as periphery.

Since the late 1940s, the United States has been the core
area in security, monetary, and commercial affairs. But the current
negotiations between European governments and the U.S. government "can be understood as part of a conscious effort by the former
to create a new nuclear or core area centered in Europe" (p. 75).
(That stake is the main one in the trend of bargaining, as well as in
alternative modes of furthering that purpose.) Morse suggests that
after World War II the U.S. government "undoubtedly struck a
trade-off" with European governments: From the beginning of the
cold war, it encouraged both European political and economic
integration and the "development of a nucleation process," and in
exchange the U.S. government "ran the security policies of the
noncommunist industrialized societies and received the benefits of
seignorage from the use of the dollar in international monetary relationships" (p. 79). Currently, however, bargaining is taking place
around three critical areas: commercial, monetary, and security.
NATO members are in a "crisis zone" with greater potential for
bargaining between the core and periphery areas. The former will
be trying to prevent the emergence of a coalition of periphery na-

tions against itself, while the latter "will be in an optimum strategic bargaining situation precisely when it is able to construct an effective coalition" (pp. 79–80). Besides, the core will attempt to strike bargains "in a variety of issue areas simultaneously" so as to gain maximum leverage, while the periphery nations will try to keep issue areas separate "to prevent manipulation."

Morse then takes up some advantages and disadvantages that each side has, noting generally the disadvantage in this sort of bargaining situation that the periphery nations have because the U.S. government "holds more strings over each of the governments than any of them . . . over the United States" (p. 81). In fact, fear of warfare, combined with the "paradoxical disutility" of nuclear force, means that Europe cannot realistically hope to develop a new core area in the near future.

However, within this entire bargaining context, a number of new phenomena have emerged that are not properly explained by traditional coalition theory. For they reflect "a fundamental change in the substance of international politics in the contemporary world: the degree to which plays for power and position are acted out in economic relations" (p. 84). Thus, the growing interdependence of NATO members has equalized the relative power that can be mobilized by individual governments: It increases the mutual linkages among nations, resulting in stalemate. There is an increase in "the blackmailing potential of lesser powers, whose stake in the stability of a system may be viewed as lower than that of the great powers, which have far more to lose as the system becomes less stable" (p. 85). Also, this great interdependence means that there is a lowered ability of any single government to achieve its goals and a greater ability to threaten others with harm.

Having touched on those elements of coercion, Morse turns explicitly to the topic of manipulation. Under conditions of increasing interdependence, there is an increased ability of any government to manipulate the internal affairs of others. So the paradox of interdependence is that a government can intervene in another society "simply by shifting the course of its own domestic policy"—and Morse gives examples. Furthermore, the same conditions that allow manipulation of other nations' domestic affairs also allow the "playing out" of domestic policies within the context of foreign

political systems. NATO governments now tend to pursue a con-
servative foreign policy precisely because of those possibilities of
uncontrolled change. Rather than directly confront such a situation, "which carries with it so many unknown factors," governments
prefer to maintain the status quo, keeping the machinery of public
affairs operating rather than "steering a course for the future."

Relations in an interdependent system are also likely to
undergo crisis (for instance, short-term flows of liquid capital across
national boundaries). Furthermore, there is an increased possibility
that crises will be manipulated, "as a general strategy of foreign
policy." Consequently, negotiations among governments normally
will tend to embrace a diversity of issues so as to reach "possible
trade-offs in reaching group decisions." But that also means, because those issues are linked, that possibilities for political blackmail
are enhanced.

Morse concludes his argument by noting that the "bargaining context is fundamentally complex and rich because the various
'layers' of the system that the members of the alliance compose are
so contradictory. They also seem to be quite stable" (p. 91). So
they are likely to endure for some time. It is clear that the "contextual aspects of the bargaining relationships . . . represent a new
form of politics. It is one to which governments have increasingly
shown awareness and with which they have so far been willing to
live" (p. 92).

There are several points to which I would draw special attention in Morse's analysis. Note he is searching for a conceptualization that will give both a reasonable interpretation of the "structure
of relationships" among NATO members—an emergent social
order, if ever there was one!—and an interpretation of the nature
of bargaining among the governments. He relates the bargaining,
its stakes, and some of its styles (potential blackmail and so on) to
the larger bargaining context. "Context" is roughly equivalent to
a set of important structural conditions that affect the bargaining.
Also important is the attention he gives to other options—to the
manipulation of contingencies and to threats of coercion, as well as
to bargaining itself—and even some hints concerning the linkages
among them. What Morse does not do in this paper (but possibly
does elsewhere) is analyze in detail the actual features of salient

types of negotiation among NATO members. Presumably, if he were to do this he would do it in close conjunction with his analysis of the bargaining context. If he did not, there would be a hiatus between those two levels of analysis.

More important, for my purposes in this section of the book, Morse's analysis illustrates how a direct focus on negotiations— *when linked* with the query of "What kind of social order am I studying here?"—can perhaps begin to answer the queries raised at the beginning of Part One. Those queries pertained to the relationships of "theory" to theorizing about social orders under inquiry and, more specifically, to the relationships of negotiation analysis to both the substantive and the more general theories. We do not know Morse's theoretical presuppositions about international order, but surely they have neither prevented a full focus on negotiations with respect to international order nor overwhelmed his analysis of the negotiations functioning "in" that order.

Chapter Eight

•••••••••••••••••••••
•••••••••••••••••••••••
••••••••••••••••••••••••

Critiquing Social Research: A Summary

•••••••••••••••••••••••
•••••••••••••••••••••••
••••••••••••••••••••••••

Carrying through with some general questions raised in the introduction about how social theorists and social researchers regard or study negotiation processes, Part One began with more specific queries about the work of researchers who are also recognized social theorists. It will be remembered that I had earlier remarked that, when faced with understanding a particular group, organization, institution, nation or society, a researcher generally must either ask "What is this all about—what is its structure of relationships?" or perhaps simply assume an answer to that question and then proceed to study whatever is central to his or her interests. But I also asserted that researchers' conceptions of social order—and their (usually) implicit assumptions about negotiation—generally lead them to overlook or misconstrue their data on negotiations; I also asserted that close examination of those data would raise some sharply critical questions both about their conceptions of social order and about some of their actual research conclusions.

The specific questions that prefaced the discussions of these researches were as follows: "Can the research actually affect the general theory (or theoretical framework) if the researcher does not see negotiation in terms of theory? What happens if the researcher sees negotiation 'in the data' but does not build theoretically on those particular data? What kind of description is offered; or what kind of substantive theory? Or, blinded by theoretical preconceptions, do researchers actually overlook the negotiations that are there in the collected data? What would happen if they, or we, would find negotiations in their data and take them seriously: How would that affect what was offered us by way of descriptions, substantive theories, and theoretical conceptions?"

With regard to these questions (and these only), how does the research discussed in Part One measure up? In general, not very well. Only Morse took seriously the idea that negotiations were at the heart of his question about (international) order. Hence, he explored the "bargaining context"—a complex of structural conditions—in relation both to negotiation processes and manipulative processes, while drawing conclusions about the nature of NATO. He has essentially given us a discursive substantive theory about the nature of contemporary international order (at least the Western part of it), subordinating his descriptions to that theory. In contrast, others of the researchers have not built negotiation into their substantive theories, although explicitly referring to or describing specific negotiations.

Riker's application of game theory to political coalition formation, for instance, does not lead him to focus more than descriptively on the negotiations that he knows quite well go into the making of coalitions. The substantive theory he offers is simply an extension of game theory. Riker's research surely does not test that general theory in any sense. My critique of his research has underscored how a sustained look at his negotiation data can reveal the multitude of structural conditions for coalition formation and behavior, to which his strict adherence to game theory and political pluralism had blinded him.

In Banfield's case, similar pluralistic assumptions are made about the necessity for negotiations among interested participants in the political process, for they must come to terms with one another to achieve some of their aims. Beyond that, there is no analysis of the actual negotiation data, which are presented descriptively, as exemplifications, perhaps, of negotiation in a pluralistic nation. They are not otherwise built into Banfield's substantive theory of political influence. Consequently, his theory simply does not take account of his own presented data.

Other researchers, concerned as they were with legitimate problems of their own, quite overlooked the negotiations that can be either discerned in their presented data or guessed to have actually occurred in their arena of inquiry. Thus, Gouldner's explanation of managerial difficulties and failure does not incorporate the ample negotiation data that he presents descriptively. After all, his aim was to modify Weber's theory of bureaucracy by careful study of an industrial firm. He is successful in that aim, but his own formulation of how industrial bureaucracy works would clearly be modified if one took into account the negotiation data from which he was diverted by his combination of functionalist stances and the aim to modify Weber.

Much the same can be said for Goffman's writing about total institutions, except that, since he makes nothing, even descriptively, of the negotiations that occur in those institutions, we must tease them out of his presented data. Goffman's interactionist concerns with combating an overly extreme structural determinism and demonstrating the proper balanced relationship between individual freedom and social constraint leave him no particular room for noting negotiations. When we take seriously those of his data that imply negotiations, his substantive theory of prison life and general theory of total institutions both require considerable modification. Interestingly enough, his interactionist concerns receive even more support then, since individual and collective negotiations surely imply even more freedom than Goffman has argued for.

Coleman's inquiry, which is concerned with the nature of business corporate power in relation to members' sense of powerlessness and little actual power, appears to flow from his more general theory about the nature of contemporary society but is, I suggested, a variant of alienation theory and mass society theory. Negotiations can be dimly sensed there in his discussion, but they are not viewed by him as theoretical possibilities; hence his substantive theory needs much modification, and his more general theory is scarcely tested by such inquiries as his into the nature of business corporations and their relations to their members.

In Blau's functionalist inquiry, which also was an attempt to qualify Weber's theory of bureaucracy, there is a mixed treatment of negotiation. In some portions of his monograph, he explicitly notes negotiations but handles them descriptively, making nothing of them for his theorizing. Elsewhere he overlooks negotiation data that are quite clearly present in his description. Again, raising questions about his conclusions through examination of his negotiation data, we are led to wonder about the adequacy of his theory of bureaucratic order and change. We can wonder also about his functionalist conceptions; but in any event, without the kind of critical and theory-focused scrutiny of negotiation processes (and other associated processes, such as manipulation, persuasion, and coercion), the functionalist assumptions cannot be much modified through Blau's kind of inquiry.

In sum, the researchers whose work is discussed in Part One do not score high on the test given them. This is, of course, a very special test, and I would repeat what I said earlier, that these are mostly and deservedly classical studies, valuable in their own right. Nevertheless they seem to have served my several purposes well. I have discussed these writings in large part to bring out the following points, which I believe are essential to any far-reaching study of negotiation. First, looking at the data on negotiations in a researcher's work can afford us a very useful critique of the theorizing done on the basis of the research itself; negotiations are not just another interesting phenomenon or special area for research. Second, if researchers are going to analyze negotiations, they need to do so in relation to questions of social order—and with an eye on their own assumptions or implicit theories of negotiation. Third, negotiation processes are entwined with other processes (manipulative, coercive), and they all must be studied together. Of course, a researcher may choose to focus primarily on one or another, but adequate research and theorizing require making connections between whatever is taken as primary and those other, temporarily or bracketed, secondary ones. All three points add to a more general one, namely that each of these researchers has raised interesting, valid theoretical problems, which I doubt can be answered—as they have attempted to do—without careful studies of a varied set of interlocked processes, including the negotiation processes.

There is a larger issue implied by all of those points. It will be addressed in the final chapter but adumbrated here in the form of a question: "Can social orders be properly analyzed without building negotiation into the analysis?" Or, put another way, "Are there any social orders that are not also negotiated orders?" Some part of my commentary on Goffman, Blau, and so on, was meant to suggest what the answers to those questions should be. In Part Two, I shall be making essentially the same claim for the centrality of negotiation processes, using a paradigm developed for analyzing them. Anyone who cares to apply that paradigm to the research writings discussed in Part One will find it applicable, I believe, as well as contributing to doubt about the efficacy of conceptualizing organizations, groups, social movements, institutions, and societies, without also analyzing their implied negotiation processes.

Part Two

PARADIGM AND CASE ANALYSES

This part of the book consists essentially of analyses of negotiation cases drawn from various research publications. The analyses will be carried out by means of a paradigm designed for that purpose. The cases to which it will be applied were chosen to illustrate the very considerable range of different negotiation processes that take place in a variety of social settings, as well as to suggest to researchers that this analytic paradigm can be useful for work in a variety of substantive areas.

Before presenting this analytic scheme, it is worthwhile recollecting some features of the literature on negotiation. Most publications are substantive in thrust, and the literature tends to be restricted to a relatively few areas, such as diplomacy and labor bargaining. Much of the discussion is descriptive, even narrative in form, or is a commentary on personal experience with negotiations. Analyses tend to be about single cases: one negotiation or a set of related negotiations. The more theoretical or analytic writings, such as those of Schelling or Ikle, are essentially attempts to build general theory on the basis of data from one or two substantive areas, rather than on comparative data from many areas. The authors tend not to detail the structural conditions under which the phenomena under review occur, either taking those conditions for granted, as in writings on bargaining theory, or handling those conditions descriptively rather than analytically. The range of consequences considered also tends to be narrow. And, since not much attention is paid to the variety of subprocesses of negotiation or to the conditions under which these subprocesses arise, not much analysis is then done pertaining to the relationships between those processes and those representing alternative modes of action (coercive, persuasive, educational, and so on).

What is needed is a theoretical scheme that can convert all those minuses into pluses; for they represent items that must, I hope to demonstrate, be incorporated into research and theorizing about negotiations and negotiated orders. As applied to the following several cases, the paradigm should also bring out important features of each case of negotiation. It should also suggest or imply what may have been missing from the researchers' descriptions or analyses. Furthermore, cues in the paradigm's application lead to remarks, in the conclusion to the book, about improved substantive and general theory of negotiations.

The key terms of the paradigm and their use in the case analyses are as follows. First, the *negotiations* themselves will be described, often using the author's own words or paraphrasing them. Included in the descriptions will be the accompanying interactions, types of actors, their strategies and tactics, some consequences of the negotiations, and embedded negotiation *subprocesses* of negotiation; for example, making trade-offs, obtaining kickbacks, paying off debts, and negotiating agreements.

Second, the *structural context* is that "within which" the negotiations take place, in the largest sense. For each case of negotiation, it will be necessary to bring out some of the salient *structural properties* that bear on the negotiation. Thus, the structural context for covert negotiations engaged in by a corrupt judge includes features of the American judiciary system and of marketplaces, while the structural context of the negotiations that occur in a mental hospital includes the properties of American medical care, the subspecialty of psychiatry, specialization among the caring professions, and the divisions of labor in mental hospitals.

I distinguish between that larger, structural context and a *negotiation context*. The structural context bears directly on the negotiation context, but the latter refers more specifically to the structural properties entering very directly as conditions into the *course* of the negotiation itself. The concept of negotiation context is analogous to the use of the term *awareness context* in a paper titled "Awareness Contexts and Social Interaction" (Glaser and Strauss, 1964; also Glaser and Strauss, 1965). Awareness context is there referred to as "What each interacting person knows of the patient's defined status, along with his recognition of the others' awareness of his own definition—the total picture as a sociologist might construct it. . . . It is the context within which these people interact while taking cognizance of it" (1965, p. 10). And, technically speaking (1964, p. 670), "The concept of awareness context is a structural unit, not a property of one of the standard structural units such as group, organization, community, role, position, and so on. By 'context,' we mean it is a structural unit of an encompassing order larger than the other unit under focus: interaction. Thus an awareness context surrounds and affects the interaction. . . . Note that ward or hospital are concrete, conventional social units, while awareness context is an analytic social unit, constructed to account for similarities in interaction in many diverse conventional units."

Just as there are many types of awareness context pertaining to interaction with respect to dying persons, so also there are many specific kinds of negotiation contexts pertaining to interaction among negotiating parties. The latter types, as we shall see, are related to permutations of the following properties of any negotiation context.

- The *number* of negotiators, their relative *experience* in negotiating, and whom they *represent*.
- Whether the negotiations are *one-shot, repeated, sequential, serial, multiple,* or *linked*.
- The relative *balance of power* exhibited by the respective parties *in* the negotiation itself.

- The nature of their respective *stakes* in the negotiation.
- The *visibility* of the transactions to others; that is, their overt or covert characters.
- The *number* and *complexity* of the *issues* negotiated.
- The *clarity of legitimacy* boundaries of the *issues* negotiated.
- The *options* to avoiding or discontinuing negotiation; that is, the alternative modes of action perceived as available.

I wish to emphasize that the final item, options, is of particular relevance in understanding both the decision to embark on negotiation and the course of negotiation itself. If the potential or actual parties to negotiation perceive that they can attempt persuasion, make an appeal to authority, manipulate political or social events, and so forth, then their choices of these alternative modes will either prevent them from entering negotiation, or if they choose that also, then their choices will affect what transpires during the course of the negotiation.

These properties of negotiation contexts are not logical constructs, but emerged from the examination of numerous instances of negotiation—including the cases reviewed here—and of writings by negotiation theorists. For those readers who are especially interested in method: In using awareness contexts, we chose only four of thirty-six possible types of context, employing them extensively to analyze interaction "around the dying" (open, closed, mutual pretense, suspicion contexts). Those types were constructed around five properties. But in the present book, whenever properties are salient in a given case involving negotiations, I bring them out in analyzing the specific negotiation context for that case. The chief consideration, in both books, is the relevance, not "logic," in developing the specific typologies or analyses of context. One must judge for oneself the fit and relevance of these negotiation contexts to the specific cases of negotiation to which they are applied. Their various permutations and clusterings constitute the explanations for the specific kinds of negotiators, interactions, tactics, strategies, subprocesses of negotiation, and consequences that will be discussed. Of course, it is expected that this list of useful properties of the negotiation context will be added to by other researchers as they do their own studies.

A steady focus both on structural and negotiation contexts and on their respective properties increases the likelihood that the analysis of specific courses of negotiation will be carefully located "within" the larger social structure. (No reification is intended.) In short, social order considerations are vital. (At the same time, those negotiations can be related to others with which they share similarities as well as differences.) Structural context is larger, more encompassing, than negotiation context, but the lines of impact can run *either* way. That is, changes in the former may impact on the latter, and vice versa. Outcomes of negotiation itself, as we shall see, can contribute to changes in negotiation contexts relevant to future negotiations. They are less likely to affect the structural context (structural properties), except as they are repeated or combined with other negotiations and with other modes of action and so perhaps have a cumulative impact. Paradigmatic application should bring out these potentialities or actualities.

Some approaches to negotiation concentrate closely on negotiations but leave unattended or implicit their relations to social structural considerations (Riker), and even sometimes to negotiation contextual considerations (Banfield, Blau). On the other hand, like many structural approaches in social science that tend not to bother with microscopic analyses of interaction, some accounts of negotiation settle for essentially narrative description or an emphasis on overall bargaining relations rather than on the bargaining itself. In both approaches, little attention frequently is paid to the *developmental* character ("course") of much negotiation, some of which will be underlined in the following case analyses.

Among those cases are those which merely yield data on negotiation, while in others the researcher is concerned primarily with negotiation itself. With regard to the first group, what the paradigm allows is an analysis of the negotiations. This deepens considerably our understanding both of them and of their relations with the substantive topics under consideration. Concerning those cases in which negotiation is centrally in focus, the paradigm helps, first, in locating comparatively the specific negotiation processes under consideration; and thus, second, it helps in assessing what has been omitted or glossed over in the author's analysis, either because of the nature of his data or because of his particular analytic scheme. The same could be said about additional cases that anyone might wish to add to this list. For both kinds of case, however, some of my own analysis will be "thin," because for one reason or other the data given us are sparse. This also means my analysis will not always give the same emphasis to exactly identical points for each case. Yet for each the paradigm allows commentary in terms of the implicit or explicit treatment of a social order, either revealed or about which assertions are being made by the researcher.

The presentation of cases follows the format of separate chapters, two cases per chapter. Cases have been paired to bring out similar or contrasting features around a central issue raised by the paradigm, with an emphasis both on structural considerations and on negotiation itself. The chapter titles should convey a sense of some of the issues: (1) continuous working relations in organizations, (2) interplay of legal and illegal negotiations in the political arena, (3) building cooperative structures, (4) negotiating compromises within social orders, (5) antagonistic negotiation within changing structural contexts, and (6) limits silent bargains, and implicit negotiation.

To bring Part One into closer alignment with Part Two, I need to make a special point here. One important property of the structural context bearing on any given set of negotiations is the respective actors' *theories* (usually implicit) of negotiation. Harking back to Gouldner's description of the manager's actions, we can see that the latter's implicit conceptions of negotiation profoundly affected such questions as when, how, about what, with whom, and how much he would negotiate. The same was true, of course, of Li Ta-Chao's actions. One of the problems with the data offered by the researchers whose work is used in Part Two is that they themselves were not particularly sensitized to actors' assumptions or conceptions about negotiation. Consequently, we are not always able to see clearly, although sometimes we can sense, the role that actors' theories play in the negotiations. The situation was, of course, quite different in the cases discussed in Part One, where it was relatively easy to discover or tease out the researchers' own assumptions about negotiation, but where, also, the negotiation data themselves were often so sparse that a paradigmatic analysis could not be nearly as full as in the cases presented in Part Two.

The ideal analysis would, then, rest on data gathered by a researcher sensitized to *all* the items listed in the paradigm. This point will be more fully elaborated in the conclusion to this book, under the section on "Further Uses of the Paradigm," in the concluding chapter.

Chapter Nine

•••••••••••••••••••••
•••••••••••••••••••••••
••••••••••••••••••••••••

Continuous Working Relations in Organizations

••••••••••••••••••••••••
•••••••••••••••••••••••••
•••••••••••••••••••••••••

*I*n this first chapter, a question that pertains centrally to organizations and that presumably is also relevant to other types of groupings will be addressed: "What does negotiation look like—what are its special features—when people are and must be in fairly continuous working relations?" Obviously, no organization can persist unless its members manage somehow or other to come to terms with each other's actions, to work with one another, even if antagonistically, in order to get done whatever needs to be done "for" or "in" or "through" the organization. While some relationships among members involve relatively routine actions guided by standard rules or rules of thumb, others may involve conflict, ambiguity or novelty, and so on.

Some theorists refer to the necessity for such processes as role taking to take place in order that "consensus" can occur (Shibutani, 1966) or that "lines of behavior" can become "aligned" (Blumer, 1969). Such generalized processes as role taking, "verstehen" (understanding), or the kinds of rational processes itemized under decision making scarcely give the flavor of what "really" happens when people are working or living in organizations. What happens involves negotiation, but it also involves coercion, threats of coercion, attempts to persuade, and appeals to authority. The appearances of those processes and their relationships are certainly not fortuitous. So each type of organization, in relation to its structural properties and those of the larger social environment within which it operates, will evidence different negotiation subprocesses that stand in at least somewhat specifiable relationships to alternative modes of action.

The two cases discussed here differ insofar as the first concerns experimental wards in a mental hospital, while the second concerns industrial firms. The former are characterized by continuous working relationships that to the actors themselves are novel and challenging, but often ambiguous, puzzling, risky, and frustrating. So there is considerable negotiation over new tasks, new roles, new functions, and new (and old) jurisdictional terrains. Among the subprocesses are the exploring of legitimate boundaries, through proffering advantages, and territorial claiming, for questions of legitimacy are frequent on these wards. In the industrial firms discussed, a great deal of characteristic "collusion," covert making of deals, is characteristic, as individuals attempt to further their jobs, aspirations, careers, and even their nonorganizational purposes through negotiating covertly as well as overtly. There are other types of subprocesses in both, such as mediating and trading off, but there is little that is characteristic of certain other kinds of negotiation where, for instance, people bargain toward the middle or make "settlements" (as in economic transactions). A key difference between the two settings is that on the experimental wards the social order is visibly in the making, the work relationships are evolving before our eyes, while the negotiations are transparently contributing toward all this development. Questions of legitimacy are intimately related to this emergent aspect of the wards, whereas in the industrial firms questions of legitimacy are related more to a relatively durable "web of commitments" that involves both legitimate and illegitimate action. In both cases, the respective researchers were faced with the difficult problem of adequately characterizing the social order of the organizations they were studying.

Case: Experimental Psychiatric Wards

In the late 1950s, several colleagues and I began a research project to determine the impact of psychiatric ideologies on the work of staff in mental hospitals (see Strauss and others, 1964). To get answers to that general problem, we found ourselves studying in great detail the interaction among staff members and between staff and patients. The case study by Rue Bucher and Leonard Schatzman (1964) discussed here is summarized from one of the publications on that research, an article quite accurately titled "Negotiating a Division of Labor Among Professionals in the State Mental Hospital." A major feature of the negotiating was the continual working out, together, of who was to do what, how, and with whom.

What was the structural context within which that negotiating took place? Its general features include the following. In the United States for about one hundred years, persons defined as severely or dangerously mentally ill were being sent to special hospitals, often operated at state expense. Care of the patients was primarily designed to be custodial rather than to cure or give therapy, since many patients were chronically ill and no effective cure or therapy for them existed. These hospitals, especially the state-administered ones, tended to be sparsely funded. The superintendents who headed them were psychiatrists or at least physicians. The personnel were mainly laypersons, with a sprinkling of trained nurses and physicians who did strictly medical tasks.

During the 1950s, there arose among psychiatrists a great argument. The detractors of these institutions argued they were merely custodial and perhaps should be done away with in favor of more therapeutic approaches. Their defenders asserted they were necessary for the custodial care of the chronically ill. During this era, psychiatrists who would previously have scorned work at these hospitals began to appear there, drawn by the opportunity to try out innovative ideas about therapy, and by the belief that not all patients there were incurable.

Psychiatry was then characterized by warring or at least contrasting ideological positions bearing on the etiology and treatment of mental illness. The two major ideologies were the somatic (which emphasized drug treatment especially) and the psychotherapeutic (which emphasized psychotherapy, with or without much reliance on drugs, except perhaps tranquilizers). A third ideological position then emerging was milieu therapy. However, those terms covered a multitude of different positions bearing on exactly what one should do when confronted by patients. Psychiatrists new to the state hospitals found they had to adapt their general positions to the exigencies of the local sites—for instance, to wards housing 150 patients.

During this era, also, psychologists and social workers were entering the service picture, with their graduate degrees, advanced clinical training, and ideologies about mental illness that were linked with the evolution of their particular disciplines. Specialized training in psychiatric nursing was, however, still relatively unknown; certainly unknown to most state hospitals.

The psychiatrists attempting to institute and administer experimental wards in these hospitals entered on their tasks with years of previous experience as physicians. They had been medical students, interns, and residents and had learned how hospital wards work—to wit, a physician as chief of service, nurses to carry out the daily operations and the medical orders. Patients were supposed to be relatively passive recipients of professional care. The standard medical aims were to care for and if possible cure the patients.

Psychiatry was also seeking a more respected place in the total medical firmament. Its status was relatively low, perhaps because its practitioners dealt with the mental rather than the medical but more importantly because it was not regarded as scientific—it really had no cures.

Many young psychiatrists who were spending time and energy on the experimental wards were venturesome, experimental, quite missionary in terms of their particular brands of psychiatric ideology, very anticustodial in stance, and yet very much physicians in their dedication to medicine. They and the other professional workers brought new ideas about treatment and care to the state hospitals and brought skills with which they hoped to radically change these custodially oriented places. Nevertheless, they came with different conceptions both of their own professional roles and requirements and of their new colleagues. They came also with different conceptions of proper—and improper—treatment and care (including psychotherapeutic and eclectic-pragmatic orientations). They exhibited varying degrees of commitment to their own professional requirements, to the treatment philosophy which they espoused, and to the institution in which they worked.

This particular hospital had a new superintendent who wished to bring the institution up to current psychiatric standards but who had relatively few resources for transforming its entrenched traditions. He chose to introduce modern psychiatry ward by ward, rather than by a massive assault on the traditionalists among the personnel. He recruited young psychiatrists by offering to each a single ward, a professional team, and considerable autonomy and freedom for organizing treatment. The teams on these "acute wards" were multidisciplinary, consisting of a psychiatrist chief, a physician, a nurse, a psychologist, a social worker, and a recreational or occupational therapist. Also there was at least one psychiatric aide (a layperson) on each team.

All five wards operated under several similar conditions: (1) "inadequate" physical facilities, (2) a patient-staff ratio in the range of 65–85 patients per team, (3) a random rotational system of patient admissions to the ward (except for sex, as the ward populations were either male or female in composition), (4) a wide range of diagnostic types but mostly "schizophrenia," and (5) an institutional mandate to organize a treatment system and to get patients discharged on improvement.

Nevertheless, each ward was different, principally in its treatment ideology, organization of treatment, and division of labor found among the professionals. In terms of the philosophy of treatment that predominated, the researchers referred to the respective wards as (1) the *radical patient government system*—a variant of the then popular "therapeutic community"; (2) the *representative system*—four arbitrarily divided aggregates of patients, each represented by a respective professional; (3) the *psychotherapeutic authority system*—following the psychotherapeutic model, but clearly under the direction of the psychiatrist chief, who had been recruited from the old hospital itself and who ran it much as any physician without psychiatric training might; (4) the *somatic system*—administered by a nonpsychiatrist physician along eclectic lines; and (5) the *unresolved system*—no dominant treatment ideology because the team was in much disarray, with a new chief and with team members each of whom had different ideas about treatment and how it should be implemented.

On each ward, the organization of treatment tended to reflect not only the professional and ideological orientations of the chief but also those of other team members. Except for the fourth ward, all chiefs were young psychiatrists who had been trained in the tradition of psychodynamic, one-to-one therapy. They had little or no experience with state hospitals, and no chief had anything but the vaguest notions of how to implement his therapeutic ideals in such an environment. They had to feel their way in organizing treatment programs, and each (including even the physician chief) had to learn how to deal with a "prefabricated" team. Bucher and Schatzman say that, although formal responsibility and authority were vested in the chief, in practice each had to come to terms with his team by negotiating with its members concerning methods of treatment and assignment of tasks. There was also relative fluidity of team composition on the wards. Various members, including some psychiatric chiefs, came and went during the teams' existences. Because they did not arrive simultaneously, the conditions for ideological and power struggle were kept alive. For example, a new psychologist assigned to a ward was not necessarily content to take over the precise functions of the preceding psychologists. So the arrival of a new team member tended rather to initiate a new round of ideological soundings, of instructions and arguments, and of negotiations over the assignment of tasks. And the total organization of treatment and the division of labor thereby underwent intermittent amendment.

The social structure of these wards was neither well crystallized—in the sense that actions were clearly prescribed either by tradition or by conventional professional title—nor "disorganized." The researchers thought it useful to think of the events that they observed as occurring within a framework of evolving social forms, whose details and rules were collectively vague and uncertain and for which few proven models of treatment or team organization existed—or were contested. While the professionals were discussing or arguing the merits of treatment forms, they also were making various claims to "essential" roles, aspiring to new ones, dumping old ones, and forcing each other to assume unwanted roles. So the researchers concluded that they were witnessing a field of negotiation and that these negotiations actually resulted in the specific divisions of labor found on these wards.

Among the salient properties of this negotiation context, one of the most striking is that many negotiations were *novel.* Of course, a fair proportion also were routine—about standard issues of work—but certainly some of the most consequential consisted of negotiations in which these professionals never before had engaged. For the first time, virtually all were thrown together with people of other professions to work as "a team." For the first time, psychiatrists were asked to operationalize their treatment philosophies. And for the first time people were about to find themselves doing tasks for which they had had no precedent in their training. These structural conditions resulted in negotiations new to them. In general, all were rather *inexperienced* at the novel negotiations that prevailed on these wards, except some had been there longer. In effect, they often had to learn together how to negotiate successfully—and sometimes they failed.

Another property of the negotiation context was that the *stakes* of the individual negotiators (for everyone negotiated) were both *common* and *very different.* What the staff members had in common was the goal of "getting the work done." However, what work ought to be done was sometimes a matter of disagreement. Beyond that, each wished to do the kind of work that would be most satisfying, whether for reasons of ease or identity or because it might further his or her career plans. What one wished to do might run afoul of other persons' goals, but it might not. Of great importance also was the matter of ideological stakes: Each professional tended to *represent* some ideological position on the question of psychiatric treatment, and many had firm convictions about implementing their particular ideologies. Sometimes their beliefs were congruent or identical; sometimes they were very divergent and even in great conflict. When negotiations over them were unsuccessful or the results were dissatisfying to one or more parties, then the personnel became frustrated, quit the ward, or found their real job rewards elsewhere.

Let us, before moving to consideration of the negotiations themselves, note one additional dimension of the context within which they took place. A striking feature of these psychiatric wards is that much of the negotiation has to do with what are or should be legitimate actions. The *legitimacy boundaries* are not covered by clear rules or conventional understandings: The boundaries themselves must often be negotiated.

Given those salient structural *and* contextual properties, here is what typically happened on these wards. Almost any task undertaken or sought by a professional was subject to review and denial. Even tasks backed by law and constitutional authority were called into question. Also, claims that had been won earlier were not insured against loss, and new ones could emerge with changes of personnel or the appearance of new ward contingencies. The claim might be to an area of competence and to particular associated tasks that might long have been successfully claimed by the team member's profession—then he was reiterating traditional rights—but the area and tasks might be quite new.

In either case, justifying rationales had to be given in negotiating for those areas of work, unless there was no contest over the traditional areas, and that was not necessarily always so. The legitimating rationales were grounded on such bases as legality (certification), appointed authority (institutional authorization), tradition, formal education (including degrees), prior experience with the task in question, current need or expediency, and a desire or wish to perform a task ("try it"). Understandably, personnel used those particular rationales that fit their respective situations.

What they judged as their situations were linked with their perceptions of the audience with whom they were negotiating. For example, on the fifth ward the psychologist was persuaded to accept the social worker's claim that on the grounds of prior experience she should conduct small-group therapy, but the ward's physician was not persuaded. The latter tended to accept only grounds of legality, appointed authority, or tradition for any professional task. As this particular dispute progressed, the social worker shifted her argument, basing her claim on knowledge by demonstrating a conceptual grasp of group dynamics. But the physician—very powerful because the psychiatrist was so new to this ward, hence uncertain of himself—neither understood nor appreciated group dynamics, so he did not honor the social worker's claim to competence.

Not all acquired tasks were gained through claiming, however: Some were proffered to particular professionals, for the team's dominant treatment ideology and current division of labor often were the grounds for suggesting that one member now undertake some specific task or handle some given area of work. If these were relatively desirable and seemed appropriate for one of the professionals, then they were offered to him or her. For instance, when the psychologist on the second ward fell behind in his "mental status examinations" of patients, he offered to teach the nurse how to do them and to share that work with her; she was delighted. On the patient government ward, the nurse was urged to engage in therapeutic contacts with patients, but she never quite understood how the team meant her to interact with patients; so then the social worker and psychologist repeatedly attempted to persuade her to hold group therapy meetings and offered to help her learn; again she could not quite imagine conducting such meetings and backed away from the proffered task. Her greatest difficulty was a lack of even minimal psychiatric language, apparently necessary to engage in such tasks. As these instances illustrate, proffers can be accepted and rejected, just as, analogously, claims can be honored or denied. The language of proffering utilizes rationales resting on such bases as ward ideology, professional pride, and individual experience.

One form of denying a claim was for teammates to do what the researchers termed "task stripping"—that is, one or more would deny another's claim to a particular task on grounds that it was inappropriate for him or her to carry out the task. These tasks usually were long associated with certain professions. Thus, on the patient government ward the physician suffered the loss of several traditional tasks, and each loss was a great blow to his professional status. First, he was not allowed to make decisions about the disposition of patients. Second, he was repeatedly deprived of his right to prescribe medications. Of course, some task stripping hardly qualifies as negotiation—only as coercion—except that in this instance the physician was not simply forbidden to do those tasks.

Teammates attempted to negotiate with him to stop and, more important, to trade the tasks for more appropriate ones. Thus, the physician accepted some proffered tasks, such as holding patient meetings, despite his initial difficulty in managing those meetings. In fact, at an earlier point, when disapproval grew intense over the physician's covert carrying on of his traditional tasks and when he was given several opportunities to resign, on each occasion he negotiated to remain as a member of the team. (The researchers note that part of his reason, however, may have been that he believed he really was carrying out *sub rosa* much of the ward's daily management.) These last negotiations, then, are complicated—he is negotiating perhaps to continue his covert manipulations but outwardly is negotiating with implicit acceptance of denied traditional claims and proffered acceptances of quite new tasks.

The complexity of issues concerning legitimate terrains and boundaries, and negotiations over them, can be underlined further. On the representative government ward, the psychiatrist chief readily agreed not to do psychotherapy with any of the patients, since, in the first place, he was not a "representative" and, in the second place, psychotherapy could not (ideologically) be given to one patient unless all patients were given psychotherapy (none was—they were given only group therapy). However, on the medical authority ward run by the physician, any professional, even the aide, could engage in psychotherapy with any patient. Thus, on one ward, psychotherapy was not subject to claims; on the other, no claiming was necessary to engage in psychotherapy, because the chief had decreed its possibility. On the patient government ward, all the major claims of the social worker and psychologist were realized; they, under the leadership of the psychiatrist chief, had established on the ward a milieu therapeutic revolution, had together established its basic design, and were in a position to dictate tasks for the physician and nurse, refusing to negotiate with them except within the established framework. The physician and nurse were forced to share unfamiliar and, for them, undesirable tasks. One consequence was a series of threats to "quit" and then the actual resignations by successive nurses, who wanted to carry out their traditional tasks and who were not willing to engage in those forced by the patient government ideology.

From the preceding discussion, additional properties of this negotiation context become clearer. The first pertains to representation: Who is negotiating for whom? Some parties are negotiating for *themselves*. Some are negotiating for the *team*. Without any stretch of imagination, we can also imagine (in some of the preceding instances as well as the following) that some parties may be negotiating for their *professions* or for some *ideological position* held within mental health professions. An allied contextual property is that negotiation can take place between *individuals* (two parties)' or can involve *alliances* (social worker and psychologist negotiate with the nurse); of course, it can also be *collective,* as when the entire team agrees to handle matters in certain ways.

One further contextual property is that many of the negotiations tend to be *linked*: They do not stand in isolation but are related rather directly to others already carried out or simultaneously going on. In order to accomplish common purposes (as well as some individual goals), it is necessary that multiple, linked agreements be reached. Indeed, if the agreements were not seen as linked, conflicts could be caused by the lack of their coordination. An example of the latter is that the physician chief on the medical authority ward neither clearly defined nor clearly negotiated the respective statuses and tasks of the new nurse and the aide, who had previously run the ward. So a conflict ensued, in which both laid claim to the management of the ward and patients. When the negotiations between nurse and aide broke down, the nurse threatened to resign. The adjudicating chief finally backed the nurse. Although there followed months of negotiations between nurse and aide over very specific tasks, the essential conflict had ended with that adjudicated victory for the nurse.

Another striking property of this negotiation context is that many of the agreements reached through negotiation are reviewed and *renegotiated*. Relationships among the staff have duration but change (including new balances of power among them), previous agreements are perceived as having undesirable consequences, new contingencies arise anyhow—and personnel leave and are replaced by new persons—for all those reasons, negotiations can be renegotiated. The new agreements reached may be the same as the old ones, but most often they are different.

How those contextual properties, plus ones noted earlier, provide conditions for the negotiations can be exemplified further by describing the evolution of the representative government ward. Its psychiatrist chief defined his function initially as one of teaching and guiding the team, but he had no prior commitment as to how to operationalize his democratic philosophy. Also, he accepted his social worker and psychologist as full partners in the therapeutic process, and they were able thereby to gain a measure of ideological leadership. The chief's philosophy also gave full sway to the development of an "intellectual union" among team members. Problems and tasks were discussed at team meetings, and assignments were hammered out in collective negotiation. Under these conditions, the traditional roles and expectations of all team members were in jeopardy. They might find themselves sharing traditional tasks with other professionals, while taking over entirely new ones that had to be done. This kind of situation proved advantageous to those professionals who sought significant therapeutic roles. But the nurse and physician also were encouraged to assume these roles. Since the representative system was evolved out of a series of meetings focused on the problem of how to treat each patient under ward circumstances, the nurse and physician took the necessary initial steps toward entering the universe of psychiatric discourse. The nurse, who learned more quickly, began coaching the physician in psychiatric attitudes toward patients. She strongly supported the idea of a representative system, never dreaming she herself might become a representative of an aggregate of patients. When the team asked her to be a representative, she was timorous at first but agreed to accept if the team would supervise her. To the physician, sharing authority and dispositional functions—even some traditional medical ones—having to submit to team supervision at first seemed a violation of his rights as a doctor; but the partial stripping of prerogatives was soon compensated by the advantages of being a representative. He and the nurse could order the services of other professionals for their own groups of patients, for instance, and could criticize or review the therapeutic programs followed by others on the team—and, singly or as allies, could enter into negotiations about how to change those programs.

I shall conclude analysis of this general negotiation context by looking briefly at the situation of the fifth ward, the one that Bucher and Schatzman call an "unresolved system." My purpose is to underline consequences of *differential stakes* and to bring out certain features of the *balance of power* that entered into negotiations on these wards. This particular ward had no single or dominant treatment ideology. The team itself was divided in its purposes and fragmented in structure. The psychiatrist chief had a psychotherapeutic orientation and was disposed to keep much control over therapy and staff actions. He "saw" patients, developed programs for each, and expected his staff to follow his suggestions and report to him on patient progress. This organization of treatment was carried on quite independently and was separate from the activities of the physician, whose orientation was somatic and whose most pressing concern was for patient census and disposition, patient control, and progress reports. The psychologist and social worker were intent on pursuing milieu therapy interests in the form of small- and large-group therapies. The nurse was the main work link for all the personnel because of her ubiquitous presence and her willingness to follow the orders or requests of all her colleagues. Given all this, team members necessarily attempted to engineer consent to their individual claims in different ways. There were alliances, but these were mostly covert or collusive in character. Also, the staff found their claims difficult not only to realize but even to articulate. Nevertheless, being persons with strong professional, ideological, or institutional commitments, they persisted in attempting to realize their claims. Unlike personnel on the other wards, who sought alliances within their respective teams, staff on this ward went far afield in search of forces to bring to bear on those who would not negotiate—even going to the hospital superintendent. They also went elsewhere to satisfy claims directly: They did psychotherapy on other wards or engaged in part-time work outside the hospital itself.

Just prior to the researchers' arrival, the preceding psychiatrist chief of this ward had left but another had not yet been assigned. In the meantime, the ward was headed by the physician who antedated the team system itself, having been at the hospital for years. The physician's authorized control over the patients and the personnel backed up his repeated claim to operational leader-

ship, but this was a forced claim, since ideological leadership belonged to the psychologist. The physician was not willing to negotiate with anybody except the psychologist, to whom he proffered a
kind of lieutenancy plus freedom to develop a treatment program.
The physician needed a working colleague, at least until the psychiatrist arrived. He regarded the nurse and social worker as
"young novices," incapable of intelligent and professional initiative.
The psychologist refused the lieutenancy but was forced into a position as team consultant. He himself did not want to get involved
and found part-time work as a therapist outside the hospital.

The claimed right of the social worker to conduct small-
group therapy on the ward was denied by the physician, as was the
nurse's claim to medical collegiality. The social worker sought to
make the psychologist an ally, but the latter refused; the nurse
proffered the psychologist the role of teacher, but he refused to give
his time. He withheld his own major claims until the arrival of the
psychiatrist. Under these conditions, negotiation within the team
came to a virtual standstill. Most claims remained pending. The
stage was set for a full round of negotiation: The physician wanted
responsibility and operational leadership to pass to another "responsible" person; the psychologist wanted an "intellectual" colleague;
the nurse wanted someone to teach her psychodynamics; and the
social worker wanted an ally to help mitigate the physician's
"arbitrary power." Both nurse and social worker were intent on
performing tasks for which they had very real and imposing models
on other experimental wards.

The psychiatrist who arrived was relatively young and quite
inexperienced in hospital psychiatry. His initial intentions were to
observe and to learn the ongoing system and then to begin assuming
operational leadership. The physician quickly sized him up as a
"boy" and grimly held onto operational leadership. While the others
saw the psychiatrist in different ways, all waited for the inevitable
contest over the chieftainship. While waiting, the psychologist,
social worker, and nurse met frequently, to find ways of helping the
psychiatrist to gain the real power. In the meantime, the social
worker made a private claim to the psychiatrist that he be allowed
to conduct small-group therapy and was granted the right to do so.
The physician could not prevent the social worker from organizing

a discharge-planning group, but he did quickly manage to discharge or transfer some patients selected for the planning group. In this way, he disclaimed the implicit claim of the psychiatrist that he could honor a claim that the physician would not honor.

Another private agreement was negotiated between the nurse and psychologist, a mutual exchange whereby the psychologist taught the nurse diagnostic techniques in exchange for her sharing some of his responsibility in this task. Much earlier, the psychologist and the physician had agreed to share responsibility for this work. The adjustment of claims on the basis of private negotiation continued until the psychiatrist was able to effect his major claim. He did this by simple assertion and action, but not until he had secured leverage from the alliance within the team and explicit assurance from the institution's administration that his claim to the chieftainship was indeed honored and authorized.

Thus, professional personnel on this team attempted to effect some of their claims by secret alliances, private agreements, and a search for power and claim satisfaction outside the ward. Their tactics also included—and we can readily understand why—denying others' claims, rejecting proffers, refusing to enter into negotiations that might lose them some advantage or give them an undesirable task, and putting off negotiation until a more propitious time—including until the arrival of a new negotiator (the chief) or a new mediating authority (the chief). On this, as on other more "organized" wards, those with little balance of power in negotiations could also act in *sub rosa* fashion to do the things that they might not otherwise get by negotiating with the principal power figure.

On the various wards, the structural bases for the power that given personnel could bring to any negotiation were, as we can see, fairly varied. Power might be associated with formal positions (as with the psychiatric chiefs) or with traditional professional bases (the high status of physicians and the relatively low status of nurses); but power was also associated with amount of specific experience on a specific ward or gained through the formation of alliances, or—more simply—power was achieved because the initiating negotiator signaled that an honored or proffered claim would help the other to accomplish his own purposes (the nurse who beat out the competing aide promised an efficient ward; the psychologists who offered to teach the nurses the things they wanted to learn). The various bases of power for different staff people shifted in accordance with changes of personnel and with the evolution of the negotiated order itself—along with perceived consequences of that order.

Summary. This case depicts groups engaged in ongoing work within an institutional setting. The negotiation relates to that continuous work and to the fact that work relationships develop and evolve over time. Negotiations may transpire between single individuals but are related to other negotiations carried out with other teammates. Much of the working together and the work itself was new for the participants, largely because of the ideological features of the work drama. Of course, there were traditional features that were related to the hospital itself, to ward organization, and to professional relationships, but many of these were affected by the novel features of the ward and its work. Hence, as the researchers came to see, a great deal of negotiation was a necessity. The many features of that negotiation, as detailed earlier, are related in determinable ways to the properties of the particular negotiation context. Said another way, the contextual conditions, in their various combinations, determined specifiable kinds of negotiations, negotiating parties and their tactics, subprocesses of negotiation, and the like.

To recapitulate briefly, a major contextual property was that many issues involving negotiation related to questions of legitimacy: What work might members of each occupational group do legitimately? Also, many consequential negotiations were novel for the negotiating parties, all of whom were rather inexperienced in these types of negotiation. Each professional tended to represent some ideological position concerning psychiatric treatment, and some of those positions were quite conflicting. The professional might also represent himself or herself, the ward team, a coalition, or a profession. Many negotiations were linked, relating to each other. Most were relatively overt; some, however, were covert, especially among persons who had little power to make their positions felt on the ward. The stakes involved in negotiations might be common to the negotiating parties or might be very different—might be linked to personal or ideological aspirations. The alternatives to negotiating would seem to have included not only refusal to negotiate or the breaking off of negotiation but also appeal to rules or authority, as well as attempts at education and persuasion, the manipulation of events, and, as noted later, even some forms of implied coercion (other than coercive threats used in the negotiating itself). The negotiation subprocesses noted on these wards included especially *trading off, mediating, exploring legitimate boundaries* via proffering advantages and territorial claiming, *bypassing* of negotiation, and—very important in this continual working out of conditions for working together—the *renegotiating* of previous agreements.

The researchers, in their attempts to characterize the most general features of ward organization—and much struck by the extent and the apparent reasons for negotiation—felt much dissatisfied with standard modes of characterizing institutional organization. They found themselves using terms that captured the predominance of negotiated agreements and action. Of course, more than negotiation was involved: Personnel did threaten to quit and sometimes carried through on the threats. Persuasion and "educating" were as much features, perhaps, as was negotiation. (Patients certainly were much persuaded and sometimes coerced.) The chiefs of the medical authority and psychotherapeutic authority wards were both strongly dominant and did not brook much opposition to their principal administrative ideas. And, of course, there were traditional rules characteristic of these institutions—the legal responsibility of the chiefs of service, for instance—that entered into the total order of these wards. Perhaps too, certain matters were nonnegotiable—ultimately, the basic ideological positions of the various psychiatrists—although the operationalization of those ideologies was exceedingly negotiable.

The researchers themselves ended by thinking of these wards as arenas wherein various personnel (and patients too) negotiated continuously in order to work together, to get things done, to reach common as well as private goals. They coined such terms as *negotiated order* to capture the flavor of the social order of these wards. Perhaps that is too strong a term, but it does suggest the difficulty of characterizing these emergent types of social forms, as encountered by those who have studied them.

As to the structural context outlined in introducing this case study: In what sense can it be said not only that this context provided general conditions for the negotiation context itself but also, in reverse, that the consequences of negotiations had a determinable impact on the larger structural setting (national or professional)? Obviously, no single negotiation or even one hospital had much impact. Yet the many such "experiments" taking place simultaneously or over a very few years must have had considerable impact—in giving new kinds of training to professionals; changing their attitudes toward professional partners, toward their own work, and toward themselves; altering their ideologies; opening up new types of careers; and so on. Negotiated agreements and actions were very much a part of that consequential ferment. Said another way, the negotiations were integral to the subsequent changes in the state of the mental health professions and their associated institutions.

Case: Continuous Working Relations in
Industrial Firms

The organizational matrix of industrial firms studied by Melville Dalton (1959) in the 1950s was perhaps not as rapidly changing, as emergent in its social order, as that reviewed in the preceding case. Nevertheless, the establishments within which he did almost a decade of field work also presented him with a most bewildering puzzle. Organizational theory at the time was picturing such places as fairly purposeful organizations, their policies developed from above and executed more or less rationally, if not always efficiently, by the echelons below. Dalton's eyes and ears confronted him with a different picture. There was much heterogeneity and clashing of group and individual purpose, with people working frequently at cross purposes and with little sense of a unitary structure.

The virtue of Dalton's monograph is that it spells out exactly that latter kind of picture in great detail and with a fine feeling for reality. Perhaps the book has not had the powerful impact it should have had on organizational theory because his own conceptualization was neither forcefully nor incisively asserted. Essentially, he was arguing against too rational a perspective on organizational functioning. He was also arguing against too literal an acceptance of the distinction between "formal" and "informal relations," then popular largely because of the Hawthorne researches and the studies they stimulated. Dalton's main theoretical argument does not appear explicitly until page 218, where it is discussed under the heading "The Interconnections of Formal and Informal Action." He does not reject the couplets of formal-informal, official-unofficial, but advocates examining closely—as he has indeed done—the interplay between these "two phases" of organizational effort. Readers who scan the book expecting to find the theoretical formulation in his final "Conclusions" chapter will discover that quite a different set of "large" issues are discussed.

In sum, Dalton's monograph was a bit short on explicit theory. Fortunately, his collecting and reporting of data were exceptionally good, so anyone can have a hand at reconceptualizing those data. My purpose is more restricted: only to utilize his data on negotiations—of whose importance he was well aware—as a source for negotiation analysis and, not incidentally, to use his own. Of course, one cannot help but ask, then, what import this later analysis has for understanding the social order of industrial firms such as those Dalton studied.

The structural context that bears on these negotiations includes at least the following major conditions: "what everybody knows" about American industry and the marketplace, the existence of management-labor conflicts within such industries, the existence of labor unions, of their agreements with both through negotiation with management and through the passage of legislation, and the differential status and social class positions and careers or jobs of workers and managers.

Turning now to Dalton's data, I begin with his comments on national agreements between management and labor. The agreements struck through bargaining between the national representatives of management and labor are supposed in due course to be implemented at local levels. However, Dalton, who had closely studied the local implementation, remarked that the national contract cannot possibly cover all the issues relevant to people at the various localities. Furthermore, ambiguity is built accidentally and intentionally into the contract. Each negotiating side sees advantages in most clauses of the final contract, although the other side may not necessarily read the clause in the same way. At any rate, the national agreement is so broad and ambiguous that when announced at the local plant it inspires more contempt than awe. Nevertheless, the negotiated contract does demand seeming adherence at the local site.

Locally, this expectation contributes to unofficial interpretations and practices as the men try to get around items written into the national contract. To do that necessitates relatively *covert* and *continual* negotiation between management and labor. That negotiation goes on within plant settings that are characterized by various properties relevant to the negotiation itself. Among them are those which Dalton himself particularly emphasizes. Thus there are cliques and friendships of varying duration and strength—within labor, within management, and involving both groups. There are complex issues to be handled that do not necessarily get solved easily by simple adherence either to long-standing rules or to labor and management identifications. In both labor and management, there are disputes over professional rights and functions. Men in management are pursuing various careers; and workingmen are much focused on their conditions of work. Both are pursuing various types of goals. And of course there is work to be done that, as we have already noted, leads local personnel—including key persons— to see the contract provisions more as irrelevant abstractions and barriers to getting the work done than as helpful for the necessary coordination of effort.

Relations at the plant level, then, are—as Dalton puts it— a blur of conflict, cooperation, and compromise initiated and guided by cross cliques. The resulting negotiation context understandably is something rather complex. More important, however, than mere complexity is the fact that the work arrangements and personal relationships that evolve within this negotiation context constitute a considerable portion of the social order of any of these plants (although Dalton does not use the term *social order*).

This negotiation context is characterized by a cluster of salient properties that, taken together, constitute conditions for the typical negotiations that take place at these industrial plants. Among the properties are the following. Many of the principal negotiators have *repeated negotiations* with each other. So they tend to be *experienced* at these particular kinds of negotiations (even though the persons whom they represent may be *inexperienced* at the negotiations). One or both negotiators are likely to be *representing* an absent party; but in fact they often *represent themselves* instead or additionally. Typically they do this covertly. In any event, much negotiation is *covert*—hidden from persons (not necessarily the represented person) who could endanger the negotiation if they knew about it. Each negotiation is likely to be part of a *series* of negotiations: Although a represented party might only be involved in the single act of negotiation, the actual negotiators have negotiated before and will do so again. Many of the negotiations are *linked;* they do not stand in isolation but depend on or involve others. Some of the negotiation is *novel,* but much of it is *routine:* it has been done before, in form if not in actual content. Some of the novel negotiation pertains to the *ambiguity of legitimate boundaries* within which some of the negotiation occurs. The *stakes* of the negotiators (or represented parties) are not necessarily mutually exclusive, but they are likely to be *different*—except insofar as each has a desire for continued relationship that will permit future successful negotiations. The *balance of negotiation power* is variable for different instances of negotiation, but threat of some kind of undesirable action (as defined by the other) often is one alternative *option* to forcing negotiation or to reaching a more satisfactory conclusion to the negotiation. Otherwise, the alternative to failed or denied negotiation is that one or both parties may fail to attain their respective aims, since usually there is neither arbitration or mediation (although see the later discussion of the "faction broker"), and certainly there is no recourse to law. Of course, the manipulation of contingent events is often a possible alternative or accompaniment to negotiation.

Now let us see how those salient contextual properties combine with each other, thus acting as complex sets of conditions for interaction within the negotiation context. I shall quote liberally from incidents vividly noted in Dalton's monograph, while making appropriate analytic commentary about the quotations. A good place to begin is by noting that, although "representation" is very salient, the men frequently represent themselves in negotiations. In Dalton's words (1959, p. 114), speaking or "politicking" for oneself was usual. "The focus for private bargaining included pay increases, desirable days off during the work week, preferred weeks of the year for vacation, a better work position, escape from restrictions applied to others, and so on." A man could negotiate for these personal *stakes* directly with the shop steward or with the griever—who desired to represent the worker—or with both.

One condition that could keep negotiation through *representatives* to a minimum—and with clear consequences—was, as one man said (p. 114): "There's no horse trading at all in our division, because the majority of workers are whites and the griever is a Negro. You won't find many whites filing grievances because they don't want a black going to bat for them or feeling that he had got something for them." Next, a union member told about how the potentially represented men attempt to negotiate over *representation*, how they may rely on "trade-off" tactics to get representation, and about the conditions under which this tactic is "now" more difficult to manage (p. 114): "There used to be a satisfactory handling of grievances before the check-off was put in. The union put that damn thing in without a vote. . . . Before the check-off, the griever used to come around to collect dues. In that way, a man had some contact with the griever. When he'd come to collect . . . you could tell him about your beef. And by God if he didn't promise to do something about it you could refuse to pay up. . . . You could make a dicker and be sure of getting something for your money. Now you're damn lucky if you can find your griever."

Next is an instance where union representation takes priority over the representation of an individual worker and where the open rejection of a proposal to initiate the latter's claim is linked with *repeated, serial,* and *linked* negotiations over "more important" *stakes* (p. 119): "A man can have a good, legitimate grievance, but the union may pass him and his grievance up to keep on good terms with the company. The union'll do it every time when there are big grievances coming up and are backed by most of the boys." The repeated, serial, and linked properties of the negotiation context lead to the following kinds of consequence—in an incident that also illustrates the characteristic horse trading—which in turn leads to avoidance of "trouble." A foreman had sent home a workman who continually had come late. The workman filed a grievance, but the superintendent answered by allowing him to return to work. The foreman asked the superintendent why. In his words (p. 120), "He handed me a line of salve about 'having to do it.' Said it 'was a small item after all' and that he 'might want a big favor from the union sometime in the future. . . . We have to trade back and forth. Sometimes we give in, sometimes they give in. That's why we never have any big trouble.' " The angry foreman, however, points up how he himself can use a canny countertactic (perhaps also threaten to use it), which consists of repeated negotiations with the union until such time as he will refuse legitimately to negotiate—and thus plunge his superior into a difficult negotiation situation (p. 120): "Well, damn that noise! If O'Brien wants to make me look like a fool everytime I make a decision, why by God he can make all the decisions. You know, two can play that game. I can give the boys every damn thing he can give them. Then when they come up with a big one what I know damn well he can't give 'em, I'll tell 'em to take it to him—that I don't want anything to do with it."

Trade-offs can be combined with representation of one set of union members rather than another—where the trade-off is fairly well known by most of the people directly concerned but kept secret from higher management (the entire negotiation is *covert*). Thus Dalton reports "unofficial bargaining" between grievers and foremen that in some sense hurt a small group while favoring a majority of those concerned. The foreman's brother was given a "gravy job," and in return the foreman liberally allowed the use of certain "bonus-fattening factors" when questioned by incentive appliers as to whether good shop practice warranted application of those factors. Eighteen men confidentially considered themselves robbed, but ninety-five had gained. This collective bargaining led to what a majority of workers in the subunit regarded as a substantial wage increase. Those who lost out were irate and made covert threats, although on occasion, Dalton notes, they received "good" jobs that they would not have received if they actually had filed grievances over the issue. Besides, if they had, both the foreman and the griever would have denied the charges.

Also, the griever had a further tactic that was immensely powerful because of his role in future negotiations for the union members: Any revolt on this particular issue would have thrown him "into a listless reverse" of stalling in regard to processing their future grievances.

Trade-offs are—as important stakes—a consequence of *experienced* negotiators who have had long-term relationships with each other, most often acting as representatives of parties absent from the actual negotiation. Many of these trade-offs are *covert*— or, if known of by superiors, are winked at—and they tend also to be connected with still other trade-offs in *linked* negotiations. Thus, some department chiefs did not want to handle grievances, so they passed on that responsibility to first-line foremen, who in turn worked out tacit exchanges with stewards and committeemen who agreed to lessen the filing of grievances. In effect, they passed on the pressures of department chiefs, Dalton remarks, to the work group itself. In return, the foremen who were involved in the agreements drove to the homes of grievers, also some of the rank-and-file, and picked up defective appliance motors and parts, delivered them to the shops for repair at company cost, and returned them. Dalton remarks that the foremen presumably got a trade-off from their departmental chiefs.

When an experienced negotiator refuses to play the game and will not try to make the trading off a smooth process, the following sort of reaction takes place. A foreman was demoted because of inability to carry out orders. He took revenge by following orders to the letter, stifling all initiative in his work, and getting himself elected to the grievance committee. "With full knowledge of techniques and personalities on both sides, he became such a figure in the union that he forced management to reckon with him on all grievances, whether he or another officer presented the case" (p. 119). In other words, even when he did not officially represent a union member, he made himself part of the negotiating process, with consequences immediately better for the claimants and worst for management, but in the end probably worse for both.

The continued relationships with concomitant *serial* negotiations between negotiators lead to, in Dalton's words, fairly complex "deals." Sometimes these involve bypassing one negotiating party in favor of another—in the following instance, someone who would not agree to the deal, in favor of his superior who would. The griever was not able to get three men promoted because they could not pass the tests legally required and overseen by the foreman. The griever therefore went to the superintendent, who had two union employees whom he wished promoted because of their uncommon ability but who lacked seniority. The two negotiators made a deal: The superintendent talked about his two protégés; the griever "agreed to the promotions if 'his' three men were given a test they could pass and if he could witness the testing of the other two. The exchange was concluded in that way." So the griever "escaped trouble with his constituents for allowing promotion of two workmen over those with greater seniority. He was exultant . . . and remarked 'I don't win 5 percent of the cases that go over Dickie's [foreman] head' " (p. 128).

The continued relationships between negotiators, which can involve complex deals, are also linked with the nature of the negotiation *stakes*—themselves linked not merely with getting the work done but also with personal animosities and friendships and the accumulation of mutual obligations through serial and repeated negotiations. Indeed, the griever, for instance, may continue to keep his representative position not only because of his many successes—followed by success at the union polls—but also because of political support abetted by his distribution of covert trade-offs. Informal leaders of shop cliques were political whips, defending "the griever's behavior, kept him informed of pertinent developments, and fought for his reelection. In return, he rewarded them with favors growing out of his bartering with individual managers. These favors were usually of a kind too rare to be granted promiscuously, hence members of the rank and file were recipients only infrequently or as they made outstanding contributions to the cause" (pp. 116–117).

Since many such arrangements are covert and there is consequent danger if the secret gets out, one negotiating party may have to promise protection for the other party via an additional, linked, covert arrangement. Note also that the accumulation of mutual obligations results in—to use Dalton's felicitous term—a "balance of favors" that very much affects the outcome of the current negotiation. Thus (see pp. 126–127), the superintendent, who had previously broken the plant rules, had allowed the griever's relative to pass a test for promotion—a fake test. Shortly afterward, two other men pressed the griever "for a similar favor. He sought to get O'Brien to allow the same arrangement. . . . After weighing the complications, O'Brien refused." Then the griever and the informal shop leaders "decided to claim that danger of accidents existed in the requirement that a man prove his skill on a new machine or in a new position without communication with others." The griever argued that workers nearby be allowed to caution the candidate if they saw him about to endanger himself and others. The superintendent still was troubled, so the griever assured him that "only more experienced workers should step forward to warn the novice and *only when genuine danger existed*. O'Brien agreed, knowing that operating instructions would be given to candidates under the guise of advice on safe procedure." Naturally, the two workers passed these tests. In return, the superintendent was given a concession—a rescheduling of workers: "After considerable review of the balance of favors interlarded with joking about what constitutes friendship, the schedule was accepted with the usual concession demanded by the union, 'that there be some flexibility in getting days off to take care of exceptional cases.' "

Because of their *repeated* negotiations and cumulative obligations, one party may have to work very hard in order to make some working arrangement actually "stick" with others who have different stakes in those negotiations. For example, a general foreman wanted to move a day foreman to the night shift and a night foreman to the day shift. But when told this by the general foreman, the latter went to the griever to cash in on obligations owing to him from previous negotiations with the griever. The griever agreed to counteract the agitation among the workers for rotation of shifts, which had been set in motion by the night shift foreman, who himself wished to move to the day shift. Meanwhile the general foreman suggested to the griever that a change might be good for everyone; the griever agreed but said nothing of his arrangement with the day foreman. The griever at first was unsuccessful in arguing against rotation with the workers, but eventually he succeeded in persuading the night workers and then won the general vote on the issue of rotation. The general foreman knew that he had been outsmarted but did not press the griever, who had previously helped him to obtain a vacation schedule that otherwise would have been difficult to get the workers to accept. That last sentence underscores what Dalton has, quite properly, called the "web of commitments" that evolves as a consequence of these typically repeated, serial, and linked negotiations.

Since much of this web consists of covert "workable arrangements" (another apt term), when the persons who have made the arrangements leave the scene, even temporarily, the consequences are apt to be awkward for those who remain. Leaving for a vacation necessitates additional, special arrangements in order to avoid those consequences—foreseen by those already experienced in them. Thus (see pp. 235–236), the supervisors "regularly operated in a network of unofficial and confidential understandings" so that their replacements were confused when following only the official guidelines of the officer who was absent on vacation. Sometimes the replacement was an enemy, so one would not want him to know about the arrangements; sometimes he was a superior who had not known about the covert understandings. The matter was additionally delicate when "informal claims were tied to issues in some critical stage." In consequence, executives were reluctant to stay away on their vacations; they would cut short their vacations or maintain continual contact via the telephone. "Those about to take the recess reflected their concern in remarks that replacements might 'gum up the works,' 'make a miscue,' or 'do the wrong thing'" (1959, p. 235). The officers were talking, of course, about covert arrangements in the making.

What may happen if the covert, workable arrangements become known to the wrong persons—and under what kinds of conditions that happens—is illustrated by the following incident. A secretary to a department head, although she had been paid off for not reporting his covert arrangements, once confided the secret to another secretary. The latter's husband was in the army, although he would be returning shortly. He had been a department head before going into the army, but the couple were uncertain he would be rehired. "So his wife, seeing the interpretation that could be made of Nevers' bookkeeping, and the consequences, hoped to have him fired and have her husband succeed him. She persuaded

Nevers' saleswoman to report him in as bad a light as possible. The officially ignorant general manager knew roughly of Nevers' techniques and regarded him as 'too good a man for the organization to lose.' Forced to defend procedural dignity, he simulated a release but gave Nevers his choice of workplace among the statewide units, vigorously recommended him, and aided him in the successful transfer" (p. 210). (That particular incident was drawn from Dalton's observations in a department store, but there are no substantial differences between what happened there and in the industrial plants that he studied.)

Here is another incident involving the opening up of what should have been a covert situation. The consequences show up clearly in the realm of executive careers (see pp. 132–133). A supervisor and a griever had agreed on additional bonus hours in order to raise the pay level of two or three jobs. But the engineers, frightened at the implied criticism of their time studies of those jobs, restudied them and said that unnecessary operations were being paid for, so they reduced the time to the original figures. The superintendent then tried to get the engineering head to change the jobs back but at first was unsuccessful. There was conflict, and the superintendent was able to get further time studies done, winning a slight increase in hours for the griever. But that victory affected his career. "His attempts to have 'smooth relations' with the union trapped him into the unforgivable sin of openly bargaining for the union with a group of his colleagues. This was not forgotten when he was under consideration for the divisional post" (p. 133)— which a competitor won.

Sometimes special steps—involving additional (that is, linked) covert arrangements—are taken in order to keep secret the original negotiations and their resultant working arrangements. If not, the consequences can be dire; but if successful the consequences can be most felicitous. For instance, the head officer wanted periodic surprise inspections and parts counts made in his departments. Two superintendents had arrangements with the department heads that only "nominal surprise" visits would occur—all arrangements having been made beforehand as to the "walking route." Also, arrangements were made with the workers to get certain parts out of the way, others cleaned up, and so on. Arrangements were also made among the department heads to move parts around, using each other's storage areas. "Thus a working adjustment" was reached. The office continued to receive "its required flow of documents, which, though only roughly accurate, allowed planning within workable limits. Able to work behind a screen of assured formalities, Bingham and Taylor escaped nervous breakdown. Friction between operation and maintenance subsided to a low level. Finally, the Milo [Fractionating Center] chiefs preserved their conception of local rights and at the same time raised morale" (p. 49).

Dalton speaks of "prefigured justifications" that act as potential tactical defenses just in case the covert arrangements might become known. These rationales consist of "logical explanations to cover essential but irregular actions." If someone were detected and questioned, "his convincing response" would save both him and the other negotiator from embarrassment and punishment. The invention of these rationales presumably is linked (although Dalton does not discuss the point) with past unfortunate experiences, when one or other of the men failed to have ready such justifying rationales. Certainly, *routinized* covert negotiation is likely to result in the preparation of such justifying means.

Not all covert arrangements are made merely because the negotiators respect each other, have nicely balanced trade-offs, or have accumulated debts to each other. A negotiation and its resulting set of agreements may be forced under threat. In these industrial plants, the person using this tactic is unlikely to threaten exposure of some other covertly reached arrangement: The whole web of commitments apparently is much too delicately balanced for that! Rather, the threat seems more likely to consist only of promising to cause someone's performance to suffer or having blame fall on him for not getting work properly done.

The following incident is revealing. For three months, a line executive had ingeniously stalled delivery of his project, hiding its completion from the impatient top-level men. Under threat from the griever of an illegal union strike, the executive agreed not to introduce change during a stipulated period of time, since the change would drop some pay bonuses to workers if the new system were applied immediately. The executive also gave in because of his margin of safety in a "circle of tightening commitments." He and the griever agreed that during the period of delay they could work out transfers of workmen "by seniority" and without pay losses for most people concerned. The executive was "in no position to refuse the demand"—his was a weak position; he was involved in a network of covert negotiations that if discovered could lead to reprisals against him. So he stalled his own impatient subordinates, kept them busy, and in the end had to prevent their leaking information to top levels through their own fear of his reprisals on them. One consequence was a severe drop in their morale.

In fact, implied threat of reprisal lurks behind a great many of the covert and even tacit arrangements. Thus, staff officers had permitted minor rule breaking by the line "in exchange for aid" from the line during crises and to delay in the application of changes already approved by top management. They also agreed to transfer of staff research funds to line accounts "in order to get more, or continued, cooperation. This last may never be expressed in such terms but is understood" (pp. 104–105). All of these agreements are "essential to prevent the line from revealing staff errors to the top." Another potential line reprisal is for the workers to "stand pat" on the rules "at a time when the staff wants evasion."

Although these threats and displays of power certainly occur, one should not overemphasize them, for a great many negotiation arrangements are made without even the hint of potential coercion. The stakes of getting trade-offs (what Dalton also calls "favor trading") are quite as important to getting negotiations carried out. And, when negotiators work together for years, trade-off "becomes simple and so unofficially acceptable that it seems natural" (p. 209).

We must also not forget that many covert agreements are made because the stakes are high—not only the stakes for particular negotiations but also those for keeping continuing relationships successfully operative. Also, the very possibility of punishment if covert negotiations become known helps both to cement relationships and to act as a condition for future negotiation cooperation. "The more 'illegal' their pact, the closer they were drawn to each other and the greater their fear of exposure" (p. 117).

That statement bears directly on the interesting question of the engendering of alliances and coalitions—even across staff-line boundaries. As Dalton says (p. 117): "Sometimes leaks led to conflict between grievers; at times there was the paradox of friction between a griever's and 'his' superintendents, on the one hand, and another griever and his allied executives, on the other hand. The friction of course arose from (1) envy of those in an alliance who successfully avoided the (national) contract, (2) demands by rank-and-file members or first-line foremen for similar benefits and free-lance dealing, and (3) horror among those few in other camps who made an end of mastering procedures and clauses and saw themselves and their labor undone by 'politics.' " So grievers who were having "poor relations with management fished for the secret of those who got on well. The same was true of foremen. Inevitably leaks occurred, denials were made, and new fronts were set up. Here, as with the alliances . . . among managers, fear of consequences and knowledge that enemies of today might be the friends of tomorrow usually prevented open breaks."

From the foregoing, it becomes clear that much negotiation in these industrial plants can be successfully carried out because the negotiators are not only *experienced* in dealing with each other but also experienced at the particular kinds of negotiation in which they engage. It is also quite evident that some of the negotiation is *novel* rather than routine: It involves new areas and putting together combinations of acts and persons that are far from usual. One structural condition for this, as noted earlier, is that the working out of differences "outside the national contract was not subject to guidebooks or officials' rules, the course of action . . . [was] thrown open to the ingenuity of participants in finding means of simulating conformity to the contract while adjusting behavior to the pressures that could not be escaped" (p. 113). Other conditions are new contingencies not foreseen, including career contingencies and evolving personal relations, as well as contingencies arising from decisions made at national levels.

But, to return to the first condition about working out differences locally (outside the national contract), this is equivalent to saying that another property of the negotiation context can be that sometimes the boundaries of what can be *legitimately* negotiated are relatively *ambiguous*. When that is so, the outcome of negotiation is more precarious and often more complex. We have seen examples of this, as in the negotiation over special promotion via rigged tests. We have also seen that much covert negotiation occurs around issues or stakes that are ambiguously legitimate or illegitimate—depending on one's viewpoint. Top-level management might well consider the working arrangements illegitimate, if they knew about them. Some lower-level executives might also—but they might not; and sometimes it is clear enough that the arrangements are "really" legitimate, providing that one is realistic about what simply has to be done in order that work can get accomplished or contributory morale be kept sufficiently high.

For instance, Dalton writes about "unofficial rewards," which are equivalent to certain kinds of trade-offs, and about "payoffs." Thus the men can be paid off very quietly: "They understood that discreet use of [company] nails, paint, brushes, plumbing and electric fixtures, and so on was acceptable as long as inventories balanced" (1959, p. 201). Sometimes the payoff was openly known—but not talked about out of bounds. The payoff can be for services rendered or for a salary that is felt to be too low—a genuine compensatory payoff. For the men who work for the executives, there are payoffs in esteem, coffee, and free meals at the executives' houses. All this greases the wheels of good feelings and morale, softens lines between departments, and keeps workers busy during the slack season, when they may get restless. The executives also got their covert payoffs, such as having their cars serviced free at the plant. However, when occasional crackdowns occurred, higher executives would call on skilled machinists from the shops instead of the usual garage personnel—that is, they would make new covert arrangements with new negotiating parties.

There was always the possibility, of course, that some people might disagree over whether or not the payoffs, or the negotiations that led to them, really were legitimate. When demands were made by a worker without sufficiently significant contribution having been made by him for a payoff, then "the 'reward' given was sometimes a disguised penalty. At Attica Assembly Company, one such aggressive person demanded a 'share' of the house paint he knew others had received. He was given all the usual bulk-purchased and unmixed ingredients—except the drying fluid. Elated, he mixed and applied the paint. When it did not dry, the accumulation of dust and insects ruined his work. He became a laughingstock without recourse" (p. 202).

When there is not even complete support for the claimant, yet that support is powerful, then we have a situation such as the following. Note that this support for the claimant derives from his good representation record and the accumulation of negotiation debts, plus the deep implication of almost everyone in a web of commitments. There was a griever, admired both by management and the union members—a great bargainer. His successful bargaining allowed him privileges to which only a minority of his constituents objected. One month he hardly appeared except to punch his card early in the morning and late in the afternoon; he even had his friends do this for him. "During the interval, he spent much of his time in the union hall attending to minor things. His actual work was to elude the demands of a minority in the plant that wanted him to process grievances, which he and the managers involved had agreed to not consider in their current balance of claims on each other. Beemer's enemies among the workers tried to bring the case before higher-ups in the union, but his friends were in the majority and blocked the action. One of his supporters commented 'What the hell. He was just resting up—having a little fun. We couldn't get a better man to represent us. He's got us more than any griever we ever had. If we had a sorehead in there, he'd never get us anything' " (p. 218).

Dalton notes occasional failures in this typical system of compensatory payoffs, because the person thinks that he is being paid exactly right or even too much. He is, in short, embarrassingly correct in his deportment. (The term *incorruptible* would not be correct here, unless one assumed that all those who agreed to compensatory payoffs really were dishonest—an assumption that hardly fits their understanding of the situation.) One of Dalton's examples is from his department store data: Because one employee refused the payoff, all her chief could do was give her deference and public praise. But in another example (pp. 212–213) it becomes apparent that resentment can arise toward such a person—not only on personal grounds but because he or she will not give compensatory payoffs and so blocks the development of normal working arrangements. One such lady, who ran the best soda fountain, aroused such resentment by not giving the usual favors at the fountain to employees that they forced the chief to check her records, "to imply that she was making errors, and to withhold the praise she obviously craved. Higher chain officials also asked her to explain her unique performance and hinted that she could not be that much superior to other fountain managers. After two years of mounting resentments, she quit the firm. The store manager regarded her as a failure because she did not understand what he could not tell her—that her margin of profits was too high and that some social use of materials, not theft, was expected. In his mind, she was too little concerned with the system's internal harmony and too devoted to formalities."

Another condition for novel negotiations, mentioned earlier, was the appearance of unforeseen contingencies—unpredicted new events. Dalton gives little data on this, except for the shifting of alliances and coalitions. However, he does show us, in one incident, the kinds of events that periodically do occur along with the resulting flurry of negotiation. The men in the chemical department began to complain about chemical vapors during the third shift. Because the management ignored their complaints, the chemists asked the workers' union to do something about the situation. The union, being interested in gaining white-collar workers, promised to act. Management objected that, because they were "confidential employees" and "part of the management group," the chemists could not belong to a union. The union asked the local health board to send a committee to investigate the complaint. Meanwhile, covert negotiations between union and management (whose nature was not known to Dalton) worked matters out: The health committee was not told that objectionable vapors were confined only to the third shift, although everyone knew this. The union told the health committee, after no vapors were discovered, that the union had been taken in by grieving crackpots and promised to ignore such complaints in the future. The union did not accept chemists as members. Management, which had speedily appropriated $35,000 to minimize the vapors, then did not use the money, although months later some slight but helpful changes were made.

One last point: Dalton only twice uses the term *faction broker*. He is referring to the rewarding of a general foreman because "acceptable to all factions, he was really rewarded as Milo's peacemaker in the clashes between operation and maintenance" (p. 233). In other words, the foreman was a mediator. We can assume that there were other instances of such mediation—just as there must be other instances of unforeseen contingencies that led to novel negotiating—but Dalton does not report many of them. Perhaps mediation is not so salient a feature of this negotiation context as that alternative form of brokerage that consists of making trade-offs in order right now to satisfy some represented party and at some later date to yield a reciprocal trade-off. That kind of brokerage, of course, involves serial (one after another) negotiations.

Summary. Despite the considerable size of the establishments studied by Dalton, a striking feature of them is the necessity for continuous relationships among their personnel. Some relationships contribute to the stated organizational goals—are "working relationships" in precisely the sense that the company officials might readily recognize them to be. Other relationships, equally durable, are organizationally illegitimate, tending to be covert—at least, hidden from certain eyes—for all the reasons spelled out in Dalton's account. (One of the great merits of his description is how well it details the apparent necessity for such covert relationships in order that both legitimate and illegitimate work might get accomplished.) A "web of commitments" grows up, continuously renewed, albeit continuously changing, evolving as a consequence of typically repeated, serial, and linked negotiations.

Dalton's detailing of what I would term *subprocesses of negotiation* is especially rich. One can easily discern, both in his data and in his own analysis, at least the following: trading off, the paying off of accumulated obligations, the covert making of deals and other kinds of secret bargains, the use of additional covering negotiations for keeping hidden the results of previous covert arrangements, the bypassing of negotiations, and the mediating of negotiations; also, a very complex balancing of accumulated favors and obligations, along with the juggling of commitments within the negotiation itself.

These features of negotiation—along with the negotiations
with whom, over what stakes, with what kinds of tactics, and what
kinds of results—were seen in the preceding discussion to be related
closely to the salient properties of the overarching negotiation context "within which" the negotiations can analytically be conceived
to occur. Among the contextual properties were the repeated negotiations between negotiating parties who have become experienced
not only in the negotiations themselves but also in dealing with
each other. These repeated negotiations are likely to involve negotiating parties who are representing absent others, although often
they represent themselves instead or additionally—usually covertly.
Each negotiation is likely to be part of a series of negotiations between the negotiators. Many of the negotiations are linked, each depending on or involving others. Some negotiation is novel, but
much of it is routine in form if not in actual content. Some of the
novel negotiation pertains to the ambiguity of legitimate boundaries
within which some of the bargaining occurs. The stakes of the
negotiators or of their represented parties are likely to differ. The
balance of negotiation power is variable in different negotiations,
but coercive threat is often built into the negotiating. Alternatives
to negotiation do not usually involve arbitration or mediation (although there may be some of the latter), or an appeal to authority,
but they probably often do involve an accompanying or substitutive
manipulation of relevant events.

In his attempt to conceptualize the structure of relationships
within these establishments, Dalton leaned, it will be remembered,
on the cementing idea of "informal relations." His detailed analysis,
however, is replete with such terms as the *web of commitments* and
overt *workable arrangements,* which emphasize the continuous relationships required to get the organizations' and the men's work
done. While there is no question at all that a full conceptualization
of social order of these industrial plants would have to take into
account such traditional items as hierarchy, authority, and the
usual terms referred to in tables of organization, it is also equally
clear that Dalton's data and its detailed analysis lead one to view
that social order as much more. These organizations may not be as
quickly or radically changing as the psychiatric wards discussed
earlier (those seemed to be changing right under the eyes of the

researchers, month by month); the web of relationships that sustains the work is nevertheless changing continuously and in the most subtle, not to say often covert, ways. The term *negotiated order* does not capture everything about the social order of these factories, but it does go a very long way in suggesting some major features of order.

What about the structural context within which negotiations and negotiative context are "embedded"? Can one say that the negotiations ultimately affect those larger structural conditions? Unlike the mental hospital case, where one could hazard that the hospital negotiations were integral to a quickly shifting psychological treatment scene, we could scarcely argue that factory negotiations, especially the covert but even many of the overt ones, have much of an impact on the national labor and management scene. That they might, however, have some consequences for changing the local institution is not too outrageous a speculation; for instance, when an especially "corrupt" covert working agreement comes to light or when management makes new rules in order to prevent the occurrence of well-known but now frowned-on informal practices.

Chapter Ten

••••••••••••••••••••
••••••••••••••••••••
••••••••••••••••••••

Interplay of Legal
and Illegal Negotiations
in the Political Arena

••••••••••••••••••••••
••••••••••••••••••••••
••••••••••••••••••••••

*I*n the preceding chapter, the issue of the legitimacy of actions that rest on negotiations—and the negotiations themselves—was viewed in the contrasting contexts of the experimental psychiatric wards (with their new kinds of jobs and work functions) and industrial firms (where "keeping the organization going" was salient). In this chapter, the issue of legitimate action will be looked at more directly, and illegality itself will be at the focus of our attention. Two related questions will be addressed here through consideration of another pair of case studies. The first question is "What does illegal negotiation 'look like'— does it have special features?" The second is "What relationship does that kind of negotiation bear to legitimate action and order?" My answers to the second question are not intended to be profound. I only wish to show that negotiation analysis has something to say about the question and perhaps can lead to its deeper examination.

To begin with a simple point: We all know there is a great

deal of corruption in American politics and public life, since from time to time it surfaces and is played up by the mass media. We are not much surprised when it appears, only at the numbers and kinds of persons or institutions caught up in the devious machinations and the downright breaking of laws. Some observers understand very well that illegality is not simply an accident, a departure from the normal state of affairs. About that, they may be cynical—meaning that they recognize the fact of illegal acts but do not condemn them. Others accept them as part of political life, if only because of the imperfectibility of human institutions, or they blame them on the nature of capitalism or on the nature of the welfare state. For some, particular laws are viewed as unworkable or as having been passed by a specific interest group; therefore, illegal acts will be violated by those who disagree with that particular law or set of laws.

What can negotiation analysis contribute to this general question of illegality vis-à-vis social order? I begin by touching base with some other cases in this book where "illegitimate" negotiations appear. A few preliminary distinctions among the types of illegitimacy found there can be useful. Thus, in antagonistic negotiation between the United States and the Soviet Union over the fate of the Balkans, the respective governments negotiated certain agreements, but then one or the other acted contrary to certain of those agreements, even making other and obviously secret agreements that ran counter to their previously negotiated agreements. Conditions for such illegitimate action may include a negotiating party who always did intend to do so or who may have been led to do so by changed contingencies or simply by a reassessment of the value of those agreements. A different kind of illegitimacy is the flaunting of official rules that, in a manner of speaking, are authoritatively "above" the negotiation. The rules permit—indeed, they may directly sanction—certain persons to negotiate with each other about certain kinds of issues. Of course, as reflected in the materials on Dalton's industrial firms, every day and at every level of an organization people are busily negotiating illegitimately around those rules. Some people are confirmed rule breakers because they believe that is the only effective way to get things done. So, as Dalton puts it, sometimes rules allow people to act effectively, while at other times rules are broken in order that people can act effectively. The case of the psychiatric hospitals suggests yet a third form of illegitimacy, that of traditional work or professional roles becoming changed through negotiation or persuasion, although the person approached may wonder about the legitimacy of the suggested role changes. Sometimes they even wonder—as did the physician with whom the team negotiated not to prescribe drugs for patients but to allow them to self-prescribe—about the actual legality both of the agreement and the negotiation itself. And, of course, there are also downright illegal acts, among them negotiations about forbidden issues (for instance, Gouldner's discussion of management-worker collusion over the state's safety rules). Whether law, rule, or agreements are broken, it is easy to see that all those illegitimate activities are intricately related with legitimate activity. In these instances, it is difficult to imagine either without the other, for they are so often tightly linked.

In the two cases discussed in this chapter, the deliberate breaking of laws is central both to the negotiations themselves and to the nature of the organizations that engage in them. That very illegality is related directly to legalized action and to laws. The two cases reflect how the illegal organizations owe their very existence to their relationships with perfectly legal organizations and systems of organizations, which in turn probably cannot be understood without also understanding those "deviant" if business-as-usual relationships. Both sides work together, whether happily or reluctantly, closely or distantly, to get the work done. The question is "What is the work, and how does it get done?" Negotiation is one mode—as always, taken in conjunction with other modes, other options.

The first case is that of the corrupt judge in the American judiciary system, who either takes or forces financial bribes. If he engages frequently in this illegal practice, then he is likely to build a durable working team. Understandably, negotiations within his organization, and between it and the outsiders, are thoroughly covert. The associated and characteristic subprocesses of negotiation include kickbacks, payoffs, payment for illegal services, stalling or false negotiating, and double-crossing negotiation. It is difficult not to conceptualize the interlocking judiciary and business systems as inclusive of *both* legal and illegal actions by representatives of those systems.

The second case considered is that of the political machine, which is able to get clients to work with itself "outside the law." As with the judge, only some of its business involves illegal actions—or at least less-than-honest transaction accomplished through political office and legislation. The characteristic sub-processes of negotiation that attend this political organization include the reaching of agreements about services rendered, kick-backs, paying off, and trading off. Many arrangements reached through those processes are, of course, thoroughly covert, and they are entwined with coercive and manipulatory actions. Understanding the implicated negotiated order is indispensable to understanding the larger phenomena—the social order—of the political machine and presumably also the social order of the city in which the members of the machine operate.

One additional remark seems necessary here about a major theoretical distinction between a nonnegotiated agreement and a negotiation. (I shall return later, in Chapter Fourteen, to this distinction.) Thus if a seller puts a genuinely fixed price on his house and does not wish to negotiate that price, the would-be-purchaser then must simply either agree or disagree on the price. Of course, he may attempt to negotiate, not believing the price is really fixed or else thinking "Who knows, he may change his mind." Similarly, when a burglar (or a corrupt judge) puts a proposition to a victim ("Do what I ask, or pay a terrible price; it's up to you"), then the victim may try to negotiate his way out of the situation—at his own hazard—or may try to gain some compromise on what he must pay; but if the other is insistent, then he faces fixed limits, and there is no room for negotiation. Another non-coercive instance—suppose someone says "Let's go to the beach today," and others agree. There is no negotiation, unless someone replies "Yes, the beach today, but the mountains tomorrow" or "OK, providing we can get back home by five o'clock." Also, it is important to realize that a past agreement can be negotiated (although not necessarily negotiated originally), if now one party or the other wants it modified. I note all this because some of the materials discussed in the two following cases (unlike virtually all the other cases in Part Two) come perilously close to nonnegotiated agreements under coercive conditions. Yet there is quite enough negotiation going on, as suggested by my discussion of their sub-processes of negotiation, to make clear that even these agreements under coercion take place within a larger texture of systematic negotiations.

Case: The Corrupt Judge

Implicit in the various powers associated with those of the office of a judge in the U.S. judicial system is the possibility of his misusing some of those powers for personal gain. Prevention of that possibility seems to rest on his inherent honesty or on his fear of governmental reprisal, as well as on structural considerations such as his having entered office owing little or nothing to corrupt backers or even to his political connections. Nevertheless, the phenomenon of less-than-honest judges is a recognizable and recurrent feature of the judicial scene. It is certainly related to the larger structural features of the American judicial system of law enforcement, as well as to that system's connection with political parties, elections, and legislative action.

It is within that larger context that one must see the phenomenon of the wayward or downright corrupt judge. Sometimes illegal "arrangements" are initiated by the judge himself; sometimes, especially if his reputation is known or suspected, he is approached by parties or their representatives eager to make such arrangements. If the judge engages in such deals repeatedly, then he will form or become part of an informal organization whose principal business it is to profit from covertly negotiating illegal arrangements.

The negotiation context is likely to include, then, the major contextual conditions of *differential but reciprocal stakes* for both parties; *linked, serial,* and *sequential* negotiations; organizationally *experienced* negotiators and *inexperienced* (although sometimes experienced) counternegotiators; *routine* because *repeated* negotiations for the organizational members, but more usually *novel* for many of the counternegotiators. Single or *few* illegal *issues* are negotiated (usually the amounts of money to pass between the parties). The *options* to negotiating are either "no business" or, especially for the client, higher costs because of going through more legal channels or risking the potential damage to a reputation.

For illustration of this type of negotiation context, we turn to the colorful and instructive case (Borkin, 1966, pp. 141–186) of Judge Albert Johnson of the U.S. District Court of the Middle District of Pennsylvania, who was investigated in 1945 by the House Judiciary Committee. The committee concluded that the judge had notoriously engaged in the barter and sale of court offices, notably in the appointments of attorneys, trustees, receivers, and similar offices and appointments, usually in consideration of a share in the salaries, fees, or other compensation paid by such appointees. The committee also concluded that his decisions, decrees, orders, and rulings commonly were sold for all the traffic would bear. The management of that considerable business—for twenty years—involved a number of people who played various roles within this informal, but none the less genuine, business concern: fixers, runners, go-betweens, cooperating trustees, referees, and officials.

Thus, in the instance of a bankrupt brewing company, Memolo, attorney for the borough (who had previously been involved in one of the judge's deals), approached Greenes (member of the judge's current informal team), suggesting that he would like an appointment as a trustee of the brewery company. Greenes passed the message to Donald Johnson (the judge's son), adding that he believed Memolo was a good man. Johnson asked if Memolo would "play ball." Greenes replied that he had done all right in a previous case, so he should "do the same in this one." In the ensuing negotiation, Memolo agreed to a 50–50 split of the trustee fees. For his services as go-between, Greenes got some payment, while the judge got the remainder of the kickback. The accountant of the brewery company agreed, secretly of course, to a similar kickback. To be certain that the judge got his proper "cut," Greenes actually accompanied the accountant to the bank; then he delivered the money to the judge's son.

In another case, which was tried in Judge Johnson's court, the federal government brought suit against a clothing manufacturer on charges of stealing cloth from the government. In his court decision, the judge proved very lenient to the defendants. His leniency had been negotiated, in a deal initiated by him. His son approached Greenes, asking him to see if the defendants' lawyer would be interested in an "arrangement." (This lawyer had previously been involved in similar arrangements.) He was. Then Johnson and Greenes drove to the lawyer's house at night. They all parked on a dark street, where the lawyer handed an envelope to Johnson containing $5,000: "You understand, this is for a directed verdict." The judge's son advised the lawyer to file a motion before his father rather than in the court of another judge in the same district. Later another $10,000 passed between the lawyer and Greenes, which the latter changed into small bills; eventually most of them ended up in Judge Johnson's bank account.

In a rather more simple type of case, a bootlegger, going through his attorney (the same Memolo involved in the first case, but now acting as a go-between), approached Greenes. For $1,250, the judge agreed to give the bootlegger a suspended sentence of one year and a day, and placed him on probation for five years; a year later, for a similar amount of money, the probation was terminated. Clearly, all parties in this negotiation were experienced in such illicit transactions.

Rather less routine were the negotiations in a case involving the tangled relations of a wire rope company and its main supplier of steel, a very large steel firm. The latter owned about 25 percent of the common stock of the wire company, which during the Depression got into grave financial difficulties. The steel company arranged for the filing of a creditor's bill by the Guaranty Trust Company; the executors of the wire rope company gave consent, thinking this was to be a friendly suit. Moore, general counsel of the steel company, arranged for a Mr. Decker to be employed as local counsel by the trust company and to file the creditor's bill for the bank. Judge Johnson then appointed his son-in-law as receiver. The steel company wished two other men as receivers, so the judge appointed them also, as well as Decker. Moore was quietly advised that the judge was personally involved in the case. In a further complication, another local judge was very upset that Judge Johnson's son-in-law had been appointed, so the latter resigned, only to be replaced by a Mr. Townsend, who was immediately visited by one son of Judge Johnson on behalf of two other Johnson sons.

Townsend agreed to split his fees, which amounted eventually to more than $17,000.

Over the next two years, the value of the wire company increased until its assets were in excess of $4 million, while its unsecured debts were about $2.5 million, the difference being available for the company's stockholders. Soon thereafter, the judge appointed Memolo as an associate counsel for the receivers, initially at $500 and later at $1,000 a month—to be split with one of the judge's sons and the remainder split with the judge's friend, Greenes. (The honest receivers, hearing of the increased payment to Memolo, threatened to quit, so the judge raised all the receivers' fees to $1,500 monthly.) Soon the judge indicated in court that he wished quick restoration of the company to its stockholders. The steel company, however, had hoped to foreclose on the wire company. Stockholder opposition to foreclosure was vigorous, although the steel company in the meantime had purchased 95 percent of the wire company's bonds at 70 percent of their face value. Meanwhile, the steel company's general counsel was attempting to find legal methods to get around Judge Johnson.

Shortly thereafter, the judge's team figured out how to turn over the wire company to the steel company, in return for an agreement. Memolo went to the steel company's legal counsel, explaining that he had arranged a deal with the judge and his son. The local counsel indicated that Moore, the general counsel, probably would decline to negotiate. But shortly thereafter Memolo proposed to Moore that the steel firm would get the wire company for $250,000. The operative device would be "administrative expenses," and Greenes would be the intermediary. Moore did decline, and for several months he and the steel firm considered alternatives to that illegal negotiation; also, the firm remained unable to eliminate stockholder opposition to its takeover plans. So Moore signaled willingness to negotiate with the judge. Memolo met with Moore in a lengthy four-hour meeting. Moore asked that Judge Johnson quickly order the disposal, through a sale, of the wire company's assets. He agreed, in turn, to pay over $250,000 to Memolo, assuming most of it would end up in the judge's hands. Within two months, the foreclosure proceedings were in rapid motion; but, since both negotiating parties mistrusted the other, it took another two months before much further progress was made.

The judge felt that if "the administration expenses" were paid in cash into a safety deposit box, with a key for Memolo and another for Moore, he would feel more secure. Moore's response was that he'd "be damned" if he'd get involved with a thing like that, adding "No one can put a gun to my temple." He was thinking, understandably, of future opportunities for the judge to blackmail his side. Then, when Memolo tried to get an actual meeting between the judge and Moore, the latter refused flatly. So the judge a few days later acted to dismiss stockholders' objections to the foreclosure; the next day the steel company bid successfully.

The marvelously covert features of these negotiations are further evidenced. To begin with, on the back of a manila envelope Moore recorded the $250,000 that went to the judge. Only he, in his law firm, knew about the secret negotiations. Meanwhile, since Moore had refused to negotiate with anyone except Memolo, the latter had told Judge Johnson that the kickback was to be $150,000; then for several years he maintained that he had not received the final, large payment from the steel company. Finally, Memolo admitted to receiving the expected $150,000 but insisted his share of the split with the judge was to be 50–50. Judge Johnson argued for 75–25 but finally agreed to 66 2/3–33 1/3. Only during the House Judiciary Committee hearings did the judge discover that he had been double-crossed by Memolo.

Ten years after the foreclosure, the case was reopened, turned over to fully legal authorities, and some six years thereafter settled. The steel company acquired the wire company, with reasonable payments to its stockholders, but all parties agreed that the steel company had not participated in any fraudulent action but rather had been boxed into a corner by circumstances over which it had "no control." The judge had long since had to resign from his office.

Although Johnson's ultimate fate has no particular bearing on our analysis of negotiation, I cannot forbear noting that after his return to private practice a local bar association elected him its president. But perhaps to its members the boundaries of legitimacy were truly debatable—however the federal government might define and enforce them.

Summary. The judge's style of negotiation illustrates the following subprocesses of negotiation: kickbacks, payoffs, payment for illegal services, stalling or false negotiating, and double-crossing negotiations by intermediaries. Some of those negotiation subprocesses, missing or marginal in the cases described elsewhere in this book, are prominent in this kind of collusive and coercive negotiation. For instance, double-crossing always seems to be a potential hazard in these negotiations when intermediaries are used; the judge, of course, attempted to reduce his risk by using his sons as go-betweens wherever possible.

Because these types of subprocesses are so characteristic of collusive negotiation, it certainly seems to have a texture or coloration different from that of covert but legal negotiation. Many of its features are closely related to the actual illegality of the stakes bargained for, along with, consequentially, the covert aspects of the negotiating among all the parties to it. The other contextual properties simply yield the variants of whether there will be particular instances of go-betweens or whether quick and easy understandings will be established because the parties have dealt with each other before.

The bearing of any given collusive negotiation on the larger structural context is virtually irrelevant: even occasional exposés of corrupt dealings or a corrupt judge lead to no appreciable reform either of the courts or American business practices. What perhaps is less apparent is that the judge's long-term working team could not exist without his perfectly legal position as a judge, along with his normal, routine, honest activities in that office. Assuming that the existence of the (slightly or very) dishonest judge is not a rare phenomenon, then it is difficult not to conceptualize the interlocking judiciary and business "systems" as inclusive of *both* legal and illegal features: agents, actions, and organizations. The option of the judge's victims would seem then to have consisted mainly of submitting to legal punishment in court, although conceivably some may have escaped that alternative by putting on some sort of "heat"—political pressure or perhaps eventually public exposure.

Case: Large-Scale Corruption—The Political Machine

The political machine is quite literally an instrument for getting things done. Its organization enables it to make arrangements at such a pace and over so broad a scope of political and business life that it seems far removed from the corrupt judge's small team. What the two instruments share is their ability to get clients—whether reluctantly or willingly—to work with them "outside the law." Of course, like the judge himself, much of the machine's focus is on accomplishing perfectly normal, honest, everyday business. Some of its business, however, involves frankly illegal operations or at least less-than-honest transactions in connection with legitimate political offices and legislation. Perhaps "honest graft" lies somewhere toward the middle of the entire range of political transactions on which the organization's existence depends. As one famous politician, George Washington Plunkett, reiterated to the journalist who was interviewing him: There is a difference between graft and "honest graft." So it was perfectly consistent for him to say openly, and with many examples of honest graft, "I seen my opportunities and I took 'em" (see Riordan, 1963, p. 3).

The negotiation context within which such transactions occur have generally the following properties: The negotiations are *linked, sequential, serial, multiple,* and frequently *simultaneous.* There are a large *number of parties* to the total negotiations and a large *range of issues* being negotiated. Negotiations occur both *between* the machine's *representatives and outsiders* and *among* its members. Both sets of negotiators are likely to engage in *repeated* and *routinized* transactions. Subprocesses include reaching agreements about "services rendered," agreeing on kickbacks, paying off, and trading off. Because so many of the negotiations and consequent actions take place within a zone of ambiguous legitimacy—if they are not downright illegal—*covertness* characterizes many of the subprocesses. Although everyone knows that a political machine is associated with a certain amount of graft and "fixing," the details of its operation are far from known except to insiders to particular deals. Like the negotiation engaged in by corrupt judges, much of the machine's has a special flavor imparted by covertness, collusion, and irregularity, if not actual illegality.

Since the nature of political machines is common knowledge, at least to social scientists, I shall offer only a few examples of negotiations typical of them, using Alexander Callow's *The Tweed Ring* (1970, especially pp. 163–181), as our source of data. (This machine's operating period was from 1866 to 1871. Modern politics has unquestionably changed in a hundred years, but the main features of its negotiated order seem remarkably unaltered, although some machines are perhaps "greedier" than others.) *The Tweed Ring* plundered New York City with such precision that it has earned the reputation of being perhaps the outstanding example of civic corruption in American municipal history. It was, in fact, the first modern political machine in New York City and provided a model for all later city bosses in that city. The ring gained control of key legislative and financial agencies, so that, in Callow's words (p. 165), every item "charged against the city treasury passed the Ring's scrutiny and was subject to its manipulation. The results were often graft, reflected in excessive charges and needless waste." The same was true for charters and franchises issued to new businesses, "and many companies, therefore, had to pay the tribute of the bribe to get them passed." All the city's financial affairs—bond issues, tax collecting, rentals on properties—were sources of lucrative graft. In effect, there was a direct relationship between power and graft. The ring had much the same sort of power over the state legislature and its business. Also, members of the business community were an important source of profit, "both as allies and victims." The business firms paid handsomely for legislation that the ring influenced. The Erie Railroad, for example, paid in thousands of dollars for "services." "Businessmen provided large 'kickbacks' in payment for receiving profitable contracts" (p. 166). Laws were even passed that threatened certain businesses with legislative extortion, and this legislation was much used by the ring.

The ring's standard tactic, however, was relatively simple and direct. Everyone who received a city contract had to alter his bills before submitting them. The levy on payment initially was 10 percent and eventually rose to 65 percent. "On large contracts, Tweed acted directly and got immediately to the point. When he was told that electric fire alarms would cost the city $65,000, he asked the contractor, 'If we get you a contract for $450,000, will you give us $225,000?' No time was wasted. The contractor answered with a simple yes and got the contract" (p. 166).

People who pressed claims against the city were handled—with stalling and implicit negotiation—by the comptroller's office.

They were kept waiting, sometimes for years, for their money. Often they sold their claim to a representative of the ring for fifty or sixty cents on the dollar. Then the new owner was quickly paid. A journalist's account in 1871 described some of the procedure this way (pp. 171–172): "Moloney sits opposite the door by which his victims enter. . . . The moment an unlucky claimant makes his appearance, Moloney jumps on his feet. . . . Bending forward, he listens to the application of the victim, and then, by a series of ominous shakes of his head and 'the oft-told tale' repeated in half-smothered whisper, he tries to convince the applicant that there is no prospect of him receiving his money for some time to come and that if he really needs it he had better go over to City Hall and see Mr. Thomas Colligan."

Tweed himself, during his investigation, described how contracts for city printing were handled, the covert trade-off being an essential element in the handling (pp. 172–173): "For instance, any department in the city, say your department, required stationery; a requisition would be made. Some young man from your department would go over to them and deliver the requisition. Jones would say, 'Well this is a very nice requisition,' and then he would try if possible to have a larger requisition made out; and, whether or not, he would invite this young man to go in, and show him a lot of fancy goods and make him presents of them and enlarge the requisition that way or else not furnish full amounts of the requisition. . . . everybody who furnished requisitions . . . received such presents. Received furniture, bridles, saddles . . . books and everything. When I say books, I mean novels—libraries."

Other standard tactics included a division of spoils among ring members through the formation of companies that sold supplies (often never used) to the city. There were also implicit payoffs to the newspapers for their calculated silence about the doings of the ring. The machine found it best to protect itself against newspaper criticism by buying advertising space "as a token of peace." Legally, the city corporation was limited to nine daily and eight weekly papers in which to advertise, but the ring advertised in twenty-six daily and forty-four weekly newspapers, plus seventeen weekly papers outside the city. Some were also given cash, so that they would not publish "things we wouldn't very much care to have made public." So Tweed occasionally had to pay actual blackmail money. However, the ring also gave explicit payoffs, giving reporters monetary gifts for Christmas and subsidizing reporters on most city papers with fees so they would write with proper discretion about politics. Also, editors were sometimes given sinecures for services rendered.

One last standard operating means: There was a legitimate demand for new streets and improvement of old ones because of the city's considerable growth during the regime of the ring. In tactics very like those that we noted Judge Johnson using, the ring routinely appointed trustworthy street commissioners through cooperative judges, with awards for commissioners charging "from ten to one hundred times as much as the law allowed for their services and expenses," although actually they were legally disqualified from being paid for their services.

Summary. All these kickbacks, trade-offs, payments, and other negotiated covert agreements were part and parcel of the multiple, linked negotiated arrangements that *constituted* the very essence of the phenomenon called the Tweed Ring. An alternative to viewing political machines as organizations is to conceptualize them as complex and interlocking sets of negotiation activities that result both in relatively stable and relatively shifting relationships among a host of interested parties. The latter include not only "members" of the machine but also hundreds of marginal recipients to "its" largesse. Whenever machines have been judicially exposed, some of their actual members have been legally punished, but in a wider sense all who profit repeatedly from the participation in the machine's negotiations are implicated in its activities. To draw the line between being "in" the organization and being "outside" of it is, at least sociologically speaking, a difficult conceptual enterprise.

Be that as it may, the modes of negotiation characteristic of machine politics clearly reflect their typical negotiation context—itself understandable only in terms of the larger structural situation within which "politics operates." Or, as Callow remarks about the Tweed Ring (p. 181), "The roads to graft . . . were paved by the very interests the ring exploited. The financial community, consumed in its own self-interests, stood to gain from the massive pump priming in city improvements. The 'open door' policy of state and city welfare deadened the voice of religious and philanthropic organizations; the newspapers, split by political partisanship and competitive self-interest, were softened by the morsels of political handouts; and the people were indifferent." These are all structural features of the political scene within which these political machines operated. Although the city machine is less prominent today and although there has been debate on whether it still exists in its old-fashioned form, nevertheless those types of negotiated arrangements surely have not altogether disappeared from American politics.

One way of conceptualizing our political life is to regard it as pulled between legal and illegal poles, the tug of war occasionally resulting in public furor whenever corruption becomes too evident. If, however, political activity is seen as carried out within determinate structural and negotiation contexts—conditions that limit and further that political activity—then the polar conception seems naive. Legal and illegal actions, negotiation included, are intricately linked. Together they make up a workable—and frequently durable, if continuously changing—web of political and social relationships. In working together thus, "things get done"—otherwise, a great many do not. In that sense, at least, the distinction between legal and illegal behavior looks very much like the distinction between ruled behavior and agreed-on behavior that breaks the rules or the agreements. In the instance of the political machine, a great many people want things to get done. They are willing to draw a fine line between legal and illegal actions. In the instance of the corrupt judge, discussed earlier, some clients are definitely cooperative, even initiating the transactions, while others would share the more general view that these particular things should *not* get done, at least not in this illegal way.

Chapter Eleven

●●●●●●●●●●●●●●●●●●●
●●●●●●●●●●●●●●●●●●●●●●●
●●●●●●●●●●●●●●●●●●●●●

Building Cooperative Structures

●●●●●●●●●●●●●●●●●●●●●●●
●●●●●●●●●●●●●●●●●●●●●●●●●
●●●●●●●●●●●●●●●●●●●●●●●●●

*W*hen organizations are built from scratch or when existing organizations come together to form a new structure that will nevertheless allow organizational existence outside the structure, we can ask "What is needed to further those ends?" Or, more specifically, "What part do negotiations play during the construction and maintenance of the cooperative structure?" We see these phenomena with great frequency in complex societies, of course. One of their characteristic features is that the respective parties share some aims but not others. If they share enough, they may wish to build a durable structure. Otherwise, the cooperation may be relatively brief and minimal in scope, and the constructed structure is not designed for a long existence. In either case, the parties not only are likely to differ in most if not many of their larger purposes but will also enter on relationships, including ones involving negotiation, with very different viewpoints. Frequently the parties come from different social worlds and even national cultures.

In this chapter, two further cases will be paired. The first,

157

which concerns Benelux, involves the building of a durable co-operative structure among several European nations. We shall follow the working together of representatives of the respective govern-ments as they build an economic union. This required and still requires repeated, sequential, and multiissue negotiations, against a backdrop of strong incentives to make the economic union work. Both the long-stretched-out, temporal linearity and the sharedness of this enterprise are especially striking. The union, although always evolving, is largely based on those negotiations, yet it represents only a portion of the total relationships that exist between or among these particular nations.

The second, contrasting case involves the building of a temporary legal structure, binding on the governments involved only until a set of actions operationalized by it (the punishment of war criminals) was completed. The specific negotiations were also sequential and involved multiissues, but the total series of negoti-ations were "one shot," like so many discussed in the literature on negotiation. Extant relationships among the governments both pre-ceded the Nuremberg trials and outlasted the temporary coopera-tive structure necessitated by the trials. The nature of this temporary organization for bringing war criminals "to justice" visibly rests on some sort of negotiated if temporary order, which must be seen against the larger ordering of relations among the respective nations.

In both cases, as will be seen, among the subprocesses of ne-gotiation are those which, understandably, include first of all the very hammering out of negotiation machinery itself, the progressive building of agreement, the ironing out of residual disagreement, and the trading off both of assigned tasks and of specific issues regarding minor stakes. In the instance of the Benelux transactions, there necessarily is periodic review and renegotiation of previous arrangements.

Case: Benelux: A Durable Structure

James Meade's account (1957) of the extended negotiations leading toward the envisioned goal of a full economic union of the Benelux countries—with free movement of people, goods, and capital among them—affords an opportunity to follow the steps, the negotiated agreements, some consequences of those agreements, the renegotiations as unforeseen contingencies arose, and some actions of the negotiating parties during the negotiations themselves.

The negotiations took place among three independent, sovereign governments—Belgium, the Netherlands, and Luxembourg. The first two were already linked into a close economic union by the treaty of 1921. The Benelux talks began during October 1943, the three governments being then in exile but very much alive in their London quarters. Beginning with those initial talks, Meade's account covers the next thirteen years of continued negotiation. By 1956, important progress had been accomplished in the direction of the "final goal of complete economic union," but excise and similar duties had not been fully unified; also, there were obstacles remaining to the movement of people, goods, and capital among the partner countries.

The first years of negotiation took place during the unsettled periods of wartime and postwar reconstruction. The initial agreements were made when other financial plans, conferences, and arrangements were being made and carried out, eventuating, for instance, in the Breton Woods conference, the foundation of the International Monetary Fund, and the International Bank for Reconstruction and Development. (Later, of course, the Marshall Plan would be implemented, and the Common Market would begin to become a reality.) So we have to realize that supranational economic arrangements were "in the air" and being forged during a period of great national rebuilding after an exhausting war. Another point to keep in mind is that Belgium and the Netherlands, and Luxembourg too, are "closely linked in historical experience, geographical position, and in language and culture" and that two of them had already had long experience in a joint venture. Nevertheless, the three countries had somewhat different economic strengths and weaknesses. The stakes of the envisioned Benelux Union were, then, very high. The task of building and negotiating the union was arduous, and progress was bedeviled by many unforeseen contingencies arising both from intranational and international developments.

The general form of the negotiation looked as follows. Once the decision to form an economic union was made, the three governments proceeded toward its building step by step. The negotiators

hammered out negotiation machinery: They decided on the requisite procedures, protocols, and general governing principles; and
they made and implemented various types of agreements. So they
met at stated intervals, having attempted actually to implement
certain arrangements. They set inquiries into motion, reported back
to each other, and proceeded "from there." They reviewed where
they had arrived at and decided on where to go next. They realized
some difficulties that they had not anticipated. They set timetables
and met or failed to meet them. At each juncture, they were working
on new agreements that involved additional or new financial and
political arrangements. By 1956, when Meade closes his account,
the governments still had failed to solve three or four key problems,
whose difficulties either had been underestimated or not foreseen.
But most problems had proven relatively tractable. The governments had also had to take into account the reactions of their varied
constituencies—domestic pressures sometimes preventing even the
implementation of negotiated agreements.

Clearly, the form of negotiation was directly affected by salient properties of this particular negotiation context. Chief among
those properties certainly must be that the three governments had
both *differential specific stakes* and an overriding *common stake:*
economic betterment, which can be best gained through a continued
cooperative venture. So conflicting interests would be muted, threats
would be virtually absent, trust would be both worked at and relatively omnipresent, and cooperative action would be highly visible
and necessary. From time to time, sacrifices would have to be made
or requested, in order to move toward the larger goals. Despite the
negotiation among *three parties,* coalitions and alliances would be
negligible or muted. Some forms of negotiation (conferences, meetings, agendas) would be *routine,* but much of the content of the
negotiations and of the resulting arrangements would be *novel.*
The negotiators would be feeling their way, albeit cooperatively.
The negotiators themselves would become *experienced,* both at the
form of negotiations and, as they met *repeatedly,* at meeting with one
another. Thus, they did not need to spend much time exploring their
respective personalities, motivations, relationships to governmental
authorities, and the like: They could proceed with relative speed and
smoothness of relationships. The negotiators were serviced by agents

who fed them information and, if necessary, by teams of experts who researched the information. The negotiators who represented the governments were often governmental officers (ministers, and so on). And there were *multiple negotiators* who met over different aspects of, or *issues* involved in, the total negotiations—at higher and lower levels as well as in specialty areas.

All the negotiations were *sequential:* except for the very first, they were all preceded and followed by others. None was to be taken in isolation, and indeed each was deliberately supposed to lead to the next ones, which indeed were often *scheduled.* No wonder much of the negotiation turned about "next steps," about reviews of past steps and current accomplishments or difficulties, and that the negotiators all faced forward in future time. Built into the negotiations were agreements to renegotiate the agreed-on terms. Also, negotiations were *linked* and *multiple,* not only sequentially but also horizontally, so to speak: one negotiation and resulting arrangement frequently depending on and feeding into one another. Another major property of the context was that virtually all negotiations were *overt.* They were "aboveboard," explicit—and so pains were taken to be very clear about every step of the negotiations, about the issues, about the agreements that resulted from each round of negotiations, and about the anticipated financial, institutional, or political arrangements that flowed from the agreements.

Unlike many negotiation contexts, this one did not turn saliently on openly employing an unequal *balance* of *negotiation power;* rather, each negotiating party tended to keep its special strengths implicit and did not bargain aggressively and overtly from strength, but kept major focus on the common stake of achieving the shared benefits of economic union. For one negotiating government to take too obvious advantage of its strength was to invite eventual destruction of cooperative effort, which among nations is at best a fragile construction. It was rendered all the more so by the necessity for coping with many unforeseen contingencies that impinged on the negotiated arrangements, which in turn needed periodically to be rethought, renegotiated, and reconstructed.

The foregoing contextual properties were, then, the principal conditions for the general strategy, range of tactics, and interactions so characteristic of the negotiation context that Meade terms the "Negotiations for Benelux." At the risk of seeming too detailed in presenting raw data, I shall quote snippets from Meade's strictly historical account to show especially both the *sequential* movement of negotiations and the *typical tactics and interactions* as the parties felt their way toward their shared goal of economic union, taking into account possible unforeseen contingencies and the probable reactions of influential segments of their nations. I shall not do much linking of these actions to specific contextual properties, since those connections should be apparent enough in this type of negotiation.

In Meade's words (1957, pp. 2–3) "this history [of negotiations] in effect opens with the signing of a monetary agreement between the Belgian and Dutch governments in London in October 1943. This agreement was a bilateral payments agreement of the now familiar type. . . . It implied some devaluation of the Dutch guilder. . . . [It was] a payments agreement under which each central bank would provide its own currency to the other central bank at a fixed rate of exchange to finance all permitted payments made by the latter to the former country . . . with the obligation to consult to see how the growth of indebtedness above a certain figure could best be prevented." The key terms for us are *agreement* and *obligation*, along with the sacrifice involved by the Dutch concession concerning its guilders. "In form, the agreement was a bilateral payments agreement of a familiar pattern. But in fact it must be regarded as something more than a purely technical arrangement to facilitate payments between one particular pair of countries . . . the two governments agreed to consult closely in the future of economic and financial policies . . . they were about to embark upon an attempt to build a close and complete economic union" (p. 4). They were negotiating with explicit focus on the future, already looking forward to the development of a shared goal.

Then (see pp. 5–7), "The second milestone . . . was the signing in London in September 1944 . . . of a convention to establish a customs union between Belgium, Luxembourg, and the Netherlands." A tariff community was "to be the first step toward a full *customs union,* and in the agreement itself it was laid down that its application would cease when the full *economic union* which the parties intended to form should come into force. But in addition to these general statements of intention the convention . . . set up some joint Benelux administrative institutions whose function it was to promote the further progress of economic union." Note that agreements were made both for intention and for implementation. These multiple agreements were also linked, to each other. "In the summer of 1945 and early in 1946 meetings took place between officials of the three countries concerned to consider the first steps to be taken in the implementation of the customs union agreement of September 1944. But it was not until April 1946 . . . that there was the first full ministerial meeting . . . to decide upon the procedure and timetable for the institution of the customs union and for the next steps toward full economic union" (p. 13). The key words for us are "first steps" in deciding on both the procedure and the timetable. These meetings "show that the governments were still overoptimistic about the speed with which . . . difficulties could be overcome. The first difficulty, which was by this time becoming clear, was the problem of the balance of payments between the Belgium-Luxembourg Economic Union and the Netherlands" (p. 14).

Then arose the first major, unforeseen contingency that would need special consideration and especially delicate negotiation: "The Belgians were . . . naturally concerned lest the special import restrictions maintained for the time being by the Dutch to protect their balance of payments might lead to the setting up in the Netherlands of industries to produce products which in the more normal long run might better be supplied by Belgium or Luxembourg. It was therefore also agreed at the Hague ministerial meeting of April 1946 that, in order to avoid the distortion of traditional channels of trade, the governments would consult each other about the establishment or development of concerns which might compete with products of the other partner" (pp. 15–16).

This agreement began to handle the contingency but was also designed not to move matters too rapidly and not to rock too many domestic boats. "It was becoming clear that this removal of the customs frontier between the Belgium-Luxembourg Economic Union and the Netherlands and, still more, the final removal of all barriers to trade between the partners involved some fairly far-

reaching modifications of domestic policies in the partner countries . . . [it] was agreed [the council] should proceed within six
months to make proposals for the unification of excise duties, turn-
over taxes, and similar levies within the partner countries, a unification which was a necessary preliminary to the complete removal of
the customs frontier" (p. 16).

Thus, more machinery and more future meetings were
agreed on. The following year saw

> (1) Final agreement upon the common customs
> tariff, (2) important and useful developments in the
> administrative machinery of the Benelux union, and (3)
> the first explicit recognition and systematic treatment of
> the great obstacle to full union presented by the agri-
> cultural problem [p. 17].

> A few weeks later, a further meeting . . . the
> ministers . . . turned their attention to the steps which
> would still need to be taken to form a full economic
> union after the institution of the common tariff. Among
> a number of [other] topics, . . . (1) It was agreed that
> before September 1, 1948, the three governments should
> submit to their parliaments legislation for the unification
> of their excise and turnover taxes—a very optimistic
> timetable for the solution of an intractable problem
> which still remains largely unsolved. . . . (2) Ministers
> now requested the Council for the Economic Union to
> draw up before July 1, 1947, a list of the industries for
> which . . . consultation should be compulsory before
> investment and development was permitted. In the end
> it proved impossible to institute any effective mechanism
> of control of this kind over industrial development . . .
> (3) It was becoming increasingly evident that free trade
> in agricultural products . . . would present very great
> difficulties in view of the divergences in agricultural con-
> ditions and policies within the three countries . . . the
> ministers of agriculture . . . should meet to coordinate
> the agricultural policies . . . this marked the initiation
> of arrangements which frankly removed a large amount
> of agricultural produce from the principles of the com-
> mon market for the three countries [pp. 18–19].

These materials suggest the range of unforeseen contingencies that now had to be considered and negotiated; old agreements also had to be reconsidered. "But even though restrictions had been maintained by the Dutch on balance-of-payments grounds against imports from the Belgium-Luxembourg Economic Union, the bilateral balance . . . was very seriously strained. . . . Accordingly, the ministers agreed that the calling of credit under the payments agreement . . . should be temporarily raised. . . . Accordingly, in June 1947 a new financial agreement was concluded. The agreement also contained provisions for . . . future repayment" (p. 21). The interaction provides a nice example of continued and sequential cooperation under difficult conditions.

There were some further products of cooperative negotiation, supplemented by several other linked sets of negotiations and taking into account public reactions to negotiated agreements (see pp. 23–24). "In August 1947, the Netherlands and Belgium signed a convention under which the Dutch government undertook to give Belgian workers in the Netherlands the same rights to social security benefits as to their own Dutch citizens, and the Belgian government undertook a similar obligation. . . . [This] raised many technical problems; and the general convention of August 29, 1947, was followed by a series of supplementary agreements applying the general principle in detail to particular parts of the social security system." Then, note the sequential steps and the meeting of timetables: "Toward the end of 1947, an agreement was reached under which excise duties on wines and on sparkling fermented drinks . . . were unified. These duties came into force on January 1, 1948, the date at which the common Benelux customs duty was put into force and the ordinary customs duties on trade between the Benelux countries were abolished. Thus there was successfully put into effect the first great step toward Benelux." And now, agreement on some very specific measures (issues) : "The ministers agreed [early in 1948] upon a system of prior consultation about industrial development and investment . . . in order to control the expansion of various industries . . . on the lines already agreed upon. . . . They now agreed upon a list of the industries to which this principle of control should be applied and upon a procedure for prior consultation about the establishment, extension, or adaptation of productive units in these industries." However, the system never worked—although the governments agreed to introduce legislative measures necessary for its implementation—because the governments really lacked enough domestic control over investment.

By the summer of 1948, the respective negotiating parties realized something more was needed than "the negative act of removing certain tax and other restrictions on the movement of goods, services, and factors of production between the partner countries" (1959, p. 25). They needed a "rather extensive coordination of domestic economic policies as well." Various agreements leading to measures that would move toward that end were made at a June conference. It was now recognized that a full economic union could be reached only if the respective currencies were freely convertible; also, the Netherlands would now need a foreign loan and all three governments agreed to cooperate in getting that loan. Also, a kind of "Now I do something for you" and "Later you do something for me" agreement and implementation was adopted, so that they could all move closer to the desired economic union. "The hope was expressed that the trade exchanges envisaged in the current trade agreement could be maintained, and to promote this the Belgium-Luxembourg Economic Union undertook to discriminate in its import program systematically in favor of Dutch products" (p. 27). And the three countries agreed, as so often before, to meet at a specified future time "to examine the progress made" on the implementation of some of the negotiated agreements.

They met in March 1949, and "A determined attempt was made to set the stage for an early introduction of a full economic union. . . . The attempt turned out to be a failure . . . but the meeting is of great interest partly because of the partial progress which it did succeed in making and still more because of the illustration which it gives of the fundamental difficulties involved in the formation of a full economic union" (p. 29). It is worth noting that this failure is not due to failure of negotiation but to intractable problems that the governments are not yet able to surmount. This same meeting, as previously agreed, was devoted to a review of "progress." They judged that enough progress had occurred so they could "lay down a timetable for the completion of the process of decontrol in the partner countries and, in particular, in the Netherlands. Thus they proposed that the end of consumer rationing and of the direct allocation of materials should be achieved by the end of 1949 with, perhaps, a continuing need for some common joint Benelux scheme for the direct allocation to users of some scarce materials from the dollar area" (p. 30). That is, they balanced one act with another in linked agreements. They also linked an agreement that subsidization of home production was to end generally by the end of 1949, while price control in the Netherlands was to be abolished by July 1950 (having already been nearly ended in Belgium). Thus all those agreements were linked, both in time and in a general coordination.

Another set of agreements is well worth scrutiny as an instance of how linked, multiple, sequential agreements are associated with cooperative give-and-take actions (some involving sacrifices) directed toward common ends—just the opposite of aggressive playing on power balances. All this was done in an effort to tackle (see pp. 32–33)

What had now become the central and basic obstacle—namely the problem of removing the restrictions of imports into the Netherlands from the Belgium-Luxembourg Economic Union, which the Dutch had been obliged to impose as part of their policy for controlling the deficit on the country's balance of payments.

The principles upon which the ministers decided to attempt to meet this basic problem . . . there was to be an initial period of preunion during which there should be a gradual and progressive freeing of intra-Benelux trade from quantitative restrictions. In order to make this possible, the Belgium-Luxembourg Economic Union was to extend additional credits to the Netherlands to enable the Dutch to import freely from Belgium and Luxembourg. The amount of these credits would be adjusted to the steps taken by the Netherlands to free imports from quantitative restrictions. Moreover, it was agreed that the Dutch should select for these initial stages of liberalization of her imports those products of which increased imports from Belgium to the Nether-

lands would help simultaneously to give increased em-
ployment in depressed Belgian industries and to enable
rationing to be abolished in the Netherlands.

These negotiations involved not only give-and-take, foretelling the
future, sacrifices, and the like; but also, rather obviously, a great
deal of investigatory activity by assisting experts and the figuring
out of complex financial detail.

Some part of such interaction also included arguing and
persuading—but always in the service of reaching some reasonable,
rational agreement. The negotiators might interact with each other,
but presumably also with their governmental superiors, with influential rational segments of population, and possibly with the
public at large. "But the ministers realized, of course, that even if
both countries achieved global equilibrium in their balances of
payments, such an equilibrium might well be subject to future
disturbances. They argued, therefore, that the final arrangements
for economic union must include some system whereby disequilibria
in the balance of payments between the partner states and also in
the balance of payments between the union as a whole and the
outside world should be quickly detected and that there must also
be arrangements for taking corrective measures to restore balance-
of-payments equilibrium when disturbances had been detected. The
measure especially recommended . . . was the use of jointly concerned commercial policy" (p. 35).

At later meetings, we see again the prevalence of "inquiries,"
the gathering of vital information that one party or another might
suggest as a necessity for rational future agreements: "At the
Luxembourg meeting, the ministers also discussed a number of
other topics, such as agricultural policy and the problems of ports
and waterways. On neither of these topics were any final decisions
reached; but new inquiries were initiated" (p. 42). That pattern
also reflected the continuing complexity of the negotiation, insofar
as both new issues and difficult recurring issues were put on the
agenda (suggested by one party or another). Indeed, we may
assume, although Meade does not go into the matter, that negotiation often took place around what ought to go on the agenda for
each meeting.

Some of the more formal agreements were marked by the signing of "conventions" and of "protocols." However, these particular negotiators only represented governments, which in turn only represented some influential publics—hence there were some snags: "The protocol of December 16, 1948, was ratified by the Dutch in March 1949, but it failed to obtain the approval of the Belgian legislature. . . . The beer duties presented a very serious problem. In Belgium, beer is a national drink and is taxed at a relatively low rate, while in the Netherlands spirits are much more widely consumed and are taxed at much lower rates. The unification of the beer duties would have involved the raising of a much higher rate of tax on the popular drink in Belgium, and the Belgian parliament was unable to agree to this" (p. 45). Just that one example of legislative refusal to back the negotiated agreements shows that some—not all—of the agreements had to pass the scrutiny of wider publics. Probably also, during the negotiation meetings some higher authorities had to be given reports about the progress of negotiations, as well as played a part beforehand in what issues would be discussed, what problems faced, what solutions might be proposed, and so on. In so complex a set of negotiations, also, one can assume that a great many sets of negotiations within each country were going on among influential and interested citizens. These negotiations, in turn, were linked to and fed into the Benelux negotiations themselves.

It is important to recognize that when the governments signed conventions and protocols they did not merely sign one large one but rather signed many smaller ones. Each act of signing corresponded to some agreement or set of agreements that, taken all together, furthered the main, shared goal of full economic union. Thus, in 1949–1950, each country signed agreements with the other, undertaking to grant social security benefits to workers coming from the other partner country on the same terms as the benefits given to its own citizens.

Yet, long after the signing of specific agreements, the negotiators were still working together solving the less tractable problems. That joint action involved persuading each other, or independently realizing, of the actual dimensions of each difficult problem. "The second major difficulty which the ministers at Ostend in July 1950

saw in the way of an early institution of the complete economic
union was the absence of a common regime for regulating trade and
payments with third countries. They decided that the aim should
be to have common and joint agreements with third countries by
January 1, 1951. To that end, as usual, they negotiated various
implementing agreements" (p. 49). The following example illustrates how the negotiations were held in subsets involving different
teams of negotiators: "On the third major obstacle to the immediate
inception of full economic union—namely, the agricultural problem—the ministers at Ostend decided that a special conference
should be called. Indeed, it had become the accepted Benelux
method that the agricultural problem should be always dealt with
by a special meeting of agricultural ministers" (p. 50). The kinds
of claims that could be made by the negotiators in light of the
special situations and problems of their respective countries, and the
way those claims were honored, were highlighted by the generally difficult agricultural problem. The kinds of domestic pressures
bearing on the claiming and honoring were also clearly exemplified: "The Luxembourg protocol had also given special difficulty to
the Luxembourg government. While Belgian agriculture needed
some protection from Dutch agriculture, Luxembourg agriculture
itself required considerable protection even from Belgian agriculture
within the Belgium-Luxembourg Economic Union. The special
problem of Luxembourg agriculture had been recognized in the
Luxembourg protocol of October 1950 in a clause which stated
that in the application of the provisions of the protocol special
regard should be paid to the special problems of Luxembourg agriculture. But this did not prove sufficient to allay the misgivings of
the Luxembourg agriculturists. As a result, at the Hague meeting
of December 1950 it was decided to give to Luxembourg agriculture
an almost complete exemption from all the provisions of the
protocol of October 1950" (p. 54). Such claiming, when met by
counterclaiming that resulted in mutual honoring, generally illustrates what we have referred to earlier as the "give-and-take" that is
so characteristic a feature of this kind of negotiation.

　　By the middle of 1952, radically new contingencies and new
issues had arisen, so that "the basic problems in building Benelux
were completely transformed." The old problem of the deficit on

the Dutch balance of payments had disappeared; in fact, the reverse was now the case. The result was that Dutch products clearly were undercutting Belgian products. Understandably, there "was very considerable pressure within Belgium to protect the Belgian industries most directly concerned." Note that the ministers now arranged for negotiations to occur not among government servants but among the very groups that had been exerting strong pressures on this particularly delicate and knotty issue: "The main idea was to obtain temporary alleviation for the Belgian producers . . . by encouraging temporary arrangements between the industrialists concerned, which would have the same effect of reducing the sale of Dutch products on the Belgian-Luxembourg market. Accordingly, in the industries concerned, the ministers decided to set up, under the chairmanship of senior officials, groups of industrialists from the Dutch and the Belgian-Luxembourg sides to promote suitable private arrangements of this kind. Governmental action was to be taken only if agreement on private arrangements of this kind could not be secured" (p. 62). At the appropriate times, the implementation of the industrialists' arrangements was then reviewed.

That concludes my quoting of the raw data of Meade's historical narrative, although he carries it forward for another two years; to present further data would add nothing to understanding the characteristic forms of the Benelux negotiations.

Summary. The negotiation context for the Benelux negotiations was quite complex, involving above all sequential, even scheduled negotiation sessions; parties with both different and common stakes; multiple and often complex issues; experienced negotiators who represented their governments and grew increasingly experienced not only about particular issues but also in dealing with each other; balances of negotiation power among the parties muted or played down; and negotiations often novel in form and content and largely overt in nature. The drastic consequence of failure of the total negotiation was failure to reach a common goal: economic union. Accompanying particular negotiations, of course, were combinations of coercive threat, manipulation of events or contingencies, and certainly persuasion and "education" on pertinent information and issues. Just because these were highly cooperative negotiations, we need not assume they were unaccompanied by those other actions. The feature of this course of negotiation that should perhaps be stressed is that it was a long, extended course of sequential negotiations that were also serial, insofar as the results of prior negotiations fed into the later ones.

Related to those contextual conditions were various characteristic subprocesses of negotiation. Among them were the hammering out of negotiation machinery itself, the progressive building of agreement, the ironing out of residual disagreements, the trading off both of assigned tasks and of agreements to take up specific issues regarding different minor stakes. Also, because Benelux involved negotiating over such a long time as well as the common aim of setting up enduring arrangements among the governments involved, additional subprocesses appeared: notably, the periodic review of arrangements (including negotiation procedures and other machinery, as well as institutional outcomes of the negotiations), and negotiating anew over relatively fixed agreements later seen to be affected by unforeseen contingencies.

Meade does not directly address the question, "What kind of a social order are these governments building together?"—he was content with writing a detailed economic history. He would possibly answer "a durable structure of cooperative relationship" in the economic, financial, and commercial areas. If so, we might agree with him, providing we quickly qualify that by noting that those areas are also deeply linked with political and even military relationships. As Morse, the author of "The Bargaining Structure of NATO" (1976), reviewed earlier, has argued, these areas are all interwoven in the contemporary Western world. Consequently, we could further hazard that these Benelux negotiations, at least in their cumulative impact, have profoundly influenced the overall relationships among the respective nations. They have been part of the changing world order within which any negotiation, now taking place among their governments, must necessarily be different from that which obtained when the building of this economic union began.

Two further points need to be stressed. First, this course of negotiation looks different from that in the next case (the Nuremberg Trials) because these negotiations were in the service of developing and maintaining a durable rather than a temporary structure. Second, much of the review of past agreements, as well as the consequent renegotiation, turned both on seeing "how things have turned out" and on the changing properties of the structural context for the negotiations—that is, on "new and unforeseen contingencies" quite aside from the negotiated outcomes themselves.

Case: The Nuremberg Trials: A Temporary Structure

A contrast to the Benelux negotiations is provided by those carried out by the United States, the United Kingdom, France, and the Soviet Union concerning the issues and procedures that were to eventuate in the War Crimes Prosecutions known to history as the Nuremberg Trials. These negotiations had features in common with those of Benelux, but their chief differences flowed from the fact that all the parties to the Nuremberg negotiations understood that they were negotiating a legal and procedural framework that would probably be entirely transitory (Alterman, 1951, especially pp. 49–100). Thus these were a one-shot series of negotiations. The respective governments would remain autonomous agents in all their future relationships with each other, under what presumably would be a world order—of alliances, coalitions, and enemies—not so very different from that which predominated down to the advent of the trials.

In the negotiations, there would be a common aim toward which the governments worked—"there was no difference or conflict among the four powers as to the ultimate aim of these negotiations"—the aim of creating an international military tribunal to indict, try, convict, and punish the major European Axis war criminals. Whatever conflicts over negotiation arose derived from differences in concepts concerning the judicial process itself, the legal procedures, what constituted a fair trial, where the trial might be held, and conceptions of substantive international law and definitions of war crimes. These differences could be expected, considering that the legal concepts and systems of each country differed considerably from those of the others. Thus the negotiations turned on those multiple and sometimes complex considerations. These negotiations were not designed to lead to continuing cooperative relationships, *except* those involved in the relatively brief period of the trials themselves.

The negotiations took place during a time when the wartime alliance had deteriorated rather rapidly and, indeed, when acrimonious negotiations were occurring or were about to occur over fixing boundaries, making treaties with conquered countries, limiting armaments, negotiating over inspection of atomic weapons, and the like. It is all the more surprising—unless one recognizes the stake the Soviets shared with the other negotiating parties—that the Nuremberg negotiations themselves were not especially acrimonious. Unlike other negotiations with the Soviet Union, there was an absence of personal attack by Soviet negotiators and of insinuations against the motives or views of other negotiators. Discussions were universally on a high plane, and the Russians showed great politeness and tact. They were stubborn on matters on which they had definite positions or on which they were under instructions from Moscow; but they were never rude. Their tactics often harassed or annoyed the other negotiators, but their manners never did. As hosts or guests during social functions, they were so gracious and genial that the negotiators from the other countries formed close personal attachments to the members of the Russian negotiating team. And neither the Soviet government nor any other government used the negotiations as "a sounding board for home consumption or for propaganda."

Besides the common stake, what were the other salient properties of this particular negotiation context? To begin with, there were *four negotiating parties* (the nations), which led to the possibility of *multiple and simultaneous* negotiations between and among various combinations of the negotiating nations. Indeed, Alterman remarks that it is quite as difficult to dissect, out of the mass of the negotiations, those representing distinctly American-Russian discussions "as it is to dissect two eggs out of a four-egg omelet. Indeed, it is more apt to say a six-egg omelet, since each . . . negotiated with each of the other three; so . . . six sets of international discussions comprised the negotiations" (1951, p. 50). So we would anticipate the *ad hoc* coalitions that formed around specific issues and then disappeared as the issues became resolved in general negotiations. Each of the four powers was *represented* by a chief negotiator, who of course reported back and was responsive to his very highest government officers. Each was supported by a team of legal experts. The chief negotiators (distinguished lawyers or lawyer judges) and the team members eventually grew *experienced,* both in these kinds of specific negotiations and with each other's styles and personalities. The negotiators often handled multiple negotiation *issues,* some of them *linked* but also handled *simultaneously.* The negotiations were *sequential* and were designed (in view of the *common stake*) to lead to a definite implementation (that is, through the final negotiation agreements to the trials themselves). The agreements also were to terminate within a relatively short time. These sequential negotiations were almost wholly *overt* and *explicit,* without the covert or collusive quality of many other negotiations among nations. They were, however, conducted in secret, confidential sessions with no press releases on details of the discussions. Often the course of the negotiation went into new territory, for international legal precedent was being set: Hence many specific negotiations were *novel,* the element of "routine" being relatively negligible. Some of the new terrain pertained to getting agreement on *legitimate boundaries* concerning the trial or the meaning of the term *war criminals*: There were arguments over what constituted a war criminal, what reasonable punishments might be, and so on. What was not very salient in these negotiations—indeed, virtually absent—was the question of *balance of negotiating power.* As in the Benelux meetings, differentials of power were muted, kept under control because of the common stake involved in the negotiations. The consequence of a failure of negotiations was giving up on reaching common agreement concerning the structure that was to punish the war criminals. This was something that none of the governments desired—so in that sense they had not much alternative to negotiation.

I now present some details of the negotiation, to bring out its flavor and to suggest how the contextual properties functioned as conditions for the evolving interaction. The so-called Yalta Memorandum drawn up by the U.S. secretaries of the Departments of State and War and by the attorney general (January 22, 1945) set forth the essence of the "American Plan." It was finally adopted, more or less, by the end of the Yalta negotiations and was carried out in the Nuremberg Trials. The memo rejected the execution of war criminals without trial or hearing, recommending the judicial process and a fair trial. "It recommended the negotiation of an executive agreement of the Big Four that would provide for the establishment of an international tribunal of a military character. It proposed the use of the theory of conspiracy to reach not only individual outrages but also the common plan of the German leaders to conduct a systematic and planned reign of terror within Germany, in the satellite Axis countries, and in the occupied countries of Europe. . . . The memorandum also contained . . . the proposal for a procedure by which the tribunal in the main trial would declare certain Nazi groups and organizations (SA, SS, Gestapo, and so on) to be criminal, as the basis for reaching the many members of those organizations in later trials of individuals. . . . This was a strange concept to Russian and French lawyers and even to British and some American lawyers, and it took extensive negotiations to harmonize views and to gain its acceptance" (pp. 54–55). The Soviet Union and the United Kingdom readily indicated acceptance in principle, and later, in San Francisco at the postwar general conference, it was agreed to meet soon to formulate definitive agreements. At the San Francisco conference, some preliminary general principles were agreed on: the trial of major war criminals rather than political disposition of their cases; the return of criminals to countries where their crimes had been committed; an international military tribunal to hear the cases of the major war criminals; a committee of four representatives or chiefs of counsel to prepare and manage the prosecution, one to represent each of the four governments. Not long after, the British invited the various governments to send representatives to a London conference beginning about June 25, 1945. The American representative, Justice Jackson, and his staff studied the draft of the British proposal, prepared a slightly revised draft, which the other governments accepted—except that the Russians suggested seventeen specific amendments. The Americans quickly agreed to fourteen, and later, in the negotiations, the rest apparently also were agreed on.

    A few days before the conference opened, the American delegation held informal talks with the British delegation. There were some differences of opinion over the probable length of the trials, the expedition of the work (as through small subcommittees)', and the number of war criminals on the respective tentative lists. Both teams agreed that each delegation should follow its own approach, hoping that they would meet eventually somewhere in middle ground. It is noteworthy that these initial talks between British and American staffs were "necessarily informal because we did not want the Russian and French representatives when they had arrived to think that the United Kingdom and the United States had undertaken any formal action prior to the start of the four-power negotiation" (p. 61). At the first meeting, the Soviet negotiator immediately proposed "that, instead of embodying the entire subject in one instrument, there should be a separate and short executive agreement with an annexed 'statute' to cover the details, such as the definitions of crimes and the rules and procedures to govern the conduct of the trials. This was reiterated by the Soviet Union in a number of conferences and was finally agreed to by the other three delegations" (p. 201).

Alterman remarks that, in both this and the subsequent conference sessions, some principal problems arose about which there were differences of view. Some had to do with perspectives on policy. Some clearly had to do with differences of legal concepts and perhaps of cultural orientations. One of the first difficulties that remained throughout many sessions was the American proposal for the conviction of groups and organizations and subsequent prosecution of their individual members. The Soviet Union was puzzled about this proposal but eventually agreed. "This acquiescence was . . . largely induced by the basic Soviet view that it was already universally known that these groups and organizations were criminal, that there really was no need to try them, but that it would not hurt to have the military tribunal put the seal of its approval on what was already universal knowledge" (p. 64).

Among the seventeen amendments presented earlier by the Soviet Union had been one about rotating the presiding officer of the tribunal. At the first session, the Soviet negotiator politely asked why this amendment had not been adopted. Justice Jackson pointed out that in the United States we did not do this and suggested that rotating the presiding officer daily or weekly would be very confusing. The Soviet Union continued to insist on the principle of rotation through many sessions. The issue was finally resolved by the agreement that one presiding officer would be elected for the first trial, with rotation for subsequent trials. (The Russians had the idea that there would be a series of trials before the International Military Tribunal, but the others had the basic concept that there would be only one trial of major war criminals before the International Military Tribunal, with subsequent trials separately held by each occupying power, in the courts in its own zone.)

"However, the major conflict of views arose out of the basic differences between the Anglo-American legal concepts as to criminal trials and the quite different concepts obtaining on the continent and in particular in the Soviet Union, Germany, and France. This first conference included a very extensive discussion of these different systems" (p. 66). These differences were major. They involved, for instance, the roles of an inquiring (investigative) magistrate, the prosecuting officer, the defending counsel, and witnesses, as well as the very nature of an indictment and how it is carried out. "In this first conference and throughout later conferences, General Nikitchenko and Professor Trainin [the Russians] showed a constant recognition that it would be necessary to select between the two different systems, to try to pick out the best elements of each, so as to create for the International Military Tribunal a system and procedure which would be expeditious and yet which would contain the essential elements of a fair trial" (p. 67).

There was also a major difference between the Soviet Union and the other parties about where the trials should take place. The Soviet Union wished the trials to begin in Berlin within the Soviet zone, or, even if the "first trial" took place in another zone, to at least have the seat of the tribunal be in Berlin. But the British and Americans, foreseeing this Soviet insistence, had beforehand agreed to resist those proposals "for obvious reasons." The final agreement was that the first trial be held in Nuremberg, provided the permanent seat of the tribunal was in Berlin.

One American proposal the Soviets rejected immediately and never accepted. The Americans had proposed that "the tribunal be empowered to appoint special masters, or commissioners, to make special investigations, take evidence, and report to the tribunal, with power in the tribunal to act on such reports. This suggestion . . . was borrowed from our familiar equity practice. Its adoption would have greatly facilitated this trial. We had in mind such special investigations as those of particular concentration camps or of other distant points where particular atrocities occurred, such as the Warsaw ghetto" (p. 69). Alterman believes that the Russians were shocked at the proposal in part at least because of their reaction to the term "special masters"—so shocked, indeed, that "no amount of explanation on our part ever enabled them to recover from their original sense of shock. In drafting subcommittee meetings, I had a great deal of discussion with Professor Trainin about this matter. The British and the French were in accord with our views that such a procedure would expedite the trial. . . . The Soviet Union never did agree to that particular proposal" (p. 70).

Thus far, then, we can see that certain difficulties that the negotiators faced stemmed variously from differing legal concepts, from differing general policies, and possibly from certain cultural differences among the negotiating parties. However, the bargaining over the several issues was polite and unaggressive, if persistent. It could be persistent because each day's negotiations would be followed by many more meetings wherein "residual disagreements" (Ikle, 1964) might just possibly be ironed out either by compromise or by victory. This relatively unaggressive negotiation was especially noteworthy because of the Soviet Union's "bargaining reputation" (Ikle, 1964).

The initial meeting (termed a "plenary session") was followed by several others. At these meetings, formal amendments, written comments, and proposals were directed to the most recent American draft protocol. Verbal explanations followed. The chief Soviet negotiator made clear that his government conceived of the trials largely as formalities. "That was a viewpoint which the British, French, and Americans had to counter many times throughout the negotiations. Time and time again the Soviets were told that heads of governments, executives, under our concept, cannot convict people of crime. General Nikitchenko was perfectly willing to go through the form of having the tribunal put its stamp of approval on the conviction, but he adhered to the view that the Nazi leaders were already convicted criminals by declaration of the

conquering powers" (Alterman, 1951, p. 72). He also disagreed
with the Anglo-American principle of complete separation of the
judiciary and the executive, and he continued to contend that the
American provision for trial and conviction of groups and organizations should be dispensed with. At another session, the American
delegation submitted a further revised draft of its protocol plus an
accompanying memorandum, making efforts to meet the respective
memoranda already filed by the other delegations.

A couple of days later, the Soviet Union presented another
draft of the executive agreement, "very brief in its terms and
eliminating any provision for trials of groups and organizations.
This precipitated an elaborate discussion, particularly by Mr.
Justice Jackson and Sir David Maxwell Fyfe, presenting the proposal for trial of groups and organizations as the very heart of our
proposals and the only practicable way in which to reach the many
members of these organizations" (p. 73). The Soviet negotiator
disagreed. But, with continuing plenary sessions on the next days,
the discussions brought the conferees closer together in principle.
They agreed then that a drafting subcommittee undertake the detailed redrafting of the agreement and of an additional part termed
the *annex*. The subcommittee worked on the new draft, agreeing on
most items, leaving the remaining for discussion in further plenary
sessions.

During one of the drafting meetings, the Soviet and French
negotiators objected to use of the term *annex* because it implied
that the addition was not an integral part of the agreement. They
suggested "statute," but the Americans felt this then implied a four-
power treaty. The Americans could not agree to that because then
the U.S. Senate would have to ratify the agreement, and the delegation did not wish to run that obstacle course. Rather, the Americans
were undertaking to negotiate an executive agreement. The
British negotiator was sympathetic to this position, and together
they discussed the issue, agreeing that a good compromise term
would be *charter*. This temporary coalition of negotiators agreed to
present the term to their Soviet and French counterparts, who in
turn agreed. So their final document was termed "Agreement and
Charter."

The important point for us about this particular negotiation was that the American delegation directly represented the executive branch of the American government and only indirectly either the Senate or the American people. So this delegation did not wish to run afoul of potential rejection of the final negotiated agreement. Another important point is that combinations of British and American—or British, American, and French—negotiators worked with each other either on compromises or on persuading another party. Thus "One of the important accomplishments . . . achieved by Sir Thomas Barnes and me, with the consistent good help of Judge Falco, was that we finally brought Professor Trainin to agreement on the . . . question of trial of groups and organizations" (p. 77). The same *ad hoc* coalition argued for having the first trial in Nuremberg, but the Soviet negotiator argued that he had no authority to make such an agreement; that is, different levels of Soviet negotiating authority had differing degrees of authority over given issues—and here he had none.

The imagery of "bargaining reputation" entered the negotiations at this point in a rather interesting way. While the subcommittee was working, Justice Jackson took a trip through Germany and heard from various military officials of the various problems they had encountered on a number of issues with the Soviet Union. Jackson returned to his own negotiations in a very pessimistic mood; he was skeptical then whether the Soviet Union would ever actually carry out written agreements. He was also disappointed because the subcommittee had failed both to get agreement on Nuremberg as the site of the first trial and to obtain a proper definition of aggressive war. Consequently, in the next sessions he went "so far as frankly to state that, unless the four delegations could promptly arrive at an agreement satisfactory to the basic concepts of the American plan, the American delegation was prepared to withdraw from the negotiations, proceed to Nuremberg, try the prisoners in American hands, and go home, leaving the other three powers to their own devices" (p. 79). This, then, was the first open threat that any of the negotiating powers had made. It was effective because the common stake was so great. "The U.K. and France were somewhat dismayed at this peeling off of the customary kid gloves of diplomacy. However, it was language that the Soviet realists understood. They, no less than the United Kingdom and

France, did not want to contemplate the withdrawal of the Americans from this international trial and they became much more amenable to reason in the plenary sessions that followed" (p. 79).

The two other big issues under debate concerned the definition of war crimes and the question of who was actually to be indicted. Getting agreement on both issues showed the teams at work, rather than just the chief negotiators, but it also highlighted the further argumentation over specific details of agreements pertaining to the issues, as well as the formation of *ad hoc* coalitions over the specific issues. For instance, regarding the indictment issue, the British and Americans had met informally before the first plenary session and, discovering some differences between themselves, agreed they would produce preliminary drafts about indictment for further consideration. When the other delegations arrived, they were too busy to get involved with the work of drawing up lists of potential criminals and had no members to assign to a subcommittee for drafting the indictment. Tacit agreement was reached that the Americans and British would proceed with the work and periodically submit the results to the Soviet and French delegations.

The British soon submitted an illustrative draft of indictment that continued to be much simpler in conception and containing many fewer names of potential defendants than did the American working draft. The Russians seemed much pleased with the British draft, but the French were puzzled about how the lengthy American materials could be reduced to an actual indictment. Shortly thereafter, preparing for second drafts, Justice Jackson felt that the British were likely to furnish nothing more than a bare outline draft, like their earlier illustrative draft, and that something much more elaborate was necessary. A number of special experts on the American staff were put to work on the final American draft. Meanwhile, General Nikitchenko had been talking with the British about how to divide up the case for presentation among the four chief prosecutors, and he tentatively suggested a division of labor: the Americans to present the general conspiracy theory and the crime of aggressive war, the British to present violations of treaties and crimes on the high seas, and so on. The respective delegations agreed his suggestions were highly practicable. At about the same time, the Russians called a special meeting and insisted on adding a number of names to the lists of defendants, including certain prisoners in their hands. The French also wished to add two prisoners. So the delegations agreed to add nine more names to the American-English list of sixteen names.

Then further, rather argumentative negotiation crystallized around the final form of the indictment. The Americans delivered an imposing document that they tried to make all delegations understand was to be considered rather as working material than as a suggested final draft. The British were much pleased with the materials; but the French soon produced a very elaborate written critique of the American materials, which they had misconstrued as a suggested final draft. They thought too much had been tied to the aggressive quality of the war. The Soviet Union expressed principal interest in crimes against humanity and seemed to argue that the whole case could be tied to those offenses. Alterman, representing the American delegation, "made quite an argument" against the French contention.

That issue, which was really left unsettled, led to the following train of events. After a next meeting, there was general agreement in principle on how the redraft of the indictment would look, and several days later a formal press conference was held. The reporters asked Justice Jackson, who had just made a reference to making aggressive war an international crime, whether the rumored reports were accurate that the French delegation did not agree with that view of war. Jackson passed the question to the French negotiating chief who did, to the great relief of the American delegation, agree with Jackson's view. There was a last flurry of argumentation and negotiated agreements when Jackson, a few days later, had some additional thoughts about the first two counts of the actual draft of indictment (British and Americans had been assigned to work on this). The British delegation fought strongly against his suggestions, but then both delegations worked things out amicably. The other two delegations still had to be sold on the redraft of the first two counts. "Meanwhile, much to the surprise of all of us, the French delegation had itself made a new and complete redraft of the indictment" (p. 92). But the Soviet negotiating team liked the British-American draft very much.

Next came a top-level meeting at which great progress was

made toward final agreement on the latest redrafts. Then Jackson
had one further thought about including the German general staff
or some recognizable category of the high command as a defendant
organization, a suggestion that the British chief negotiator argued
against so vigorously "that a number of members of his staff later
apologized to me [Jackson]," but the French and Soviet Union
voted in support of the American position. The Americans, with the
help of a knowledgeable British intelligence officer, worked out a
formulation to define the German staff and high command group;
this was presented at the next plenary session and adopted. But
another last-minute proposal made by Jackson, to add additional
defendants from among German industrialists, was opposed by the
British, who were supported by the other two delegations, who
again decided the specific issue by formal vote. They all voted
against the proposal because they believed it would delay the beginning of the trial. By then, time was moving in on the delegations:
The pressure was on to get the trials going as soon as possible.

   Summary. The negotiation context for the Nuremberg negotiations was quite complex, much like the Benelux negotiations,
with which it shares many features. For both, contextual conditions
included sequential and scheduled negotiation sessions, as well as
experienced negotiators, representing their respective governments,
who became increasingly familiar both with each other's negotiating
styles and with this specific type of negotiation. Many details of the
negotiation were novel, as were the issues, which sometimes proved
quite complex and which included the question of the legitimacy of
the trials themselves. The balances of negotiating power were muted
or played down. However, the details of the Nuremberg negotiations were kept largely covert from the larger public, although they
were known by the respective governments. Negotiation itself was
quite necessary, for the only option to it was to forgo the common
aim of holding trials—at least, as a cooperative venture—of the war
criminals. Accompanying the particular instances of negotiation,
of course, were combinations of open or covert coercive threat, the
educating of each other to national legal or political perspectives,
and the persuading to positions; possibly, too, there was a certain
amount of manipulation of events, such as the fast production of
working drafts or their production as cast in certain forms. A fea-

ture of these negotiations that should be especially stressed is that they were sequential, leading up to a legal-procedural structure; prior negotiations thus led systematically into later ones.

Various subprocesses of negotiation were related to the Nuremberg set of contextual conditions. Among them were the hammering out of negotiation machinery; the progressive building of agreement; the ironing out of residual disagreements; and the trading off of necessary tasks. Missing, by contrast with the Benelux negotiations, were the periodic review of arrangements and institutional outcomes, as well as the renegotiating of previous arrangements in light of new contingencies—missing precisely because the Nuremberg arrangements were designed to be temporary or nondevelopmental. An important subprocess was that, unlike Benelux, there was much covert coalition building concerning positions to be taken on next-step negotiations (although not on general positions taken throughout the total sequence of negotiations, for that, if known, would probably have destroyed the fragile bases for four-power cooperation here).

Suppose one asked, "What is an appropriate characterization of the social order that undergirded the total working group of four-power representatives as it designed the war criminal trial procedures?" What would be an approximate answer? Despite the continual daily and hourly building of working relationships through negotiation and other processes, one can easily discern many traditional features of international order, including a machinery for allowing formal negotiation among nations and negotiators.

Of course, there also was some manipulation of events during the meetings themselves, as well as plenty being done by the respective governments with regard to the meetings (domestic announcements, propaganda aimed at international audiences)—and all of this occurred within a larger structural context of contemporary events that involved not only further manipulation of contingencies but also threats of coercion and the actual use of force.

If we ask how the Nuremberg negotiations affected that larger structural context, especially in the long run, the answer seems "precious little." The international order that has emerged since the end of World War II owes nothing discernible to the relatively harmonious but impermanent working relationships that constituted the Nuremberg negotiations. However, the trials themselves did set a precedent with not entirely negligible consequences for international relations, insofar as the issue of "human rights" entered two decades later into both the Helsinki agreements and Carter's American foreign policy initiative in the late 1970s.

Chapter Twelve

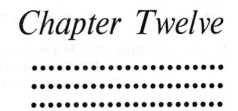

Negotiating Compromises Within Social Orders

*T*he dictionary defines *compromise* as an arrangement for settlement by mutual concession. Popular conceptions of bargaining emphasize this particular form of negotiating toward some middle ground, usually involving money or at least financial equivalences. That particular literature on negotiation that leans on economic theory also tends to focus on this specific form of negotiation. As many of the foregoing case analyses demonstrate, however, this kind of negotiation process either may be absent or may be much complicated by and subordinated to other subprocesses of negotiation.

One might assume that the structural conditions that further such compromise bargaining are primarily economic ones, including the possibility of moving toward the middle because money itself is divisible. That is too simple a conception of what is at issue. In the first place, this negotiation subprocess occurs only when there is a recognizable and relatively stable social order, with explicit rules about bargaining. Everyone, for instance, is familiar with the contrasting situation wherein, say, American tourists are trying to bargain with Arabs but do not understand the Arab rules about bargaining toward middle ground. The bargaining either breaks down, or the seller teaches the buyer his rules and requests that they be followed.

While much compromise bargaining is of a one-shot nature, taking place between strangers, undoubtedly that process becomes more complex when those making the transaction have done so before and thus are building other relationships into and around this specific transaction. Consider now what might happen if the bargaining were entirely subordinate to a web of relationships and carried out between negotiators who have an eye not merely on the money at stake but on the common stake each has in the web of relationships. These social order aspects of compromise negotiation tend to be much neglected in the negotiation literature based on economic theory. Yet those aspects are vital to our understanding of those negotiations.

In the two cases presented in this chapter, I take up this type of negotiation, using portions of the analyses made by the authors. The first case is much the more complex of the two. It concerns bargaining over bridewealth among the Labwor, as described and analyzed by an anthropologist (Abrahams, 1968). Since the negotiation takes place within an ongoing system of clan and family relationships, it is preceded and will be succeeded by a history of previous and future negotiations, about bridewealth and other stakes, and, of course, is covered by conventional rules. Furthermore, the specific transactions between the fathers involved are embedded in and precipitate a thick texture of simultaneously occurring negotiations among numerous other relatives and clan members. These negotiations constitute subprocesses and appear essential to the continuance of family and clan social orders.

The second case concerns the bargaining that transpires between insurance company representatives and persons who claim compensation for medical injury incurred through automobile accidents. The bargaining in this instance seems rather simple in contrast with the bridewealth negotiation. Perhaps it appears simple (although the actual interaction can be fairly complicated) because it takes place only until the settlement is made or refused and because the claimant rarely engages in many such transactions, although the insurance company, of course, engages in a multitude of them. The negotiation between the respective parties is of a one-shot nature; nevertheless, there is a social order of some kind "within which" the interaction occurs, always in reference to explicit or implicit rules of procedure, notions of equity, and the like.

Finally, in each of the cases we have the opportunity to see in some detail the beginning, development, and conclusion to its principal subprocesses of negotiation.

Case: Clan Intermarriage and Bridewealth Negotiations

The anthropologist Ray Abrahams (1968, pp. 203–214) gives the following relevant information about the background for decision making on the transfer of bridewealth among the African Labwor. The Labwor are divided among a number of named, exogamous, patrilineal descent groups, which they call *kaka* or *ateker* but which Abrahams refers to as "clans." The clans vary a great deal in size. The events that Abrahams describes involve the marriage of a man from a smaller clan to a woman from one of the larger clans. The members of each clan are to a considerable extent localized, many senior males having homesteads or being within calling distance of each other. Marriages between members of such neighboring clans are common, although the form they can take is limited by certain rules, such as who cannot marry whom.

The senior members, rather than the couple, are mainly in charge of the formal arrangements for the marriage. Marriage is polygynous. Most marriages take quite a long time to arrange and are rarely broken once arrangements are well under way. There is always a transfer of bridewealth whenever the arrangements are made. Generally, the man himself or his father or other jural guardian is responsible for the necessary wealth to be transferred; and the girl's father and his full siblings, plus some of their dependents, tend to form the minimal group who may share by right in bridewealth paid for her. Clansfolk and others may, however, help a man to pay bridewealth if they want to, and often they do. Thus it is not unusual for a mother's brother to provide a head of cattle to help a young man marry. Nowadays, bridewealth typically consists of an agreed number of cattle, distributed among the bride's kin according to a fairly clear-cut customary pattern. Agreement over the transfer is reached during a series of negotiation sessions.

The particular sessions discussed here happened to be a bit more conflictful than usual, because after initial arrangements the man began to change his mind, and after impatiently waiting for some time the women's kinsmen put on considerable heat to have the previous agreement fulfilled. The negotiations began with the bridegroom's father (William) issuing an invitation for the bride's father (George) and his people to come to his homestead on November 25th to "see" the bridewealth cattle, which he had assembled in his kraal. Before coming, George and his younger brother drew up a written list of demands. As is customary, these were divided into three main sections pertaining to family, clan, and mother's kin. Different numbers of cattle were to be given (seventy-three in all) to the various receiving persons. Thus, the father's younger brother was to receive seven cows; the mother's senior full sister was to receive one.

After preparing the list, George and about thirty men, consisting of close fellow clansmen and others, including two friends, set off for William's homestead, which was nearby. A female contingent, largely composed of the wives, followed shortly thereafter. All were greeted by William and various members of his homestead, also by numbers of his clanfolk and affines who had come for the occasion. After a while, George and his male companions were invited over to see the cattle. All the men then sat down for the proceedings, in separate groups. So did William's wives (also a separate group). The visiting wives mostly watched from the verandas of the neighboring huts.

Before continuing the narrative, note the contextual properties that have already entered into this negotiation situation. We know this negotiation will involve no great novelty; it is *routine*, at least in the sense that it is covered by sets of rules or conventions. Although this is a *one-shot* negotiation (these same two persons will marry each other only once), nevertheless the two clans will have (and even the two families may have) negotiated previously over bridewealth transfers. And the clans will do this again: So this particular negotiation is only one of a *sequence* of similar, even possibly *linked*, negotiations by the same negotiators. But, if not they, at least others watching the negotiations will be *experienced* both in the form and the content of the negotiation and guarding the conventional rules of procedure and equity involved in the negotiation.

Now let us continue with the narrative. Once the people were arranged properly, William was given the prepared list of demands, which he read. Then he suggested that the 500 shillings originally paid as a kind of token, when the marriage arrangement first was made, should count, along with an additional 100 shillings, as four head of cattle. After a bit of discussion, his point was accepted. George then told William to start bringing out the cattle from the kraal. William brought out one cow at a time in front of George's group, naming the proposed recipient as he did so. In effect, he was giving counteroffers, since what he gave to each person was not necessarily identical with what George had proposed.

Before he had fully completed his disposition of cattle, a variety of dissatisfactions were voiced—for instance, the girl's mother complained strongly that her sisters had not been allotted cattle, since there were obligations to them for cattle that she had been given when their daughters had been given in marriage. William gave way, at least partly, to some of these claims. The total number of cattle offered up to this point was thirty-eight, compared to the seventy-three originally requested. Finally, an ox with a bell tied around its neck was given to the bride's mother; this payment marked an important stage in the negotiation, since this animal is always the last to be driven out of the kraal.

Abrahams summarizes the proceedings up to this point: a relatively formal presentation of a series of demands for cattle by one party, followed by a series of offers (and nonoffers) in response by the other party. Complaints about some of these responses resulted in the making of supplementary offers, but not all complaints were successful. This honoring and rejecting of claims was not yet contested further. According to conventional understandings, there was time later to do this.

The routine or conventional character of this particular negotiation context, as well as the great experience of the negotiators, meant that further contest over claims would take place within what were understood to be reasonable or *legitimate boundaries.*

Outrageous claims either could not be made or could legitimately
be rejected; conversely, legitimate claims ought to be honored, or
cause should be shown for not doing so. There was still another
important contextual property: *Multiple negotiators* were present.
The people who expressed dissatisfaction, making complaints about
William's counteroffers, were *also* negotiating. They engaged in one
negotiation after another, as well as sometimes simultaneously.
What is especially interesting is that sometimes they were negotiating in their own behalf and sometimes they were *representing*
someone else. So this negotiation context was further complicated
by the fact that the negotiators might be agents representing others'
claims. Even William might be regarded as representing his household; but certainly various members of George's party could be
conceived of as representing others' claims. They might also be conceived sometimes as representing George's household—and perhaps
his and their clan.

The matter of representation was, in this particular negotiation context, quite complex, as we shall see. During this specific
phase of the negotiation, representation was made for brothers who
were not yet adult; by the girl's father on behalf of his friend
Andrew, who, although present, had no formal right to demand
a beast; and, as touched on earlier, by the girl's mother on behalf
of her sisters to whom at previous marriage arrangements she had
incurred debts.

The girl's group was next invited to continue the discussion
in the hut of the groom's mother. This invitation was accepted.
George's party then narrowed down to his brothers, the girl's eldest
full brother, her mother and her mother's brother, and various of
her own and her mother's clansmen plus some of their wives.
(Matrilateral links form an important part of the system of kinship
and marriage among the Labwor.) On William's side were his
brother and some other clansmen with their wives, including the
groom's mother, the groom's mother's brother, and some of William's other affines. The ensuing discussion was less formally organized than the preceding one; also, because of the conflictful history
of this particular set of marriage arrangements, the discussion was
more acrimonious than is usual. A number of claims were raised and
discussed, including the ones about friend Andrew and the bride's

mother's sisters. For the first half hour, it seemed to Abrahams that no progress was being made: Neither side seemed willing to yield on any point of consequence, and there was much hard bargaining. George's youngest brother Jacob was particularly obdurate about his claim for all six cattle originally demanded for him.

During the early stages of this discussion, we can see another set of representatives in action: two senior men who represented the respective clans. They counseled acceptance of the proffered cattle on the general grounds that marriage was a good thing, and a bride joins people together. As clansmen of the respective negotiating parties, they were entitled to be present, and since they were speaking as senior clansmen their opinions carried extra weight. Also, neither was closely enough related to George or William to be personally involved either in receipt or payment of the bridewealth. Hence they could act as mediators. (Another structural property of the clans contributes to their particular type of representation: Different roles are assigned to the clan and to its various constituent segments. As Abrahams notes, this tends to guarantee that this "useful sort of participant" will be present during the negotiation.)

When a deadlock seemed to have been reached, eventually a variety of participants on both sides began to make more "practical gestures," and this changed the tone of the proceedings. The mood gradually became friendlier and more cooperative, and when Abrahams left, two and a half hours later, it was clear that a basic agreement had been reached with only small details needing to be finished off. By this time, too, the gathering had begun to turn into a jovial beer party, with singing and shouting that continued on for several hours. What Abrahams has referred to as practical gestures included the following. George's friend Andrew reluctantly agreed that the beast in question should go to George's elder brother (who was not present because employed away from the village). The latter clearly got his share because of a legitimate claim; while Andrew's gesture was related to his continuing relationship to George. In another deal, two male kinsmen of George's announced they would be willing to do without their share—Abrahams notes that one was in debt to George, which may have influenced his decision. Clearly, the *major stakes* of getting the bride married *and* the clans (and families) into agreement operated in this forgoing of shares (possibly also in George's incurring future obligations to the kinsmen in question).

These major stakes also operated in a few proffers of cows by various clansmen. Thus William's brother promised one for George's younger brother. Some of the clansmen's proffers were also influenced by the continuing relationships between the two clans and preceding intermarriages. A cow was offered to George's second sister by the brother and guardian of the groom's first wife, who in turn was a fellow clansman of the recipient. Again, William's son-in-law, who belongs to the bride's mother's clan, offered 100 shillings for George's younger brother. And—even more entangled in clan relationships!—Rupert, a clansman of George, who himself was promised a cow, offered to contribute 100 shillings to George's elder brother's share; he did this because he was married to William's daughter. George himself eventually announced that he was in favor of the marriage and said that if Jacob, his youngest brother, persisted in making an issue over his share then he would give his own portion to Jacob. (His action is so customary that it has a name, *Konyo koror*, meaning, "Helping the beast owned by the son-in-law.") This left Jacob in an untenable position—he was beyond reasonable bounds—so eventually he accepted the three cows offered to him. George added he understood that still other dissatisfied persons might ask him for redress after the marriage.

In short, because of the importance of the major stakes involved in the negotiation, clansmen both of the bride and the groom were allowed, and expected, to proffer—but only after the bride's father had completed his own proffering. And George, even though he is a major, not a minor, negotiating figure, could also proffer to members of his own clan. Note also that all those who proffered actually did so themselves. Because present as members of one or both negotiating parties, they could contribute to the final settlement. According to the conventional understandings that operated in this negotiation context, each could make financial proffers without consultation with the person or group represented through his or her action. The only *option* for all participants to this negotiation was to block, or allow to be blocked, the marriage itself—marriage or not marriage, flat acceptance or rejection—by both sides. No appeal to any higher authority, such as a court or board of arbitration, was possible.

One additional point about the negotiated payments (the total payment was forty-three cows and forty-seven sheep and goats): clearly, there were conventional judgments being made as to reasonable amounts to be given to the various recipients. Analogous to the settlements in insurance negotiation (in the case discussed next), where claims are paid by a kind of standardized equivalences, here the various kinsmen and clansmen could only make conventionally reasonable claims and would receive only reasonable payments. The *boundaries of legitimacy,* then, covered not only the total amounts that passed from one clan to another but also the amounts that passed to (and from) particular participants.

What about the consequences of this type of negotiation? Abrahams notes that George's offer was significant, since it reflected the development of ties between him and his new affines, which completed and might even conflict with those between him and his agnates and other kin. To that we can add additional consequences (other than that the marriage could actually take place). Some people received wealth, others lost some. Some clansmen incurred obligations, others were paid off for previous ones. Continuing relationships between the respective clans were furthered—both through the transfer of wealth and the marriage—but an additional minor relationship was also added via linkages between the two families. (Since there had been conflict between the two families, the negotiation somewhat affected their relationships—"somewhat" because Abrahams notes that a tragic testimony to the strength of the conflict was the suicide of the bride about a year later, after a quarrel apparently involving her husband and his first wife.) Also, various persons were put into new relationships with others through the product of the negotiation; that is, the marriage itself: The bride became a kinswoman by marriage to numerous others, and so on.

This range of consequences pertains to the central question of what relation this kind of negotiation (or this particular negotiation) has to the social order of the clan and/or family. The specific (one-shot) negotiation certainly alters some relationships between clans and families, just as the type of negotiation continually builds

those relationships and in turn sets the basis for the development
of further relationships not directly concerned with marital relationships. Whether any particular instance of bridewealth negotiation
much affects the intrarelationships of family or kin or clan presumably depends on some additional variables, such as whether
certain kinsmen are drawn more closely or further apart—by
gratitude or anger—because of the course taken by the negotiation
and its associated payments. It is quite clear that intrafamily and
intraclan relationships are affected by the incurring and paying
of debts. So, in general, we may conclude that this type of negotiation "functions" to sustain *and* alter both the interrelationships
and intrarelationships. Insofar as it does, we can speak of this type
of recurring negotiation as part of the social orders of the clan
and family. Apropos of the duality of the sustaining and altering
of those social orders by negotiation, the anthropologist-sociologist
Pierre Bourdieu (1977, pp. 56, 204, and 235) has made interpretations of bridewealth bargaining that are virtually identical
with mine:

> The ritual of the ceremony of presenting the
> bridewealth is the occasion for a total confrontation be-
> tween the two groups, in which the economic stakes are
> no more than an index and pretext. . . . It was not
> possible to give an account of matrimonial exchanges
> unless, in addition to the purely genealogical relation-
> ship between the spouses, one established the objective
> relationship between the position in the social structure
> of the groups brought together by the marriage, the his-
> tory of the economic and symbolic exchanges which had
> occurred between them, and the state of those trans-
> actions at the moment when matrimonial negotiation
> was undertaken, the history of that negotiation, the mo-
> ment at which it took place in the lives of the
> spouses . . , its length, the agents responsible for it,
> the exchanges to which it gave rise, and in particular the
> value of the bridewealth, and so on. In other words,
> the study of matrimonial exchanges cannot be separated
> from the families' economic and social history, of which
> a genealogical diagram gives only a skeleton. . . . the

apparent issue at stake in matrimonial negotiations, conceals the total circulation, actual or potential, of goods that are indissociably material and symbolic. . . . The amount of the payment, always of small value in relative and absolute terms, would not justify the hard bargaining to which it gives rise, did it not take on a symbolic value of the highest importance as the unequivocal demonstration of the worth of a family's products on the matrimonial exchange market and of the capacity of the heads of the family to obtain the best price for their products through their negotiating skills.

It is worth reemphasizing that much of the form and procedural detail of these negotiation proceedings is governed by tradition and convention—these proceedings being governed more or less as past ones have been and as more or less, ones in the future. However, the word *govern* is slippery; it can be interpreted not only in the determinate sense but also merely as signifying the operation of sets of conventional agreements that have been reached through negotiation in the past on how generally to conduct such proceedings as the transfer of bridewealth in association with marriage. Those *past* negotiations have perhaps been forgotten, and only their products remain, looking now like firm conventions (or the Labwor may possibly regard them as conventional agreements, while outsiders may err in conceiving them as above and beyond the phenomenon of negotiation).

Summary. By way of brief summary of the case: the general, common stake of the negotiating parties is to achieve a marriage with relative speed. But, the parents of the prospective bride and groom have mutually exclusive stakes—one party's material gain is directly associated with the other's loss. As in the accident settlements discussed next, these two properties yield a characteristic subprocess of bargaining from extreme positions toward a *compromise middle* with the usual offers and counteroffers, rejections, and final agreement. Yet other important contextual properties also help to shape the total negotiation interaction. Because this one-shot negotiation actually is part of a sequence of similar and even related negotiations, the multiple parties who get into the act of negotiation are responding to past and future transactions. Also, when they negotiate they are representing various others, and all such representations are openly recognized. The rapid sequence of offer and acceptance by multiple negotiators not only is in reference to past and future but also is related directly to the total settlement reached by the two clans and is related to the specific exchange between the two fathers of the prospective couple. And the contextual property of "this negotiation as one of a sequence of similar ones" means that the general flow of negotiation events moves in accordance with conventionally routine steps, procedures, and phases. Hence, while the subprocess (reaching a settlement through bargaining to a compromise) does occur, actually a more accurate phrasing is that what occurs is a *collective enterprise* in which multiple negotiators engage in numerous serial negotiations that add up to the final group settlement. Also, we can observe other subprocesses at work. Insofar as there is transpiring between various negotiators much *paying off* of previous contractual obligations (or delaying or abjuring getting paid off), there is also a kind of *forfeiting* (paying or giving up payment) because of persons being in certain status relationships. Paying up and forfeiting clearly involve individuals only as representatives of social units (clans, kin statuses), and negotiation processes refer not only to the present negotiation situations but also to past and future ones and to the perduring relationships that run through those situations. There was also some *mediating*, which was especially visible when the senior clansmen stepped into the proceedings. Affecting some of these negotiation subprocesses were persuasion and maneuvering of contingencies (for instance, the woman's kinsmen put on pressure to get the stalled negotiation going again), and possibly coercive gestures. Many of those other actions are highly conventionalized or at least fall routinely within the conventional rules of this particular collective enterprise of the Labwor.

Case: Negotiation Between Insurance
Companies and Claimants

Until the passage of no-fault legislation, now becoming more general, any American in recent years who could prove he or she was injured through the negligence of an automobile driver could claim recompense. Nineteen out of twenty such claims were settled out of court through a process of negotiation between the injured persons (or their lawyers) and the representatives ("adjusters") of insurance companies. Approximately half of the injured persons represented themselves, without lawyers, in this negotiation over claimed damages to themselves (Ross, 1970).

Such negotiation is relatively simple. For the claimant, usually, it is a once-only affair, albeit not necessarily a routine matter, while from the viewpoint of the insurance company, such negotiation is frequent and routine. Many claims are being processed simultaneously, meaning that many negotiations are being carried on simultaneously, but few of them are of earth-shaking importance to the company itself. The consequences may be far greater, understandably, for the claimants.

Abstracting from a careful study of insurance company practices (1970, especially pp. 136–175) by H. Laurence Ross, let us first look at some relevant properties of the structural and negotiation contexts—especially the latter, since the former are more obvious. The three insurance companies studied are large and well established, and all deal in other lines of insurance besides automobile insurance. They have branch offices in various regional centers, to which are attached "house adjusters" who deal with claimants to bodily injuries. Although the formal law of negligence requires a close, individualized look at each claimant, each company has an interest in processing the aggregate of claims as quickly as possible. This has eventuated in simplifications that make the task manageable despite constituting departure from handling each case on its merit. Indeed, just to manage the processing—let alone speedily—seems to require such simplification of investigating, evaluating, and negotiating claims. Thus, investigation is greatly simplified by making assumptions about liability based on the physical facts associated with each accident. There are rear-enders, red-light cases, and stop-sign cases. Evaluation frequently consists of merely applying the local formula "multiplier" to the bills incurred through an injury.

Over each adjuster, there is a supervisor. Typically, cases are reviewed periodically, the supervisory conference being based

on the claim file kept at the office. The adjuster has considerable
control over the information he places in that claims file, so that,
in effect, supervision cannot be very strict. The adjuster's discretion
as to what to place in the file is affected by certain pressures. One
such pressure is to close the case quickly—a supervisor noted,
"When we put the money in the reserve, that's money we can't
use. The sooner we dispose of that file, the better off we are"
(p. 60). The pressure on the adjuster to close files expeditiously is
greater than to close them cheaply. "The adjuster's economy is
judged on a case-by-case basis, where special circumstances are
always relevant. In contrast . . . efficiency in closing files is judged
on a total case load basis." Open files can lead to complaints that
go over the head of adjusters to supervisors or to managers; but
few files actually closed ever give further trouble to the adjuster.
Mainly the adjuster has to be certain that the payment he suggests
to the company will satisfy the supervisor. He does this principally
through his actual control of materials fed into the file.

After receiving a case, the adjuster must investigate it, evaluate the liability of the claimant, and then, if need be, negotiate
with him over the amount of recompense to be paid by the company.
If this can all be done on the first visit—"a first-call settlement"—
then the claims department and the adjuster, as well as the claimant,
will find this a very desirable settlement. In routine cases, settlement
is relatively easy: The adjusters often claim to predict liability with
considerable accuracy just from initial notice of the accident, presumably because of the simplification procedures. The routine case
most often is a whiplash or neck sprain, with great emphasis on
the cost of medical services as a basis for estimating value. The
serious case is characterized by the claimant's more serious injury—
"residual impairment" or "disfigurement"—where potential value
in front of a jury is the basis for estimating how much the company
should pay the claimant. Serious cases tend to be investigated more
deeply: Their evaluation is far less mechanical and conventional,
and payments are much more generous.

The negotiation context within which the adjuster and the
claimant negotiate a settlement typically involves several salient
properties. A very important one is that the parties usually share,
to a considerable extent, a common goal—that is, they have a

common stake in speedily reaching agreement through negotiation. Both want to get the settlement over with quickly. Neither wishes to go to court, since that involves both time and expense as well as being somewhat risky as to desired result. Even a routine case is apt to cost each party several hundred dollars more than a negotiated settlement. Costs include those of the courtroom—court costs, jury fees, document fees, and the fee of the trial lawyer—as well as various costs in preparation for the trial. None are recoverable even if the case is won. Hence both parties prefer a settlement through negotiation. This preference is furthered by the desire to avoid the delay involved in a court trial. That delay can vary from just a few months to several years. For the claimant, delay means no compensation until after the court trial; meanwhile, because of his injuries his living expenses may be increased and earning power decreased.

Ross's study indicates that the adjusters ordinarily regard delay as a nuisance and attempt to minimize it. (Nevertheless, since delay is more costly to the claimant, he wants it less.) As for the anticipated risk of a court trial, the claimant is aware that the jury may well follow the judge's instructions regarding contributory negligence at face value and so render a verdict against him. However, to the insurance company the jury system seems to make the formal law a claimant's law in the matter of bodily injury claims: so the company also prefers not to face court trial.

In consequence of the *joint interests* of claimant and insurance company, over 95 per cent of all bodily injury claims are settled through negotiation. Even when the claimant is represented by an attorney, the majority result in negotiated settlements. It is important to note that the negotiating parties need not discover their common stake in negotiating, for either they know it before the negotiation or else the more experienced adjuster alerts the claimant. They do not need to engage in elaborate exploration of the other's motives for negotiating.

Despite their common stake in avoiding a court trial, both also have very different stakes insofar as what one gains monetarily through the negotiation, the other will lose. Thus, their monetary stakes are *mutually exclusive*. It is that particular difference that brings about the usual tactics of sequential offers and counteroffers, until some compromise "figure" is reached. As Ross remarks, first they reach a "settlement range"—the range within which compromise seems reasonable or possible—and then finally an actual sum on which they can both agree. Another contextual property pertains to the *options* available. For the insurance company, the alternative to no agreement is *denial* of the claim itself (or of the claimed amount). Both the company's and the claimant's options are to *threaten* or *actually to take the case to trial*. (Alternative means—such as overt coercion or appeal to other authority—are not feasible.)

If the claimant really expects payment but the adjuster evaluates the claim as really inadequate, the latter may deny the claim, but generally only does so when the objective damages and the claimant's attitude suggest that the claim will not be put into litigation. Ross remarks that the adjuster, like the "con man," must skillfully handle the denial situation so that he wins the claimant's acquiescence to the justice of no payment; otherwise, the claimant may take the case into court. A claimant may, of course, threaten to litigate unless satisfied with the settlement figure, but Ross does not give us much data on that tactic except to hint occasionally that claimants can be so "unreasonable" that adjusters may prefer attorneys who "know the score."

Several further contextual properties help to explain the relatively simple character of the typical negotiation between adjuster and claimant. Negotiation only directly involves *two parties* (indirectly, of course, it may involve the claimant's friends and kin). Of course, whereas the claimant represents *himself*, the adjuster is a *representative*. This might make the negotiation more complicated, except that the adjuster has relative autonomy from his supervisor since he controls the information about each case that the latter gets to read. The *issues* about which negotiation takes place are neither complex nor numerous. Rather, they are relatively simple and deal only with how much money is approximately equivalent to the claimed bodily damages. As we have seen, most cases are *routine* and can be settled speedily by the adjuster with the application of rather mechanical procedures of evaluation. For more serious cases, he may have to investigate more thoroughly and balance many more pertinent factors; even so, the actual issue being negotiated is relatively simple. Even the "serious cases" do not present remarkably novel types of negotiations for the adjuster. For him, the negotiations themselves are relatively routine, although to the claimant the situation might appear quite exceptional.

The claimant is usually quite *inexperienced* with regard to the content of this negotiation over claims. He has never before had to bargain over injuries due to some automobile driver's negligence. On the contrary, the adjuster is, unless a novice at his trade, quite *experienced*. (If a novice, then he goes around asking the advice of more experienced colleagues about his cases, until he gets confidence in his own estimations—then his negotiations come more quickly to a close.) The adjuster's experience in these negotiations gives him a greater *balance of power* in the negotiating situation. Many claimants are naive, having only vague knowledge concerning their rights to recover damages. They are certainly less experienced in the specific tactics that are effective in negotiating over their claims. One consequence of the adjuster's experience is that he can close off routine cases quickly, fairly easily persuading claimants about proper settlement or persuading potential claimants that their claims really are not genuine. Thus the negotiation is rendered relatively simple.

Another very considerable consequence of the experienced adjuster and the inexperienced claimant is that the latter tends to receive a lesser settlement than otherwise he might—and less than if he had hired an attorney to represent him in negotiating with the adjuster. In Ross' study, the average unrepresented claimant received a settlement of approximately $250. Claimants represented by solo lawyers receive about $1,500; if represented by a legal firm, then around $2,225; if by a member of the negligence group, the American Trial Lawyers Association, almost $5,000. Some of the differential between unrepresented and represented settlements unquestionably results from the lawyers' selectivity concerning their claimants—those with minor injuries or problematic liability are less likely to obtain legal representation. Ross believes that much of the discrepancy, nevertheless, is due to the inexperience of the claimants in this particular negotiation situation. As he says, either they play the "game" very badly, or it is replaced by a different game substituted by the adjuster.

A few tactics commonly used by the adjusters are as follows. The claimant is asked to document his losses, and after the specific items are added up the adjuster asks, "Is there anything else?" If not, the adjuster offers a settlement, usually by filling out a draft and release. When the claimant signs those, he has, in effect, often settled for much less than the company is prepared to pay, because even questionable liability cases can support more than the payment for general damages listed by the claimant. Inexperienced claimants do not realize they have a right to ask for "special damages" or do not know enough to talk about "pain and suffering" so as to get higher payments. However, an inexperienced claimant sometimes asks for too high a payment; then the adjuster informs him and presents a counteroffer.

These negotiations are relatively uncomplicated because they are *one-shot* affairs. Considerations of continuing relations between the negotiating parties are totally absent. Even if a trial is insisted on by the claimant, its loss does not threaten the loser's reputation—either in general or concerning bargaining specifically. The negotiation's one-shot character is, of course, linked directly with the inexperience of the claimant and the relative strength of the adjuster in each negotiation. (It also relates, less directly, to the degree of control that the adjuster has in comparison with negotiating the conditions under which "terms" will be renegotiated.) The settlement is once and for all: for a past event and present (or past) associated expenses.

Despite the convergence of mutual interest on the settlement through negotiation, occasionally a case is taken to trial. First, there is no other place for the two parties to go—they cannot negotiate with other parties in lieu of an agreeable negotiation between each other, as in certain other types of negotiation situations. Honest differences in assessing the expected value to be gotten through litigation do exist and are more likely to occur as the size of the claim increases and the processing costs decrease in relation to the amount at stake. Ross and others have shown that proportionately more large cases do go to trial. However, "manifest disagreements" between experienced negotiators (usually when lawyers represent claimants), for small amounts of money, sometimes do occur. Following a student of labor-management negotiation, Carl Stevens,

Ross suggests three other sources of failure that seem to apply in bodily injury claims negotiations. First, negotiation can fail despite a large area of agreement. Both parties may make offers that they know the other would prefer to no agreement, but they are not accepted because each party is waiting for the other to accept the alternative offer. If a deadline is involved, as through the filing of suit papers, the case may go to trial. Ross believes this situation perhaps occurs in many cases involving small amounts of money that evolve into litigation. A second possible cause of failure is the undiscovered area of agreement: There is a range of values that each would prefer to no agreement, but they do not know this. They have not made the relevant proposals because they fear a concession might be interpreted as weakness, or they believe it is necessary to save some concession for later stages of the negotiation (as during trial), or they may fear their best offer may concede more than necessary to obtain agreement.

Still another possible cause for failure is "incompatible commitments"—although the parties prefer to yield rather than go to trial, the price of yielding has now increased in terms of resources or reputation. However, strong and credible commitments appear only very infrequently in the claims situation, and when they do the company will sometimes change its negotiator. The company is represented by a defense attorney, or a claims manager, or someone from the home office. These people may attempt to continue negotiations. Ross concludes that the large number of cases settled during the pretrial period partly may be explained by the new representation, plus perhaps the more realistic appraisal and professional camaraderie that may distinguish attorneys from adjusters.

Summary. Among the principal properties of this case were a general, common stake (to settle as quickly as possible and out of court) and a mutually exclusive stake (one party's gain is the other's exactly corresponding loss). These two properties together give the negotiations their characteristic subprocess—reaching a settlement by bargaining from extreme positions toward a compromise. Like the preceding case concerning Labwor bridewealth, the bargaining here includes the characteristic offers, counteroffers, and final acceptance—or final rejection if one party decides to go to the adjudicating body.

The remaining negotiation properties give much of the substance and variation in tactic, interaction, and consequence (and these, of course, differ from those of the bridewealth negotiation). Those properties include the following: The option exists for adjudication (court trial); the negotiation is one-shot; the procedure is routine for one party and, if exceptional for the other, at least not novel in form; the agent represents a company, the claimant represents himself; one party is more experienced than the other; there is a single issue (how much money is given or received); and the balance of power generally is quite unequal, favoring the agent. These properties, as we saw, are reflected in the characteristic interaction, in the various tactics, and in the general run of monetary consequences for the respective parties.

When an experienced lawyer is "slotted into" the interaction instead of the usual inexperienced claimant without relationships with the insurance business, then the flow of interaction and tactic and consequence varies correspondingly. The lawyer often is as experienced as, or more than, the adjuster at these negotiations. Also, his balance of power in the negotiations is higher than the usual claimant's, because of his professional status, and his threats to go to trial are more credible. Hence he usually makes better terms than if he were not in on the case. On the whole, however, the general character of negotiating to reach a settlement through compromising toward the middle is not appreciably different when a lawyer is involved. Nevertheless, the lawyer's structurally approved role in these accident cases points up how structural and contextual conditions affect their principle negotiation process.

It is easy to imagine other conditions that would change some of the features, at least subsidiary ones, of the negotiation interaction; for instance, (1) a lawyer or an agent who is also a claimant, (2) a claimant who also has insurance in the same company, (3) a very experienced claimant (or lawyer) dealing with a very inexperienced agent, (4) a foreigner to whom this kind of negotiation is entirely novel, (5) an obdurate kinsman who makes the claimant hold out for more money or even talks him into going to court, (6) a disgruntled agent about to quit the company, (7) or even conceivably an agent who wants to strike his own sexual bargain with the client. Those variations may not in fact occur very frequently, but they point to how the negotiation might correspondingly vary.

One-shot negotiation such as this hardly can have much impact on relationships between company or agent and the claimant. Likewise, although an agent's relationship to his company might be affected by a good or poor negotiation performance, the company itself scarcely could be much affected by specific negotiations. Conceivably the claimant's family might be affected by the outcome: by no money or little money, or by the psychological impact of a court trial, or even by changed relationships between spouses if negotiations seemed to go badly.

So, in respect to the larger question of how these particular negotiations impact on the larger social context, one could answer, "Not much." However, there is the potential influence of cumulative negotiations. Actually, they may have had some influence on the current movement to promote legislation changing accident (medical) insurance to "no-fault" insurance. As of now, the negotiation arena has changed correspondingly, with the insurance companies probably attempting to negotiate with legislators, or persuade them, to attain legislation less costly to themselves than the laws recently passed. It is just these kinds of structural changes that will either eliminate the specific kind of negotiation studied by Laurence Ross or change some of its relevant contextual properties.

In any event, the settlement of accident claims occurs within a larger structural context of legislative and conventional rules pertaining especially to notions of equity. So again, as in the first case in this chapter (clan intermarriage), considerations of social order are central to understanding what looks, on the face of it, to be essentially economic negotiation. Like all other types of negotiation, these too are ultimately political in nature.

Chapter Thirteen

•••••••••••••••••••••
•••••••••••••••••••••••
•••••••••••••••••••••••

Antagonistic Negotiation
Within Changing
Structural Contexts

•••••••••••••••••••••••
•••••••••••••••••••••••
•••••••••••••••••••••••

*I*n this chapter, the emphasis will be on two issues: first, the nature of negotiation between highly antagonistic parties; second, how that negotiation is affected by changes in structural conditions bearing on the negotiation—that is, by a changing structural context. These issues are entirely separate issues, but since they often occur together, it makes analytic sense to consider them together, as in the cases discussed in this chapter. In most of the preceding cases, the respective structural contexts were, during the actual courses of the negotiations studied, either relatively stable or taken as such by the researchers and by myself. Benelux was an exception, but the negotiation there was highly cooperative.

A structural context that is changing in one or more of its properties can drastically affect the negotiations: These properties include the implied stakes, the guiding strategies, the associated tactics, the numbers of participants, the issues, the combinations of

208

negotiation and alternative modes of action, and the alternatives to negotiation itself—in short, virtually anything and everything can be affected by the changing structural contingencies. Then, as we look at adversary negotiation taking place between very antagonistic parties, we also see that they seek to take advantage of those changing contingencies. Indeed, one aim of their negotiating, or choosing of alternative modes of action, is to change the structural contingencies more or less permanently in their own favor.

In the first case, concerning the Balkan countries, the Soviet and American governments negotiated with each other, not altogether in good faith, while acting manipulatively, coercively, and persuasively within a wider political, economic, and geographic arena, in efforts to gain greater respective national power. Insofar as the respective governments were "working together" at negotiating, they were doing so in a very minimal sense, because their stakes in the negotiation were radically different—even opposing. Also, they had different balances of negotiation power—power within the negotiation itself—that kept shifting over the duration of the total negotiation. One differential stake at least, that pursued by the Soviets, was masked or hidden from the Americans. Negotiations were sequential and linked with other negotiations, some actually more important than those specifically taking place over the Balkan issues. The negotiators represented their governments, and to some extent the American negotiators sometimes represented "the American public" or at least influential sectors of it. Multiple, linked issues were being negotiated during the sessions.

The second case depicts what happened, over a number of decades, among various ethnic groups in Kenya as they struggled for position and power. As the structural context bearing on that struggle changed, so did the nature of the negotiations among the various groups. We shall see how salient properties of that context, as they changed, affected in turn the negotiation contexts "within which" the negotiations both occurred and occurred in relation to alternative or supplementary modes of action. Among the important properties of a structural context is the balance of power among those who will be negotiating. Of course, there is no simple, direct connection between the structural balance of power and the balance of power within the negotiations themselves. Power to coerce, to call on the resources of authority, to persuade, and to manipulate is not necessarily equivalent to bargaining power itself. Every student of diplomacy recognizes that powerful nations are not able always to exert their power commensurately within certain negotiations; and the ability of homeowners to hold out against powerful real estate interests illustrates the same point. It is the specific property of power within negotiations, as it shifts in response to the changing of structural balances of power, that will be the central focus in discussing the Kenyan case. The data that will be drawn on afford a clear picture of those shifts, whereas the data used in the Soviet-American case are more suited for revealing both the quick shifts of power balances and their apparent manipulation by the respective governments.

Case: The United States and the Soviet Union: Negotiating over the Balkans

The story of the Balkan negotiations, in the words of Ethridge and Black (1951), "is the story of the first important lessons learned by the United States about the postwar trend of Soviet policy." We need not expect anything like accuracy here; yet taking the Ethridge and Black account "straight" yields, I believe, a revealing comparative case. The course of negotiations was protracted, difficult, increasingly antagonistic, and marked by mutual distrust, and it contained elements of false rather than genuine negotiation. It was also linked with a shifting of balance of power between the respective great powers within the Balkans—due both to efforts by each and to changing contingencies—and hence involved a shifting balance of power within the negotiations themselves.

Structurally, the situation was this: At the war's close, central and western Europe lacked, for the first time since the defeat of Napoleon, "the organization and power which for so long had served to counterbalance Russian influence" (1951, p. 181). After Germany's surrender, the United States was still preoccupied with winning the war against Japan and evinced little interest in the Balkans. The predominant assessment of Soviet intentions in high American governmental circles was optimistic. According to the dominant American view, the charter of the United Nations would provide a framework within which the affairs of the Balkan states could be handled satisfactorily. There would be free election of governments, and these governments would participate in the United Nations, taking advantage of financial assistance then available from the International Bank for Reconstruction and Development and the International Monetary fund. Furthermore, after V-J Day popular demand led to rapid demobilization and to the sudden discontinuation of Lend-Lease aid, which had become one of the chief instruments for U.S. foreign policy and U.S. relations with the Soviet Union. However, to American officials a sustained American interest in foreign affairs after V-J Day seemed unlikely. As events turned out, "the Russians" did not intend to continue cooperative relations with the allies, at least as far as the Balkans were concerned, but did not intend openly to indicate this. They began to work toward gaining "complete dominance" (or at least considerable control) over the Balkan states. Quite possibly, Ethridge and Black note, the Soviet Union may have underestimated American interest in the affairs of the Balkans because initially the Americans displayed little interest there. Also structurally relevant in this situation, of course, are the different goals of the respective nations and their mutual mistrust: The Americans began with more trust but soon lost it; the Russians apparently never had any illusions about trust. And, finally, a most important structural property of the situation—the Soviet Union had military preponderance in the Balkans and so entered the negotiations in a relatively strong position.

The Russians' strength increased because of events entirely extrinsic to but directly bearing on the negotiations. Indeed, Ethridge and Black conclude this is why the Soviet Union continued to delay during the negotiations and to feign some sessions that constituted false rather than genuine negotiation. Much of the negotiation turned on questions of *legitimacy* concerning the acceptance of the Yalta Declaration or its rejection. The negotiations were presumably to end in the free elections of Balkan governments. Actually, those negotiations as a whole got linked with quite other and more important negotiations, to the detriment of the American position on the Balkans.

Probably the Soviet government felt it could gain its ends

with coercive and manipulative actions, along with a pretense at
negotiation; but perhaps also it could not at first refuse to negotiate,
because other important issues were much involved, and thus associated aims would be endangered. For the Americans, the negotiations, even at the very close, represented proper behavior; also,
because of international public opinion, when the Americans saw
they had little bargaining power then at least continued negotiations
meant that something might be gained when linked with negotiations about other and more important issues. The failure of these
Balkan negotiations, along with the effect of actual Soviet actions in
the Balkans and elsewhere, had great consequences: Among them
was the formulation of the Truman Doctrine, "which made resistance to Communist aggression the cornerstone of American policy"
(p. 181).

In October 1944, direct negotiation between the British and
Soviet statesmen had arranged for a division of predominant influence: the Russians in Rumania, Hungary and Bulgaria; the
United Kingdom in Greece; and both, equally, in Yugoslavia. This
arrangement was intended as binding only for the transitional
period before Germany's defeat. The U.S. ambassador in Moscow
was only an observer at this particular set of negotiations. At Yalta
in February of 1945, the Western allies opted for a general statement of principles that served the purpose of establishing broad
postwar objectives for United Nations policy in the liberated states.
Ethridge and Black believe that the Western leaders did not work
toward getting specific and detailed agreement because it might
have tended to work to Soviet advantage in the Balkans, as the
terms of the armistice agreements with the Axis satellite states already had demonstrated. So the Western leaders at Yalta agreed to
a "declaration on Liberated Europe," affirming the right of all
peoples "to create democratic institutions of their own choice" and
noting the principal areas in which the liberated states would require assistance.

The ability of the United States and the United Kingdom
to implement the objectives of the Yalta Declaration began before
long to decline rapidly. Their weakness showed up as early as the
Potsdam conference held in July and August 1945. And when the
Council of Foreign Ministers, set up at Potsdam, met in London in

September and October of that year, it became apparent that there was a crisis in American-Russian relations regarding the Balkans. "In London, the time had come to draft the permanent settlement [peace terms], and the full extent of the divergence of policies now became apparent. . . . It was . . . the question whether, in the language of the Yalta Declaration, the Balkan states should have governments responsible to the will of the people" (p. 182), established through free elections, or should become full-fledged satellites of the Soviet Union. The Americans stood firmly behind the principles underlying the Yalta Declaration, and there were heated debates between the respective parties. "The breakdown of the conference insofar as the Balkan problem was concerned resulted from the refusal of Molotov to admit that the representative character of the Rumanian, Bulgarian, and Hungarian governments could properly be questioned. For ten days, the foreign ministers wrangled . . . without being able to achieve agreement on anything more important than a few of the technical details of the proposed peace treaties" (pp. 182–183).

The United States did have a strong pressuring tactic at its command: It could recognize or refuse to recognize the new Balkan governments. And soon the Americans were able to use that tactic. In the midst of the foreign ministers' conference in London, U.S. Secretary of State Byrnes "suddenly provided dramatic demonstration of the American viewpoint." He would recognize Hungary in return for a pledge of free elections. The pledge was given promptly, and the government was recognized not long after. Two days later, the satisfactory elections were held. But the main argument among the ministers pertained to Bulgaria and Rumania, where the local Communist Parties had "been most flagrant." At the conference's close, Byrnes had decided to withhold recognition until the conditions of the Yalta Declaration had been met. He then announced the appointment of the Ethridge Mission, which was to conduct a survey of political conditions in Bulgaria and Rumania. The mission, then, was to be an instrument for gathering information necessary for continued negotiation and policymaking. Moreover, "American opinion was scarcely prepared to support a vigorous challenge to Soviet influence at this time, and the secretary believed that it would be necessary to build up a background of publicly

acceptable evidence before such support would be forthcoming"
(p. 184). Byrnes went outside the ranks of the U.S. State Department and appointed as his special assistant an experienced jour-
nalist-publisher who could be viewed by the public as responsible
and objective. The mission initially was conceived of as an instrument for reporting, not for negotiating, but soon it was realized that
the mission could be a powerful instrument of pressure on the
Soviets. The members of the mission spent two weeks in Bulgaria,
one week in the Soviet Union, and ten days in Rumania. Priority
was given to Bulgaria, because a forthcoming election had been
scheduled.

Without going into the details of the Bulgarian situation, it
suffices to say that the mission was interested in whether free elections really would be held or whether "the elections would only
confirm the Communist-dominated regime in power and prolong
indefinitely the deadlock reached during the London conference"
(p. 185). Earlier information in August had convinced the American and British governments that an election "certainly would fail to
meet the demands of the Yalta Declaration . . . [so they] made a
major diplomatic effort to convince Moscow that the election
should be postponed and its procedure reconsidered. This determined
action, taken shortly after V-J Day when the relations of the Big
Three were still relatively cordial, produced remarkable results.
Acting through the Allied Control Commission, the Russians de-
clared that they found no objection to the postponement of the
elections. With it was postponed also the crisis in American-Russian
relations over the recognition of Bulgaria" (p. 190).

So the American-British persuasive tactic worked—temporarily. Whatever reasons lay behind the Soviets' agreement, they
presumably believed that time was on their side concerning their
increasing power in Bulgaria. When the Ethridge Mission reached
Bulgaria in November, a new election date had been set for November 18, 1945. The mission concluded from various kinds of evidence
that "The decision regarding the Bulgarian election had been
reached not in Sofia but in Moscow . . . [and] since the local
authorities were in such agreement that the decision lay in Moscow,
it was decided that the Ethridge Mission should proceed to the
Soviet capital to explore the possibilities with regard to the Bul-

garian election" (pp. 191–192). The only reason to hope that such late negotiations might succeed was that the Soviet government might regard nonrecognition of Bulgaria as undesirable, as did the American government. If the Soviets were convinced that the United States would not recognize a government elected under existing conditions, a compromise might still be reached. "Any such compromise would of course only postpone the date of a showdown in Bulgaria between the Communist-led Fatherland Front and the agrarian and socialist opposition leaders, but there was reason to believe that the position of the latter might be strengthened by such a postponement" (p. 192).

The American proposal was turned down by Vishinsky, who, however, used a countertactic. "The one possibility which [he] . . . left open was that Moscow might be willing to accept postponement if a request for advice on his question came from Sofia, as it had in August. This was no more than an elaborate formality, since no request would be forthcoming in any event without Soviet consent, but it was a face-saving procedure which had proved successful three months earlier" (p. 194). The U.S. State Department sent a strong note to the Bulgarian government, reminding it of the conditions defined in the Yalta Declaration and concluding that there was no reason to believe that the scheduled elections would result in a representative government. The election was held anyhow, with the Fatherland Front winning an overwhelming victory.

The situation in Rumania was somewhat different, because the local Communist Party was not strong enough; thus they had "to rely more exclusively on direct Soviet support . . . hence had made compromise more difficult. . . . The prospects that an eventual election would be free . . . were nevertheless not bright" (p. 199). In any case, Moscow insisted, for each country, that the Yalta Declaration was being implemented. "It was still a year before the Cominform was to unveil 'peoples' democracy' as a transitional form of government designed to transform the satellites into socialist states of the Soviet type" (p. 200). The general tactic was to talk the language of democratic coalitions among parties, with Communists eager to cooperate with agrarians, liberals, and socialists. (So the Ethridge Mission was generally welcomed to each country with flowers, banquets, and cheering crowds!) At any rate, the mission's report to Byrnes was so critical that "its publication as originally planned would have been something of a shock to the prevailing view of American opinion, which was still optimistic regarding the prospects of cooperation with the Soviet Union" (p. 202).

The time for open political conflict had not yet arrived, since Byrnes had shortly before agreed to further discussion among the foreign ministers, in Moscow. So it seemed best to Byrnes not to release the report as long as any hope remained that friendly negotiations might result in a Balkan settlement. It was decided, however, to use the report in the ministerial discussions. Those discussions covered much more ground than the Balkan problem: The issues involved the peace treaty procedure, the plan for a commission on atomic energy, and the settlement in China, Korea, and Japan. The Russians agreed to hold a peace conference, agreed to a commission on atomic energy in the U.N. framework but made no substantial sacrifice to the American viewpoint on the Far Eastern issues. "Yet to the general Western public these seemed like real gains, for it was still hoped that once a formal peace settlement had been agreed to the processes of economic recovery would restore political balance" (p. 202). However, the Soviet concessions had been purchased at the price, it is very important to note, of a substantial increase in Soviet bargaining power in eastern Europe. The compromise reached at Moscow regarding Bulgaria and Rumania "provided that the Communist-dominated regimes . . . should be broadened by the admission of an additional two representatives of the democratic opposition parties in each country" (p. 203). This did not prevent Communist-led coalitions from winning relatively quickly—but not before the United States had recognized Rumania. The United States did refuse for two years to recognize Bulgaria— it had not yet given up on nonrecognition as a means of diplomatic pressure.

By the summer of 1946, when it came to drafting the peace treaties in Paris, "It became increasingly clear that these negotiations would offer no opportunity to win back the concessions which had already been made to the Soviet point of view. . . . The peace treaties were signed [on February 10, 1947, but] marked no advance . . . in the Western effort to establish representative government based on free elections in eastern Europe" (p. 205). The Americans and the British did manage to get articles written into the treaties on the enforcement of human rights, but these never could be implemented—any more satisfactorily than were some provisions of the Yalta Declaration. In 1947, it became increasingly clear to the Americans that they had failed "to preserve [even] a degree of political freedom in the Balkan states through the implementation of the Yalta Declaration. The substance of this freedom had been bargained away in the hope that such concessions might win Soviet cooperation in what appeared to be broader and more significant fields of international endeavor" (p. 204).

The last phrase is of great importance: The American (and English) stakes in the Balkan negotiations simply were not as great as those involved in other negotiations about issues deemed more important. Both sets of negotiations had become linked, to the detriment of the American and British aims in the Balkans. The upshot was the Truman Doctrine: Power was to be met with power.

Summary. This particular course of negotiations is much like many others reviewed and analyzed in the literature on negotiations. It fits very well with the concepts of such analysts as Schelling and Ikle, with their emphases on coercive threats, coercively tinged persuasion, masked aims, and maneuvers within and outside the negotiation itself, with delaying tactics utilized while the parties wait for contingencies to break or actually bring them into being, and so on. This is all so familiar that it scarcely seems necessary to discuss how the specific negotiation features relate closely to the specific contextual properties described at the outset of this section or to the more general structural context of "world events" and "international relations" of that postwar era.

However, it is worth mentioning some of the subprocesses characteristic of these negotiations over the Balkans, since those are not so well brought out in the literature, and since they contrast with many discussed elsewhere in this book. These include (besides those characteristic of the creating of temporary operational arrangements) *renegotiating* the actual implementation of agreements *after* their actual *violation* or *failure of implementation* by one or other party; *exploring priorities of the new issues* as they arise because of contingencies external to the negotiations; *renegotiating over progressively appearing contingencies*, some maneuvered by either party; and *negotiating with an eye to public impact,* including impact on one's own countrymen, the other's countrymen, and citizens elsewhere. Of course, there was also *false negotiation* by at least one party, although both parties seemed sometimes to negotiate in good faith.

As for the impact of such negotiations on the larger structural context, recollect Ethridge and Black's assertion that this story pertained to the first important lessons learned by the United States about the postwar trend of Soviet policy. That assertion may or may not be true, but certainly the negotiations at least contributed to the American public's, if not the government's, perspective on "what the Russians are up to." How the negotiations affected the structure of Soviet-American relations because of the Soviet reception of the negotiation, one cannot tell from the Ethridge-Black narrative.

Subprocesses such as renegotiation after the violation of an agreement and false negotiation are, of course, related to the extremely antagonistic stances of the negotiating parties toward each other. On the other hand, the need to renegotiate is related generally to the other major factor illustrated by this case study; namely, the changing structural context within which the negotiations occur over time. As noted in the introduction to this chapter, the two governments each attempted to alter elements of that context so as to shift the balance of power in their own favor. If they could do that, they might not require recourse to negotiation or might be able to negotiate with greater bargaining strength. Or, if the structural context shifted independently of their own maneuvering, that too would affect the calculations and actions of both parties. By contrast, in the next case, which concerns Kenya, the structural changes occurred with infinitely less speed, so that the researcher can speak of changes occurring "over the decades." These changes correspondingly affected, over the long run, the nature of the negotiations among Kenya's ethnic groups.

Case: Kenya: Ethnic Negotiations

David Rothschild, whose "Racial Stratification and Bargaining: The Kenya Experience" (1976, pp. 235–254) will be utilized next, begins by noting that an interracial bargaining situation prevails when the leaders are prepared to engage in tacit or direct negotiations: The parties have divergent and often conflicting interests but also have "the common need to avoid mutual damage and . . . secure convergent goals" (p. 234). Negotiation, then, pertains centrally to both *common* and *different stakes*. Rothschild remarks that, "when racial rankings are frozen" and political and economic power resides in the hands of a racially exclusive elite, then there is little negotiation among the groups. But when group power is sufficiently dispersed to make "mutually beneficial" there will be more negotiation—and it may function to speed the "process of restratification, allowing adjustments to occur swiftly with increases and decreases" (p. 236) in the relative strengths of the respective groups.

During its late colonial period in the 1920s, Kenya was "rigidly compartmentalized and stratified"—European settlers in the usual overwhelmingly privileged position, Asians in the middle-level status, and Africans socially at the bottom and doing unskilled tasks. These rankings, with few exceptions, were largely fixed and unchanging. Under those structural conditions, there was little scope for interracial bargaining. Such bargaining did occur, however, between the two top groups over certain *limited issues,* such as representation in the legislative council. This bargaining took place under the egis of third-party (governmental) control. As the Asians gradually achieved better organization, they competed more successfully "for the favor of the administration" (both in Kenya and in Britain). One consideration was that the local administration, under pressure from London, carefully retained a monopoly of influence for the European settlers.

So all through the 1920s "hegemonial bargaining" (Rothschild's term) took place between the *two* most powerful racial groups, through the *mediation* of the governmental third party. From Rothschild's discussion, it would appear that the negotiations were not so much carried out between the Asians and the Europeans as between each group and the government—with the latter generally having greater power in those transactions. The government was negotiating to maintain the status quo in Kenya; while the Asians were seeking small gains through negotiating. The

Europeans were using the negotiations to maintain their relative position against the Asians. In this structural context, *issues* about which negotiation could occur were relatively few, and it appears that not many were negotiated simultaneously. It is not altogether clear either whether or not most negotiations were kept relatively *covert* from the other interested racial group, although that seems probable. It is not clear either what the important negotiation subprocesses were, but there seems to have been some *trading off* with regard to stakes. That is, the respective parties aimed at gaining at least some portion of their respective stakes (no upsetting of the colony's apple cart, small gains, and the maintaining of positional status). The Asians and Europeans had to compromise in their trade-offs because of their lesser *bargaining power* vis-à-vis the government—"lesser" both because of their competition with each other and because structurally the government was more powerful than they were.

By the 1950s, the rigid political, economic, and social stratification system had undergone a process of change. The three-tiered structure continued, but Africans and Asians increased pressure on it as a result of the development of increasing "consciousness of and indignation" over their status, powerlessness, and lack of benefits. The Europeans began to lose some of the "moral certainty" that underpinned these racial rankings. Both Africans and Asians became more effectively organized. By the late 1950s, all of this began to alter the old balance of political power, thereby affecting the Europeans' social and economic prerogatives.

"As African power achieved near parity with the entrenched Europeans, Kenya entered . . . a *direct bargaining* stage" (p. 239). The racial leaders communicated openly with each other in order to reach a mutually beneficial agreement, although of course self-interest drove them to do so. The degree of convergence varied in each according to the balance of *negotiating power* ("configurations of power"). This period of direct bargaining continued through the end of that decade and into the next "when the spokesmen for the three major races jockeyed [through negotiation, manipulation, and persuasion, at least] for a meaningful say in, even control of, the main institutions, as well as for future guarantees of property and civil liberties" (p. 239). The non-Africans reluctantly and slowly yielded to African demands, securing concessions whenever possible. In this *multiissue, linked,* and doubtless *serial* and *overt* negotiation, under those conditions of shifting structural power, the Africans were gaining increasing power within the negotiations themselves. As a result, a "trade-off occurred between legal and constitutional concessions to non-African interests . . . and the acceptance, with certain limitations. That is, they were negotiating [the boundaries of acceptable and legitimate negotiation] of African self-determination" (p. 239). We can assume, also, there were subprocesses such as negotiations for forming coalitions between the Europeans and the Asians and possibly some even between the Asians and the Africans.

During this era, the governmental administration provided a mediating framework that allowed diplomatic action, supervising "the search for interracial accommodation." It had little choice other than employing a costly policy of repression. The British government, then, played a strong game since it could "delay independence, devolve powers upon territorial authorities, and provide aid and support for British nationals" (p. 240)—that is, it could manipulate and threaten coercion, as well as enter into side negotiations and even into direct negotiations between the racial groups. (We can assume that they sometimes did this with coercive threats.)

With the official transfer of power—independence—to the Africans, the bargaining situation was fundamentally redefined. The stratification system crumbled, first politically and then economically and socially. The Europeans, however, still remained powerful but less visible as of 1976, and the highly skilled Asians were still indispensable. These structural conditions have led to what Rothschild believes is a third or *tacit bargaining* state in interracial encounters, in which "quiet transactions" are characteristic. Now that the British government and its local administration are gone, and now that there is majority African political control, little room is left except for "tacit exchanges" among the racial groups. All negotiating parties now recognize "the mutuality of benefit from a reconciliatory course." But agreements need not be stated or explicit. The racial groups "must accept a given line of action in order to maximize convergent interests" among them. Again there was (and is) a major *trade-off.* There was a silent agreement for the Africans to tolerate the affluent strangers in their midst "provided they contributed to economic well-being" and "acquiesced, in good faith, in their own demise when their services were no longer deemed essential" (p. 242).

The specific *stakes* over which negotiations occurred included property rights, citizenship, and allocation of resources. Rothschild believes that direct bargaining was precluded by the disparity of *balance of power* inherent in each situation. Thus tacit bargaining was a "means of ensuring the persistence of the existing structure through an implicit recognition of reciprocal interests under present time-place circumstances" (p. 242). Later, at a further stage, when structural conditions continued to change, presumably the characteristic negotiation processes would also change.

Rothschild's analysis, sophisticated though it is, is unquestionably oversimplified, since he treats each negotiating racial group as a homogeneous unit (although his analysis of the government often distinguishes between local and London administrations). Undoubtedly a multitude of accompanying negotiations were occurring within each racial group, along with associated alternative modes of action to negotiation. Nevertheless, Rothschild's paper allows us clearly to see a three-stage shift of structural context, and the associated negotiation context, as changing conditions for the evolving types of negotiation subprocesses.

During the first stage of hegemonial bargaining, the principal subprocess was a trading off, with the government's mediating as a necessary accompanying process. The negotiating was mostly covert and took place not only between the two principal ethnic groups under government supervision but also between each and the government itself. The European elite's dominant privileges and general position were nonnegotiable. During the second stage of direct bargaining, the chief subprocesses included trading off, negotiating over legitimate (no longer frozen) boundaries, coalition formation, and mediation. The negotiations were now more likely to be overt and occurred among all three ethnic groups over a multitude of issues. During the third stage of tacit bargaining, there was continued trading off but over different issues, involving the negotiation of different stakes from those previously concerned.

The negotiation processes, then, were part and parcel of Kenya's social order during each period. There existed not merely overt and silent conflict, or manipulation done openly or behind the scenes, or rule by coercion and coercive law—negotiation, too, was integral to the social order of Kenya during each era. In Rothschild's account, we are also given a glimpse of negotiation flowing back on the structural context itself during each period—"glimpse" because the impact is neither traced nor can it be divorced from the coercive action that was certainly pervasive during the first two stages, and the immense manipulatory and persuasive actions that undoubtedly were characteristic of all three stages.

The similarities between the Kenya case and the preceding one of American-Soviet negotiation are suggested by this chapter's title, "Antagonistic Negotiation Within Changing Structural Contexts." As the structural context changes, it cannot but affect the negotiation context and thus the associated and specific negotiations. In the relatively brief negotiation over Balkan issues, both parties attempted either to change properties of the structural context itself or to cash in during the period of the negotiations on structural changes that were occurring independently of their own maneuverings. In the protracted period of the intermittent Kenya negotiations, there was some attempt by the weaker ethnic groups to change the structural conditions that affected their lives, but there were much more effective attempts by government and European elite to maintain the status quo. However, every change of structural condition might mean renewed negotiation, and thus those changes were watched closely by the respective ethnic groups.

Chapter Fourteen

●●●●●●●●●●●●●●●●●●●●●●
●●●●●●●●●●●●●●●●●●●●●●
●●●●●●●●●●●●●●●●●●●●●●

Limits, Silent Bargains, and Implicit Negotiation

●●●●●●●●●●●●●●●●●●●●●●
●●●●●●●●●●●●●●●●●●●●●●
●●●●●●●●●●●●●●●●●●●●●●

*I*n this chapter, an important topic will be addressed, partly through case analysis. The topic is the relationship of negotiations themselves to nonnegotiated "limits," which are often relatively fixed but sometimes temporarily or permanently alterable. In thinking about that relationship, I have found it helpful also to think about "silent bargains" and about implicit negotiations.

The negotiations depicted and analyzed in preceding sections have primarily been explicit: transactions openly carried out between parties who recognize their own negotiating. Some of these negotiations have also been quite complicated in the numbers of parties involved, the kind of negotiating procedures used, the numbers of negotiation subprocesses transpiring, and so on. But it is not the complexity that I wish to emphasize here—only the complexity in relation to the explicit character of those transactions. However, negotiations can also be implicit, their products being tacit agreements or understandings.

Some negotiations may be very brief, made without any

verbal exchange or obvious gestural manifestation; nevertheless, the parties may be perfectly aware of "what they are doing"—they may not call this negotiating *bargaining,* but they surely regard its product as some sort of *worked-out* agreement. Other negotiations may be so implicit that the respective parties may not be thoroughly aware that they have engaged in or completed a negotiated transaction. If the latter kind of agreement gets broken by one person, however, the other is sure to experience some feeling, whether surprise, disappointment, annoyance, anger, or even a sense of betrayal or exploitation, but possibly also relief or unexpected pleasure.

A most important consideration about implicit negotiations is that life in groups, organizations, institutions, and societies cannot conceivably go on without tacit agreements and the more or less implicit negotiations that often lead up to them. Perhaps this assertion is most easily checked by thinking of intimate relationships, as in families, where there seem to be many tacit understandings, both negotiated and nonnegotiated (just "simple" agreements), reached with a minimum of discussion, rational calculation, and open bargaining. Often they rest on subtle gestural interaction. Reaching such understandings and making such tacit agreements do not occur in a social order vacuum; they occur against a backdrop of explicit agreements (some of them negotiated) reached in the distant or recent past, as well as (family) rules that for some (family members) may have been partly negotiated as well as imposed from above. Of course, in both formal organizations and families, there may be coercive relations that are very much part of the structural context that pertains to both implicit and explicit negotiating. For both kinds of negotiation, a social order is a necessity.

To say, as one sociologist has, that in organizations there are not only overt negotiations recognizable by the participants but also an "everyday covert implicit substratum of negotiation" (Morgan, 1975) can, however, be confusing unless we are very clear about what that implicit negotiating is *not* likely to be about. Here the concept of "limits" is esssential, and some examples pertaining to them will be useful. Suppose, for instance, that there is a law against bathing nude on the beach. Individuals could break that law, which represents constraining limits on behavior. However, if they broke it covertly, as at night, they might go unscathed; if they broke it openly, they might be punished. In either event, the law remains unchanged. On the other hand, a group of people might repeatedly test that law and, by that means and by an ensuing campaign, seek eventually to get a less restrictive law. Or they might test it out to see if the enforcing policeman will, for this one time, make an exception. In none of those cases is negotiation necessarily involved— at least, not obviously. However, a person or group can also get an exception to the bathing law providing they agree—in negotiation with the police—to some limitation on their behavior, such as "but no mixed bathing," or "OK, but down there at the very end of the beach." The limits of that law are thus temporarily stretched, but the law as such is not affected by the negotiation.

In a rather subtle fashion, one can see how limits are tested and stretched, usually without actual negotiation, in the following instance—subtle because the testing is often uncalculated and its cues are so gestural. In hospitals, when patients are dying a "ritual drama of pretense" often gets set up (Glaser and Strauss, 1965, pp. 64–78) whereby both patient and staff know the patient is dying but pretend otherwise, both agreeing to act as if he or she were going to live. Either staff or patient can initiate this pretense, and it ends when one or another cannot or will not sustain the pretense any longer. The researchers who studied this phenomenon remarked that they once visited a specialty hospital where every patient was terminal and care was efficiently organized but where nobody talked about dying, although the patients were well aware of impending death and some doubtless wished to talk about it. Usually, hospital staff would rather not bring dying out into the open, so if the patient introduces the subject the personnel will set limits by ignoring, reprimanding, or chiding ("don't think of such things"), thus setting up or continuing the mutual pretense. The patient agrees to this, not necessarily because he or she fears punishment but sometimes because there is tact or genuine empathy for staff "embarrassment or distress." In turn, if the patient wishes the pretense sustained, he or she will reject the staff offers to talk about impending death or act as if it were imminent. There need be no actual talk about any of this, for, as the researchers remark, it is remarkable how a patient can flash cues to the staff, inviting the staff to talk about his or her destiny. The staff may accept such a request but may decide it is better not to talk lest the person "go to pieces." The person then may pick up their signals, agreeing to the initiation or continuance of the mutual pretense—that is, the staff's definition of limits.

The researchers refer to these instances of mutual pretense as "silent bargains." These may be bargains, but often there has been no bargaining. Rather, one party or the other has set limits, and the other party willingly or reluctantly has agreed to abide by the limits. Sometimes a dying patient does not wish to so abide and will upset the staff by refusing to allow the nurses to perform their usual routines on his or her body, thus forcing the staff-imposed limits. Again, that is not negotiation.

However, one might maintain that some negotiation goes on within the limits and in supportive relationship to them. This possibility is suggested by the researchers' description of how both sides work at maintaining mutual pretense by adhering to implicit rules: staying away from topics likely to lead either to the forbidden ground of the patient's death or to events touching on the far future; or, if something happens or is said tending to expose the fiction that both parties are attempting to sustain, then each pretends nothing has gone awry. Each shares responsibility for maintaining the pretense. The major responsibility may be transferred back and forth, but each party must support the other's temporary dominance through his or her own action. So, while the research account does not clearly focus on or depict negotiations, apparently the parties do make subtle, on-the-spot gestures that we might interpret as implicit negotiations (silent bargaining). These negotiations are essentially trade-offs between staff and patient, each respecting the other's stakes in the game of mutual pretense—but only up to the limits set by whoever was more powerful in setting those limits. On the other hand, this use of the term *negotiation* might appear to be stretching its meaning too far. I would not argue the point. The main issue is rather that actions are being taken with respect to nonnegotiated limits imposed or signaled by one side and agreed to directly by the other. These kinds of silent bargains, then, would seem to pertain to agreements that are not much brought into explicit discussion and that represent limits *within* which negotiation can go on. Sometimes, as noted earlier, they go on in *support* of the limits, or they temporarily *stretch* the limits.

Precisely that kind of interpretation seems applicable to what Morgan (1975), in his study of rule breaking in the service of individual autonomy within an industrial firm, calls "implicit negotiation." In his major case study, he notes that, although there were clear rules concerning workers' "time," there was also much implicit negotiating by individuals on a daily basis about the exact times of their checking in, checking out, taking lunch or coffee breaks, and so on. They did not talk about the negotiating or negotiate openly; they just did it, whether occasionally or regularly. Some stretched those times more and some less. (All this was quite aside from overt bargaining about the rate at which work should be accomplished.) In official terms, this rule breaking was regarded as a "large-scale waste of time." Then why were the workers allowed to persist? One possibility suggested by Morgan is that the management was using the recognized leniency as "a bargaining counter" held "in reserve for more strategic occasions." But he concludes this was not entirely what was at issue.

Using the equivalent to my term *limits*, Morgan remarks that, while the waste of time was seen and to some extent was used by management as a bargaining counter, the situation was not as much "in the control of any one set of persons" as that description might suggest. "To say that management could use elements in the situation in the more overt processes of negotiation is not to say that it was fully able to choose whether to have these elements in the first place nor was it necessarily the case that the workers responded to them in these terms" (1975, pp. 222–223). What Morgan is really most interested in arguing is that strict rules do not govern workers' actions and that indeed workers possess a certain amount of autonomy even under contemporary capitalist working conditions. Mostly, the daily struggle occurs "implicitly or explicitly" over relatively small issues such as time. Sometimes workers win, sometimes not. Morgan wishes, like Dalton in our earlier case (see Chapter Nine), to show that there is plenty of leeway in organizational functioning.

We may certainly agree with Morgan's main contention,

while still questioning whether his interpretation of "implicit negotiation" is adequate. A more accurate interpretation is that there is a great deal of testing of the managerial rules by individuals (perhaps also by groups) and much daily stretching of those rules "in fact." Some of that testing is calculated; some only represents how individuals feel on a particular day, at a particular moment, and knowing the rules are stretchable they stretch them. Yet the rules stand: They do not seem to be challenged either directly or permanently through daily flouting or stretching. Whether or not we should call this "implicit negotiation" is, again, not the major question. Rather, we probably should be asking how strict limits are made less strict; how respective parties manage to live with each other; and how, not incidentally, they get their respective work done. Sometimes this involves explicit negotiation; sometimes it certainly involves implicit negotiation; and sometimes neither, but only other forms of interaction.

Case: Geriatric Wards and the Silent Bargain

I turn now to a full case study that illustrates and perhaps will additionally clarify the points just made. The materials are taken from a monograph depicting and analyzing what happens when hospitalized patients are in pain (Fagerhaugh and Strauss, 1977, pp. 181–192). One of its chapters deals with elderly people housed in nursing homes and geriatric hospitals. In industrial nations like the United States, elderly people near the close of their lives are likely to be sent to public or private institutions by their kinsmen who for one reason or another find it difficult or impossible to house or care for them at home. (It has been hazarded that other contributing factors are tight housing conditions, the disintegration of the extended family, and changed relations between the generations.) Public expenditure for this housing and care tends to be relatively minimal, at least in the United States. Those who work at these institutions are neither among the best paid nor the most trained personnel, for the medical care given there tends not to be exciting nor would it be especially rewarding to highly trained health personnel. Often these places are referred to as essentially "custodial," meaning that medical care is minimal—suitable for people who are incurable and many of whom are dying. The accommodations may also be minimal.

The low social value assigned to the elderly, which results in the niggardly allocation of funds to these institutions, means that staffing usually is not plentiful when measured against the large amount of physical work needed to keep patients relatively comfortable and their health stabilized. The limited resources encourage tight scheduling and routinization of tasks in order to "manage" the large numbers of patients. Efficiency is sought not so much on the basis of a patient's "needs" as in accordance with the required work as perceived by the personnel. Everyone's life is organized into daily and weekly routines: times for rising in the morning, for prebreakfast washing, for feeding, bathing, toileting, walking, napping, and so on. The staff's major work revolves around maintaining both hygiene and bodily functioning of their charges. The volume of "body work" is very great, since many patients are disabled; it is also physically demanding and often carried out by teams of personnel. This teamwork in turn requires further coordination, scheduling, and routinization.

After the first weeks or months, an elderly patient tends to have few visitors. Often the geriatric institutions are distant from the homes of kinfolk, or sooner or later the kinfolk move elsewhere. Besides, many patients are visited with decreasing frequency and often are abandoned by their children, spouses, and friends. The pervasive loneliness and social isolation characteristic of these locales are striking, although frequently a process of isolation actually precedes the institutionalization, and the latter only heightens the person's isolation.

Pain may be a part of the picture. A very great proportion of the elderly suffer from some degree of chronic pain or discomfort. Of more concern, however, to most are undoubtedly their increasing bodily deterioration, the closeness of death, and the general problem of coming to terms with those issues. Nevertheless, there is pain, whether chronic or temporarily at peak. Working with elderly people in pain involves tasks such as moving painful joints or other bodily parts or assuring the elderly that they must endure whatever pain derives from their bodily maintenance, since bedsores and other complications must be prevented. Also, because of the routinization of work, requests for pain relief tend not immediately to be responded to, so patients must endure pain—without undue expression of it—until the next prearranged time for moving them or until after mealtime. But pain is also minimized by staff members who handle the elderly bodies gently, allowing the patients to move at their own speed, utilizing such measures as propping pillows. Over time, the personnel, who tend to be a stable work force, get to know individuals rather well and so understand what comfort measures are likely to be effective or what modes of interacting make a person more cooperative and seemingly less focused on pain.

On the other hand, as the patients become increasingly isolated from the outside world, they increasingly rely on the personnel for social contact as well as for many other aspects of "living." Hence, a statement commonly made by personnel: "We're the only family for him." Over the years, then, their lives become intertwined. Often the patients live vicariously through the staff members' lives: They are interested in the staff members' families, what they do on days off, and so forth. In turn, the staff engage in a number of touching and even passionate acts designed to brighten the lives of their charges: They bring favorite dishes cooked at home; wash the patients' personal clothing, also at home, where it will be less likely to be damaged; and shop for items desired by the patients. The latter's dependence and vulnerability encourages gratefulness for small favors and compliance to the personnel's dictates. Gradually, the elderly learn to "fit" into the institution and adapt to its routines, accepting at least outwardly such statements of personnel as "We're one big family and like a family we have to get along with each other. Each of us has to give and take and meet each other halfway." The researchers believe that this imagery helps to persuade the aged to endure their considerable pain and other complaints in silence, as they balance merely covert or minimal expression of pain against good relations with the staff. "In effect, there is a trade-off, in a silent bargain between the two sides" (1977, p. 189).

That bargain is glimpsed even more clearly when the issue of social isolation is considered. The first priority for many, if not most, of the aged is social contact, and the staff members also clearly recognize that loneliness and social isolation are major problems for the elderly. Many personnel remark on the relationship between a patient's perception of pain and his or her anger and frustration at being abandoned to these institutions. So part of the silent bargain is a mutual concern with lessening the patients' isolation, an isolation that the staff recognizes and wishes to assuage. Since this also has very high priority for the patients, it furthers the tacit agreement that each side will act properly, carrying out its side of the agreement.

Of course, the phrase "its side" is a simplification, since the staff is a plurality and there are multitudes of patients. A veritable host of such transactions are transpiring daily, while the individuals themselves are building mutual histories of transactions with each other. This web of cumulative interactions—some consisting of explicit negotiation ("Wait until later and then I will do . . . ."), but much being neither implicit negotiation nor negotiation at all— of course is a vital aspect of the proffering, assigning, adapting to, adopting, accepting, honoring, and asserting—and no doubt also denying and rejecting—of important identities and activities by patients and staff alike. In that sense, the entire tangle of negotiations and other interactions helps to maintain, and certainly does not unduly disturb, the limits to behavior that are essentially imposed by the more powerful of the two parties; that is, the personnel working on these wards.

Neither does it, understandably, disturb the larger structural context outlined earlier. This relatively powerless segment of the population is more or less tucked away where it is not too visible to those who live in the real world outside and does not affect them. Inside the institutions, there are daily slight alterations in the staff-imposed limits: Either side may initiate the alterations, sometimes through negotiations, whether explicit or implicit, but sometimes by other means. Thus the personnel can tighten the rules by coercing or simply by denying requests through citing "the rules" and other tactics, while patients can get the limits stretched by requesting, persuading, and covertly manipulating—although not often by any coercive tactic. Insofar as negotiation occurs within the limits of those rules, basically it would appear to be in the nature of trade-offs pertaining both to the work (patients are involved as partners in the work) and to agreements on what each regards as his or her appropriate identity—or at least as close to "appropriate" as can be achieved. All this is done within a relatively stable, routinized organizational context, whose negotiation dimensions include, besides the generally imbalanced negotiation power, repeated and sequential negotiations; largely one-to-one negotiations, where negotiators represent themselves, with relatively simple issues negotiated; relatively clear legitimacy of issues; and fairly unstated but understood respective stakes. If closely studied, the biography of relationships between any patient and specific staff member would show implicit and explicit negotiating mixed with the other modes of action just mentioned—the mixture undoubtedly changing over time as the relationship itself changes.

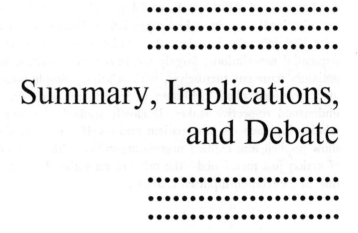

Summary, Implications, and Debate

What has been the central argument of this book? What data and interpretations have supported the argument? And why should there be argument at all, rather than a straightforward presentation of data and theory? Answering that general line of questioning allows a quick summary of the book's contents; it also allows, in a later section, focused consideration of both pertinent and not so pertinent objections raised by critics of a "negotiated order perspective." Engaging in that debate should help to fill in whatever detail may be missing elsewhere in these pages, as well as to correct any further misreading of what is implied in this approach to the study of negotiations and negotiated social orders.

Summary

In this book, negotiation has generally stood for one of the possible means of "getting things accomplished" when parties need to deal with each other to get those things done. Negotiation is not merely one specific human activity or process, of importance primarily because it appears in particular relationships (diplomacy, labor relations, business transactions, and so on), but is of such major importance in human affairs that its study brings us to the heart of studying social orders. As argued in the preface to this book, a given social order, even the most repressive, would be inconceivable without some forms of negotiation.

The implication is that social orders are, in some sense, always negotiated orders. The phrase "in some sense" is a guard against asserting that negotiation explains "everything," for it is always found in conjunction with other processes, other alternatives to getting things done—notably coercion, persuasion, manipulation, and the like. Most research on negotiation has either focused rather narrowly on substantive areas of negotiation, such as those just mentioned, or, if taken as a relatively universal phenomenon, nevertheless tends to approach the phenomenon from relatively rationalistic, efficiency perspectives (as in game theory or in the work of economists who have written about negotiation). I have argued that issues of outcome, efficiency, decision making, and the like are secondary to issues pertaining first to how negotiation is related to other modes of action and second to varying kinds of social order.

I have also argued that larger structural considerations need to be explicitly linked with microscopic analyses of negotiation processes. Negotiations always take place within social settings. The various structural conditions of the settings affect the actions of the negotiating parties, the aims they pursue through negotiation and alternative modes of action, their tactics during the negotiations, and, undoubtedly, the outcomes of the negotiations themselves—which in turn may affect not only future courses of action but also the social settings themselves.

Furthermore, if negotiations are indeed relatively universal, then our conceptualizations should deal with the whole range of the phenomenon or at least with their great variation. That implies the need for examining a variety of structural contexts and their associated courses of negotiation. It also implies that either a general theory of negotiation should be developed or that at least (as I have done) a paradigm should be offered that other researchers can qualify, amend, add to, and work over, so that eventually a theory of negotiation might get developed.

A subsidiary argument was that researchers' conceptions of social order—and their usually implicit assumptions about and theories of negotiation—generally lead them to overlook or misconstrue their data on negotiations; also, that close examination of those data would raise some sharply critical questions about both their conceptions of social order and some of their research conclusions.

In examining the research of a number of well-known social scientists (Goffman, Blau, Gouldner, Banfield, Riker, Coleman, and Morse), whose perspectives included functionalism, political pluralism, interactionism, and so on, the following questions were asked. "Can the research actually affect the general theory (or theoretical framework) if the researcher does not see negotiation in terms of theory? What happens if the researcher sees negotiation 'in the data' but does not build theoretically on those particular data? What kind of description is offered—or what kind of substantive theory? Or, blinded by theoretical preconceptions, do researchers actually overlook the negotiations that are there in the collected data? What would happen if they, or we, found negotiations in their data and took them seriously? How would that affect what was offered us by way of descriptions, substantive theories, and theoretical conceptions?"

With due respect to their other virtues, these researches generally did not score high on the special test offered by my questions. I concluded that my scrutiny had supported the following points. First, looking at the data on negotiations in a researcher's work can afford a very useful critique of the theorizing done on the basis of the research itself; negotiations are not just another interesting phenomenon or special area for research. Second, if researchers are going to analyze negotiations, then they need to do so in relation to questions of social order—and with an eye on their own implicit theories of negotiation. Third, negotiation processes are entwined with manipulative, coercive, and other processes, and they all must be studied together, although the researcher's main focus may be on one or another. I concluded, too, that each researcher had raised interesting and valid theoretical questions, but I doubted whether those could be answered without careful studies of a varied set of interlocked processes, including the negotiation processes. The larger issue implied, of course, is whether social orders can be properly analyzed without building negotiation into the analysis. Or, said another way, are there any social orders that are not also negotiated orders?

In Part Two, I addressed that issue, attempting to cast doubt on the efficacy of conceptualizing about organizations, groups, institutions, and so on, without also analyzing their implied negotiation processes. Part Two—the longest and perhaps more important section of the book—consisted essentially of analyses of negotiation cases drawn from various research publications. Eleven cases were presented, paired in six chapters, to bring out similar or contrasting features around a central issue raised by a paradigm, with an emphasis both on structural or social setting considerations and on the negotiation itself: (1) negotiating working relations in organizations, (2) legal and illegal negotiations in the political arena, (3) negotiating cooperative international structures, (4) negotiating compromises within social orders, (5) antagonistic negotiations and changing structural contexts, and (6) organizational functioning and the silent bargain.

Clearly, a considerable variety of social settings and the associated types of negotiation were examined. The organizational scale of the cases varied greatly, the negotiating parties ranging from individuals and small groups to large nations. The settings varied from face-to-face ones to those that are international, from relatively simple or routine ones to the most complex and unpredictable. Time scales also varied greatly—from immediate transactions to those occurring over long periods of time.

In analyzing those cases of negotiation and their embeddedness in social settings, a paradigm was utilized. Its key terms include *subprocesses of negotiation*, of which examples were making trade-offs, obtaining kickbacks, compromising toward the middle, paying off debts, and reaching negotiated agreements; and *structural context*, "within which" negotiations take place in the largest sense. Hence for each case of negotiation it is necessary to bring out some of the salient *structural properties* of the social setting. (One important structural property consists of respective parties' theories of negotiation, which bear on the negotiation.) The term *negotiation context* refers specifically to the structural properties entering very directly *as conditions* into the course of the negotiation itself. The many specific kinds of negotiation contexts pertaining to interaction among negotiating parties are related to permutations of the following properties of any negotiation context:

- The *number* of negotiators, their relative *experience* in negotiating, and whom they *represent*
- Whether the negotiations are *one-shot, repeated, sequential, serial, multiple,* or *linked*
- The relative *balance of power* exhibited by the respective parties *in* the negotiation itself
- The nature of their respective *stakes* in the negotiation
- The *visibility* of the transactions to others; that is, their overt or covert characters
- The *number* and *complexity* of the *issues* negotiated
- The *clarity of legitimacy* boundaries of the issues negotiated
- The *options* to avoiding or discontinuing negotiation; that is, the alternative modes of action perceived as available

I wish to emphasize that the final item, options, is of particular relevance in understanding both the decision to embark on negotiation and the course of negotiation itself. If the potential or actual parties to negotiation perceive that they can attempt persuasion, make an appeal to authority, manipulate political or social events, and so forth, then their choices of these alternative modes will either prevent them from entering negotiation, or if they choose that also, then their choices will affect what transpires during the course of the negotiation.

When introducing this paradigm, I argued that a steady focus on both structural and negotiation contexts, and on their respective properties, would increase the likelihood that the analysis of specific courses of negotiation would be carefully located in relationship to the larger social structure. (No reification was intended by the term *social structure*.) In short, social order considerations were vital to any analysis of negotiation. Also, we could see that the structural context is larger, more encompassing than negotiation context; but the lines of impact might run either way. That is, changes in the former might impact on the latter, and vice versa. Outcomes of negotiation itself could contribute to changes in negotiation contexts relevant to future negotiations; although they are less likely to affect the structural context except as repeated or combined with other negotiations and other modes of action, perhaps thereby having a cumulative impact.

I further argued, there, that some approaches to negotiation tend to concentrate closely on negotiations themselves but leave unattended or implicit the relations of negotiations to social structural considerations, and sometimes even to negotiation contextual considerations (as shown already in Part One). On the other hand, like many social science approaches that tend not to bother with microscopic analyses of interaction, some accounts of negotiation settle for essentially narrative description or an emphasis on overall bargaining relations rather than for an analysis of the bargaining itself. In both approaches, little attention frequently is paid to the developmental character of much negotiation, some of which is underlined in the case studies of Part Two. An additional richness was added to the paradigmatic analysis insofar as each case illustrates somewhat different combinations of subprocesses of negotiation that are explainable by the type of negotiation under examination.

Further Uses of the Paradigm

In this section, I wish to supplement the earlier discussion of the paradigm's use for analyzing and commenting on other people's data. Here, the first question might be "How can the paradigm be useful to researchers whose main concerns are not with negotiation in general, but either with negotiations in a given substantive area or only with that area itself?"

First, the paradigm can sensitize them to possibilities in their data that otherwise might go quite unnoticed. Thus they can become sensitized to negotiations, actors, interactions, tactics, subprocesses of negotiation, and consequences that have been overlooked or left relatively unanalyzed in the data. Second, grasp of the paradigm can force them to analyze the negotiation aspects of their data. Researchers will ask themselves if they have enough data on negotiation and along various contextual dimensions. They will be forced to compare the kinds of negotiations being witnessed or interviewed about, as well as the range of negotiations being studied, to other kinds that they know about—to the end of forcing themselves to think more intensively and systematically about the former negotiations. Systematic pursuit of negotiation data should force consideration of relationships between the negotiations under study and the major substantive matters under study. That is, analytically speaking, the researcher will have to relate the negotiation properties to other substantive properties.

A third use of the paradigm is that it can help researchers discover which contextual properties of negotiation are salient for their specific substantive materials. Once a researcher senses that certain properties are relevant, "fit" the reality of the data, then a systematic exploration of the implications of these contextual properties will check out the researcher's sense of their fitness.

A fourth use of the paradigm pertains to its possibilities as a predictive guide. What I have in mind is that, if the researchers begin to grasp the general structural properties of the substantive areas under study, they will begin to make informed guesses about the most salient contextual properties of negotiations and about the associated negotiation events; that is, they will make better predictions about negotiations and their outcomes. Conversely, there is a feedback from the negotiation materials to phenomena other than negotiation. During the course of the research, then, there is a crucially important interplay between achieving an increasingly better awareness of relevant structural conditions and getting more accurate predictions about the negotiation phenomena. Or, as reiterated throughout this book, insofar as the researcher is interested in social order, he or she must be concerned with negotiated order.

In the early stages of a study, a researcher is handicapped by how relatively little he or she knows about the structural conditions bearing on the phenomenon under study. It takes time to know them. The researcher has not been around long enough to be familiar enough with what everyday events may signify, or for important events and behaviors to have transpired, or to have hit on the most important documentary data. And the researcher certainly has not yet done sufficient data analysis to have the kind of grasp of structural conditions that will lead to relatively accurate predictions about negotiations. So the more structural conditions one can anticipate, the better the predictions about the main features of both the associated negotiations and the variations in their patterning. The kind of paradigm offered here should help researchers in their theoretical sampling (Glaser and Strauss, 1967) by forcing them to ask "What would happen if . . . under this or that condition?" Then they must look for or inquire about that "if."

One difficulty about predicting outcomes accurately is that the structural context may change, thus changing the relationships of negotiation to alternate modes of action among which actors may choose, as well as changing the elements of the negotiation context itself. That condition of long-run and often radical change does not eliminate the probability of relatively accurate predictions about negotiation outcomes; but, presumably, the more unexpected the radical change, the less accurate the prediction. (This issue will be discussed apropos of general theory in the next section.) Despite those changes, the paradigm should be of continued use. By directing attention to the relationships of current structural properties to contextual properties and by periodically requiring soundings about changes in either context, clues can then be found about new directions of change—with their consequential impact on the outcomes of negotiation and on alternative modes of action.

Another issue: "Is there a difference in procedure between the researcher who is interested primarily in substantive negotiations and the researcher who is interested primarily in a substantive phenomenon and so concerned with negotiations only as a means for better understanding it?" Their principal procedures are probably the same. The differences have to do mainly with their major focus—with implications for their respective apportionment of time and effort and for how detailed and elaborate their respective analyses of negotiation itself will be.

On this latter point, an example will perhaps be useful. In a study titled *Military Lawyers, Civilian Courts, and the Organized Bar* (1972), a legal scholar, Raymond Marks, traces what happened when the armed forces decided to attempt an experimental program for expanding the nature and scope of legal assistance to servicemen and dependents. This program raised a problem because special permission was required in the various American states for "foreign lawyers" to practice in the local courts. Marks shows that, as the result of varied kinds of negotiations, the program got implemented in a considerable variety of ways in the different states. Marks is primarily interested in the outcomes of the negotiations (that is, what finally was permitted or arranged), rather than in the negotiations themselves. Nevertheless, he offers considerable information on the negotiations. The detail and clarity of his discussion of the negotiations depends less on his interest in them than on the ease or difficulty which the armed forces encountered in making arrangements and on the amount of compromising they had to do in terms of what they had originally requested. In fact, this researcher has more data on negotiation in his files than he cared to analyze, since negotiation was distinctly secondary in focus. He obtained as much on negotiation as he did in part because it was clearly a part of the primary topic in focus. One implication of his unanalyzed negotiation data—and the data of other researchers in similar situations—is that if he cares to analyze those data he could certainly write separately about the negotiations themselves.

      Turning to a fifth potential use of the paradigm, one implicit in various cases reviewed in Part Two, the paradigm can be useful to researchers who are interested in how negotiated order is destroyed or even prevented from forming. I have in mind not the specific structural conditions that prevent successful, linked negotiations, but the strategies and tactics of parties who are not necessarily involved directly in the negotiations. An instance that springs vividly to mind is how the fragile alliance that made Allende the head of the Chilean government for a short while was undoubtedly destroyed not simply by the course of events or the falling out of the various parties to the coalition but also by an effective combination of various modes of action: use of force, threat, persuasion, manipulation of events, money, various resources, and also, undoubtedly, covert negotiations among the various parties who wished to see the Allende alliance destroyed. The ability and the desire to break up or prevent a given order is, of course, not confined to political affairs. The paradigm can remind us that we should not be in-

terested merely in successful or unsuccessful negotiations and how
those are managed but also in the wider structural and contextual
issues in any substantive area we study. Some case analyses presented earlier undoubtedly suffered because the respective researchers did not offer (they rarely do) good data on how opponents
outside the negotiation situation attempt to play those related
antagonistic games.

In rounding off the suggestions made in this section about
the further uses of the paradigm, it may be useful to emphasize
again that a vital part of the concept of structural context is that of
the negotiating parties' "theories of negotiation." Hence all of my
suggestions also direct researchers to gather data on those theories.
One of the considerable deficiencies of studies of negotiation to date
is precisely either that researchers fail to collect data about those
theories or, if they do have some data bearing on them, that they do
not analyze their significance. I urge the necessity to do just that.

Is a General Theory of Negotiation Possible?

What about the use of such a paradigm for those who are
genuinely interested in a general or "formal" theory of negotiation
per se? Before attempting to answer that question, I should state my
position on the possibility of formulating general theory, for I have,
after all, insisted we must take into account that negotiations take
place within changing structural contexts—within historically
changing social orders. The question of whether general theory is
possible has been variously answered by different scholars. Some
take extreme historical positions, denying the possibility of universal
propositions about social life. Others, such as Simmel and Weber,
whose discussions and formulations of general theory continue to
stimulate social scientists, nevertheless had a profound respect for
historical matters. However, many contemporary social scientists
apparently believe that, regardless of the particularities of historical
moment, the formulation of general theory is entirely feasible.

Concerning the possibility of negotiation theory, my own
view is related to the distinctions drawn earlier between structural
and negotiation contexts. I have argued and attempted to demonstrate that the features of a specific negotiation context cannot be

properly analyzed except in conjunction with a clear specification
of the relevant structural context. In a historical perspective, structural conditions, including actors' theories of negotiation, do
change, and therefore new types of negotiation contexts do evolve—
while old ones may disappear, should pertinent structural conditions
vanish (for example, in the Kenya case and the Li case). This
means that old contextual properties of negotiation may disappear,
while new ones emerge and while their combinations with each
other also change. The changes brought about by "the workings of
history" do not at all signify that a general theory of negotiation is
impossible. They only mean that no such theory can ever predict all
the future permutations of negotiation context. This kind of theory,
however, can predict by theoretical sampling (Glaser and Strauss,
1967) the possibility that such combinations may emerge at a
future time ("What if this property were to change to . . . ?"). It
can likewise predict backward in time, directing us to look for
times long vanished but concerning which we may have good data,
when different types of negotiation context were in operation from
those to which we are now accustomed.

I turn now to the original question: "What about the uses
of the paradigm, as developed in this book, for those who are
genuinely interested in a general theory of negotiation?" Several
answers are possible, according to the interests of different groups
of scholars. First, there are those who while doing substantive research find also they can contribute to a general theory of negotiation. They would do this in entirely conventional ways. Thus, they
might elaborate sections of the paradigm that are sparse or under-
developed—as by working through the implications of an additional
negotiation contextual property, by following out in more detail a
property already noted by me or any other theorist, by focusing
intensively on different subprocesses and types of negotiation interaction, or by treating the same ones more elaborately. Another
conventional and entirely necessary possibility is to qualify the
formulated theory, since some of its parts are inadequate or inaccurate. Those qualifications can, of course, be either minor or
very considerable.

Researchers whose chosen concerns are with the development
of substantive negotiation (whether labor bargaining, economic

transactions, diplomatic negotiation, and so on) are currently more likely to make major contributions to the development of a general theory of negotiation; but certainly any researcher into substantive phenomena might make a useful contribution, provided he or she is interested in that particular theoretical enterprise. Perhaps the latter researchers can then make very interesting contributions precisely because their data will be drawn from nontraditional areas concerning the analysis of negotiation.

Finally, another group of social scientists might be interested in general theory of negotiation for its *own* sake. I envision that their elaborations and qualifications of a negotiation theory would proceed by further theoretical sampling of data from extant negotiation literature in many different substantive areas. This secondary analysis could greatly—and probably quickly—help to further a general theory. For instance, someone might be interested in elaborating the contextual property of the negotiator as a "representative" and hence do theoretical sampling of varied data concentrating systematically on various properties of representativeness itself.

As a brief illustration of how that might work, I offer a few beginning steps for such an analysis. First, there is the question of *who* is being represented. The negotiator can represent himself, another person, a group, an organization, a faction in the organization or a majority group, a government, and so on. (Note that the government itself represents another "party"—but that is an additional complexity.) Second, in *what relationship* does the negotiator stand to the represented? Is the negotiator appointed, commanded, elected, self-selected, and so on? Third, we must ask about the *recognition* by the represented, of the representative: Do they know or understand, are they aware when they are not being represented? Fourth, if they know, do they *agree* to such representation or do they not, and to what degree? Fifth, of which or how much of the negotiator's actual negotiating interactions are the represented parties actually *aware?* How quickly do they become aware? What control do they have over his or her actions? Are all of the represented or just some of them aware? Sixth, *how many parties* are actually represented by the negotiator? If more than one, are their interests, for any given issue being negotiated, in conflict, not connected, commensurate, and so on? Does the negotiator actually know the details accurately? Do the respective parties recognize all the details? All these questions and more should immediately suggest to the theorist-researcher questions about resultant strategies, tactics and consequences. For instance, there may be a struggle among members of an organization to have certain persons represent them in negotiations, and that struggle may be different in established structures (such as labor unions) from the struggle in more emergent ones (say, in black organizations during the late 1960s); of course, these struggles will bear differently on representativeness in ensuing negotiations with outsiders.

Turning to the relationships between the negotiators themselves concerning their representativeness, one could look at the forgoing questions in reverse. Thus, what does each know about the representativeness of the other? How accurate or incorrect is their assessment of that representativeness? How accurate is the presentation of his or her own representativeness by each to the other? Are they suspicious and discounting, or do they take the other's presentation at face value? Or, more specifically, there are such questions as "How clear is it whom the other is actually representing? Does he really represent himself rather than those he is supposed to be representing? Can he be induced to represent himself rather than them? At least on this particular issue? Is he representing some faction rather than the whole organization (government, group)? Or is all that, or some of that, unclear, ambiguous, clouded?"

Those questions can lead to a fairly complex issue of analyses, when one considers that the larger analysis must also include the strategies, tactics, consequences, and so forth pertaining to those questions that the negotiators themselves are asking about each other. For instance, how do the negotiators check out whether they can induce the others to double-cross or sell out their represented parties? Whom can the negotiators choose to represent themselves in checking out both that particular possibility and the consequent negotiation about the double-cross? My suggested questions about representativeness are, of course, only initial steps in an inquiry about that important contextual property of negotiation, but I believe that thinking about negotiations along those lines—and collecting the necessary comparative data—would take us along the path toward a general theory of negotiation.

One could analyze the cases presented in Part Two systematically for "representativeness" or for any other contextual property itemized in the guiding paradigm. Then the analysis would have to be done in terms not of each case as such but in terms of their total theoretical yield. I did not choose to do that in this book. To build a general theory would take many more cases of negotiation and a determinedly comparative stance toward those data. I have wanted to put my emphases elsewhere.

Debate

The general line of argument in this book was implicit in two previous publications by my colleagues and me (Bucher and Strauss, 1961; Strauss and others, 1964) although, as noted in the introduction, it was not nearly as fully developed as here. Since then, the "negotiated order theory" (or "perspective" or "approach"), as it has come to be termed, of the study of organizations and social order has gained adherents. In consequence, certain aspects of it were further developed or explored (Bucher, 1970; Bucher and Stelling, 1969; Stelling and Bucher, 1972; Hall, 1972; Morgan, 1975; Farberman, 1975; Martin, 1976; Gerson, 1974, 1976; Maines and Denzin, in press; Denzin, in press; Busch, 1977). The approach has drawn severe criticism, although mixed with some appreciation of its virtues, by Benson and Day (1976) and Day and Day (1977; see also Roth and others, 1973). Here is a succinct summary of the critique (Benson, 1977, p. 12):

> Negotiated order theory . . . is a process-oriented perspective stressing continuous emergence of organizational arrangements out of the ongoing interactions of participants. Proponents . . . argue that organizational arrangements are continuously being negotiated through the day-to-day encounters of participants. The arrangements reached through negotiation are seldom stable. . . . While some (Hall, 1972) have recently extended the negotiated order argument to

deal with large-scale negotiations (for example, nations),
most of the work has dealt with microprocesses of interaction between participants. We do find in this perspective, however, a processual conception of organizational
life and a tendency to undermine confidence in seemingly
fixed features of the organization. . . . Day and Day
review much of the negotiated order work and develop
a critical stance toward it. They are particularly critical
of its failure to deal with historical origins and larger
institutional arrangements and of the consequent implications that everything of importance is currently negotiable. Thus, while the negotiated order analysts have
effectively challenged the static view, they have fallen
into the error of disregarding structural limits. They
have emphasized the small-scale adjustments possible
within the limits imposed by more encompassing structural arrangements and have not dealt convincingly with
the latter. The negotiated order theorists have a basic
difficulty in grappling with social structure, which in
their framework concerns the relations between distinct
contexts wherein negotiation occurs. While it may be
true, as they contend, that negotiation is present in all
social situations, the structural problem is to grasp the
relations between situations—the ways in which some
negotiations set limits upon others.

That kind of criticism reflects the efforts of social scientists
who are trying to reach some mediating position between extreme
structural determinism and a view more open to human beings'
control of their own destinies. Structural determinists would doubtless criticize a negotiated order perspective much more harshly,
regarding negotiation as a relatively minor phenomenon when
measured against more determining factors such as social class, the
material conditions of life, and so on. Or, in the words of one
Marxist who read an early version of this book, "The *important*
things are always nonnegotiable." Negotiation would be similarly
dismissed or at least downgraded by other types of determinists:
biological, psychological, cultural, and economic. If held dogmatic-
ally, those positions are impregnable, so that there can be no

genuine debate. However, the assertions of the partly appreciative critics afford an opportunity for correcting misapprehensions about my line of argument. I am not at all concerned here with correcting misreadings of the earlier publications, but only with getting on with the work of studying and building theory about negotiations, negotiated orders, and social orders (for countering arguments to Benson and Day and to Day and Day, see Maines, 1977, in press; Gerson, 1977). To that end, the following discussion is organized in terms of typical critical objections to "negotiated order" and what I believe are appropriate answers to each of them. The objections are grouped into the two following sections: first, those representing misapprehensions or misunderstandings of the position; second, those representing clear divergence with the position.

Misapprehensions. First, let us deal with the objection that negotiated order research seems to apply almost wholly to microscopic interaction rather than to macroscopic-structural problems. ("The corollary of its utility in dealing with microprocesses is its inadequacy for handling large-scale structural problems and reorganizations"—Benson and Day, 1976, p. 11 of ms.) Leaving until the following discussion how efficacious the negotiated order approach might be for handling large-scale structural issues, it is clear that the data cases reviewed in Part Two of this book have included negotiations carried on between or among units of very large organizational scale (for example, nations). The analytic paradigm had no less applicability to these negotiations than to those that would strike observers as relatively microscopic in character (for example, between the corrupt judge and his victims or the insurance agent and the claimant). If temporal scale is also a measure of large-scale structural problems and reorganizations, then the paradigm is equally applicable to those extending over months and years (for example, the case studies of Benelux and of Kenyan interracial relations).

Second, the objection that negotiation order researchers assume that social order, or organizational relationships, are everchanging, unstable. ("The arrangements reached through negotiation are seldom stable and often represent merely surface agreements which mean different things to different groups"—Benson and Day, 1976, p. 12 of ms.) In a general sense (see later discussion), I would assume that social order is ever-changing, but certainly there is no need to debate the quite differential stability and instability of specific social orders. Indeed, negotiation may contribute both toward their stability and toward minimally disruptive change (for example, in the first stage of the Kenyan case or in the Labwor bridewealth negotiations). This misapprehension may partly have come about because of the following kind of reading of the negotiated order position: "Proponents . . . argue that organizational arrangements are continuously being negotiated through the day-to-day encounters of participants" (Benson and Day, 1976, p. 12 of ms). Of course, in some types of organizations, some (not all) arrangements are under fairly daily negotiation; in other types of organizations, not at all.

Third, the criticism has been made that negotiated order theorists emphasize cooperative relations to the neglect of coercion and conflict. (The "conceptualization of negotiation and bargaining which is presented suggests a cooperative and usually smooth process involving temporary disruptions in normal routines, new tacit understandings, and so forth, with little actual domination or oppression emanating from different cases of power within and without the organization"—Day and Day, 1977, p. 131.) The negotiated order perspective certainly has not hitherto explicitly focused on coercion ("power" will be discussed later); but, of course, in this book it has been an important issue (see also Farberman, 1975). A concentration on conflict between organizations of every scale has been central to virtually all negotiated order publications. In the case studies of Part Two, conflict appears as differentially overt, antagonistic, endemic, or essential to relations between or among negotiating parties.

Fourth, it has been said that negotiated order is taken as a complete explanation of social order. ("In general terms, the theory of negotiated order violates the dialectical principle of totality. A limited slice of social reality is abstracted from its context. It is then seen by some as a general theory of social order, ignoring its partial and temporary character"—Benson and Day, 1976, p. 14 of ms.) The position taken in this book is that there is no social order without negotiated order; that is, negotiation is part and parcel of any social order. That is *not* the same as asserting a theory of negotiation could explain everything about any given social order. To assert that would be not merely presumptuous but patently foolish.

Fifth, critics charge that the negotiations perspective deals with the "subjective," naively accepting the perspective of participants under study. ("The most basic difficulty with the theory of negotiated order is that it reflects a limited, partial perspective in identification with a specific set of actors in a particular type of situation . . . analysts . . . have built a theory of order which corresponds to the constructed world of the actors"—Benson and Day, 1976, p. 10 of ms.) My answer to this objection will be partial here because it is more fully developed later; but for a beginning I shall flatly assert that nobody espousing a negotiated order perspective has ever ignored structural considerations, has ever taken over uncritically the constructed world of the actors under study. In any event, the paradigmatic analysis in the foregoing pages certainly takes both actors' viewpoints and structural considerations into account. The paradigm is meant to ensure that the researcher will do just that. Some of the confusion here seems to turn on the critics' noting that much of the negotiated order research was carried out through field observation and on a misreading of that research stance as consequently yielding "a very strong tendency for the participant observer to embrace only the participants' own interpretations of certain situations" (Day and Day, 1977, p. 134). That would in fact be very poor field research. This criticism is confounded by the observation that most research done by negotiated order researchers has involved only field work. That assertion is only partly true (Farberman, 1975; Denzin, in press), but criticism of field workers for failure to "verify interpretations by means of using additional sources of data such as records [and] documents" (Day and Day, 1977, p. 134) is quite different from criticism directed toward the adoption of participants' biases. I naturally concur that any and all sources of useful data should be tapped.

A subsidiary and related misreading is that "The adoption of the participants' view also exposes us to the risk that the negotiated order may be seen as a permanent rather than a precarious reality. Participants may take for granted the persistence of their social world even in the face of its imminent demise" (Benson and

Day, 1976, p. 13 of ms.) Of course, participants often do just that.
That negotiated order analysts may do that is most unlikely, and
the criticism runs, in fact, contrary to the second objection considered earlier.

Sixth, critics remark that not everything is negotiable, as
negotiated order analysts claim. ("The tendency is to treat all
aspects of society as negotiated and in some degree negotiable. In
this respect, it suffers from . . . a failure to deal with emergent
levels, breaks, and so on, beyond which some features become fixed,
determinant, resistant to change"—Benson and Day, 1976, p. 13
of ms.) Of course, not everything is either equally negotiable or—
at any given time or period of time—negotiable at all. One of the
researcher's main tasks, as it is that of the negotiating parties themselves, is to discover just what *is* negotiable at any given time. This
point leads into the very important topic of "limits" and their discovery, discussed hereafter.

Divergent Positions. The major objection raised against the
negotiated order perspective pertains to its presumed inability to
come to grips with matters of relevant social structure. There seem
to be several dimensions, or aspects to this criticism, which for the
sake of clarity should be separated. I shall outline each briefly and
then summarize the whole set of related issues (the quotations are
from Day and Day, 1977, p. 134).

First, there is the criticism that negotiated order research
rather ignores the social setting within which negotiations are studied.
(There is "only a rather restricted effort to show how the world
outside . . . impinges upon what goes on inside" the organization.) This objection is a severe one. It is not directed so much
against an inadequate locating of the negotiations within a social
setting as against an inability to relate the setting analytically to
consequent negotiations. Furthermore, this criticism implies that a
structural analysis that takes into account only the properties of the
organization itself, or the negotiating parties, is not sufficient.

Second, it is said that the social setting includes not merely
the immediate locale but also large-scale national impingements.
("As a direct consequence, we gain very little insight as to how the
larger structural features of American society influence and perhaps
predetermine the limits of the negotiations under investigation.")

In short, studies of negotiations must take into account very large
macroscopic influences. The search for those influences cannot stop
at the more immediate doorstep of the organization or organizations being studied.

Third, critics state that the macroinfluences include historical ones, not merely contemporary ones. ("Similarly, most of
the case studies conducted from this perspective represent limited
attempts to understand the broader historical forces at work in our
society.") Worse yet, the very emphases of negotiated order theorists on temporality and contingencies "lull the reader into believing
that" the perspective "does in fact incorporate a wide-ranging
historical analysis."

Fourth, critics claim that negotiated order advocates fail to
come to grips with the vital issue of power. (They do not "critically
examine the hard reality of power and politics and the influence
they exert upon negotiative processes . . . we are told that power
is situational and contingent in nature and, as a result, power
relationships have to be explained in light of the broad sociohis-
torical context in which they are found. This sounds fine but . . .
this particular type of analysis is never forthcoming. Instead, specific
events and interactions are explained only by nebulous references to
their origins in previous negotiations.")

And, fifth, can the negotiated order approach handle the
issue of constraints—or does it assume that humans are all too free?
Can the approach specify the limits to negotiation, or do the limits
either seem relatively unbounded or, at any rate, not specifiable?
Those questions, of course, are related to the queries about whether
negotiated order can handle structure and large-scale problems.
("The set of structural limits within which negotiations occur
always lies beyond the reach of the theory. Likewise, the process
through which those limits might be overcome remains out of
reach"—Benson and Day, 1976, p. 11 of ms.; and the previously
quoted sentence: "We gain very little insight as to how the larger
structural features of American society influence and perhaps
predetermine the limits of the negotiations under investigation.")

Researchers in the criticized tradition have clearly pointed
to the limits of particular kinds of negotiation: For instance, Freidson (1967) noted how the limits of negotiation are affected by the

type of hospital in which it occurs; Bucher and Stelling (1969) noted that negotiation tends to be overt in professional organizations but is often covert in industrial organizations because of fear of the negotiating parties that they will be discovered, and Bucher (1970) notes that in medical schools various constraining features affect the strength, direction, and character of negotiation processes. My paradigmatic analyses have underlined both the constraints (concerning types of negotiations, subprocesses, tactics, and stakes aimed at, and so on) and the structured limits to negotiation (so often utilized in conjunction with the alternative modes of action).

These issues, then, involve the following relevant impingements on negotiation: (1) the organizational setting with its intra-organizational properties, (2) the external setting "within" which the organization is located, (3) the large-scale setting (for example, national), (4) historical as well as contemporary considerations, and (5) power, dominance, and political considerations.

I do not believe it necessary to argue that the paradigmatic analyses offered in this book are safe against the criticism that they have failed to take those considerations into account. Of course, analyses of particular cases may be lacking in one regard or another, primarily due to the data made available in a given case, but in general the paradigm is designed to focus attention on precisely those issues called to attention by the critics. (They are quite correct in underscoring those analytic necessities but have not been altogether accurate in their assessing of previous negotiation order literature.) I would not claim these are the most comprehensive analyses possible, but surely they represent a good beginning effort.

The nub of the debate lies in the question of where the analyst or theorist chooses to put his or her structural emphasis. Preconceived notions of social structure or of structural relevancies may lead to criticizing others for not giving due weight to considerations of social class or stratification of technological factors, or national character, and so on. That kind of argument does not lead anywhere except to fruitless debate and acrimony. It is, of course, entirely desirable that every careful structural analysis—of negotiation or anything else—be qualified by equally careful succeeding researches. If a critic, friendly or otherwise, can show that an important structural consideration was omitted, show its rele-

vance, even to the negating of other claimed considerations, then
that criticism certainly represents progress.

The related issues of power and politics are currently very
much alive in American scholarship, as is also the perceived relevance of history for social interpretations. I would certainly agree
that anyone interested in negotiations ought to pay close attention
to what is implied in these considerations: Some of the major thrust
of my argument has been aimed at taking negotiation research in
exactly those directions.

Part of the problem in the debate over the value and meaning of negotiated order rests on different conceptions of social
structure that are held by people representing different traditions of
social science. Structure certainly means something different to
functionalists, neo-Marxists, structuralists, interactionists, and presumably sometimes even to different scholars in the same tradition.
Listen, for example, to Peter Manning criticizing, in a recent article
(1977, p. 45 and p. 57), Blau, Parsons, and other functionalists'
versions of structure, which of course emphasize the primacy of
rules, norms, goals, and the like: "The most serious omission of
organizational action studies associated with the functionalist perspective . . . is the lack of clear explication of the process by
which goals, formal procedures, or rules are translated or transformed by organizational practices. . . . The study of rules as
they are continuously negotiated in interaction is one basis for understanding organizations as acting units. . . . Rules are . . . resources to be used tactically by participants, and by so doing participants negotiate the limits upon organizationally sanctionable
rules." Or listen to Pierre Bourdieu's vigorous attack on various
forms of structuralism (1977, pp. 17 and 22):

> Talk of rules, a euphemized form of legalism, is
> never more fallacious than when applied to the most
> homogeneous societies . . . where most practices, in-
> cluding those seemingly most ritualized, can be aban-
> doned to the orchestrated improvisation of common
> dispositions: The rule is never, in this case, more than a
> second best intended to make good the occasional
> misfirings of the collective enterprise of inculcation. . . .
> The place which a notion as visibly ambiguous as that

of the *rule* occupies in anthropological or linguistic
theory cannot be fully understood unless it is seen that
this notion provides a solution to the contradiction and
difficulties to which the researcher is condemned by an
inadequate or an implicit theory of practice. Everything
takes place as if, fulfilling the role of a refuge for ignorance, this hospitable notion which can suggest at once
the law constructed by science, the transcendent social
norm and the imminent regularity of practices, enabled
its user to escape from the dilemma of mechanism or
finalism without falling into the most flagrant naiveties
of the legalism which makes obedience to the rule the
determining principle of all practices.

Structurally oriented critics of the negotiated order perspective certainly do have at least implicit commitments to what structure
"really is." Those commitments are noticeably different than those
of the people they criticize—and vice versa.

A clearly stated version of structure that I generally agree
with has been expressed by Elihu Gerson (1976, p. 276):

My approach rests on the assumption that both
social order and individuals arise in and through a
process of ongoing negotiation about who shall be whom
and what order shall pertain. These negotiations may
take place on relatively small scales or on large scales
(through the activities of many people over a large area
over a long period of time). In fact, we have a general
situation in which smaller-scale negotiations are continuously taking place in very large numbers *within* the
context of the larger-scale arrangements which are
changing more slowly and less visibly to participants.
The larger-scale arrangements appear to individuals at
particular times and places as "givens," the "system,"
the "natural order of things," even though on a larger
scale (that is, macrosociological and historical) perspective shows them as changing, often "rapidly." Occasionally, there are "revolutionary" periods in which cumulative large-scale changes become evident to individuals
over relatively brief periods of time.

Elsewhere (1977, p. 15 ms.), Gerson adds, " 'Structure,' therefore, may be conceptualized simply as larger-scale and/or longer-term process."

To that, two things should be added. First, a proviso for the practicing social researcher: Structure is not "out there"; it should not be reified. When we talk about *structure* we are, or should be, referring to the structural *conditions* that pertain to the phenomena under study. Those conditions surely do obtain but they just as surely need to be discovered and analytically linked with their consequences. Simply to assert their relevance is to mistake dogmatism for the completely different and often difficult work of demonstrating relevance. I repeat: If someone disagrees with someone else's analytic linking of structural conditions and their consequences, then the requisite task is to qualify, supplement, or negate—by work, not by assertion. (David Maines, in press, has similarly argued, when countering the Benson and Day and the Day and Day criticisms, that "the negotiated order theorists actually impose more stringent requirements on structural analysis. They insist that the analyst specify the kinds of objects and activities for which a given structure is a 'structure.' This is a much more demanding mode of analysis than that which usually passes for structuralism.")

A second and related point is one formulated previously by Barney Glaser and me (1967, pp. 239–242) and one that we have both utilized since as a guide to research and writing theory (Glaser, 1976; Fagerhaugh and Strauss, 1977); it is exemplified in this book both in specific places and by its general thrust. That formulation is termed *structural process,* in order to emphasize the following (condensed) points. One of the central issues in sociological theory is the relationship of structure to process. Ordinarily, sociological analysis does not join structure and process as tightly as in the concept of structural process. Structure, then, tends to be treated as relatively fixed—because structure is what is, certain processes can occur. Or, inversely, because the major goals involve certain processes, as in a factory, the structure is made as nearly consonant with the processes as possible. New processes are conceived of as leading to new structural arrangements; while innovations in structure similarly lead to associated processual change.

But structure and process (as well as interaction) are related more complexly than in that kind of conception.

Thus in the study of "dying in hospitals" (Glaser and Strauss, 1965), where structural process was exemplified, we remarked that during a given phase of a dying trajectory (a course of dying) a ward could be quite a different place from before. For instance, when the staff's morale ("sentimental order") has been profoundly disrupted, the structural elements that can be called on are not quite the same as before; some no longer exist and may never again exist. If afterward an equilibrium is reached, it is a moving equilibrium, with the ward calmed down but forever at least a somewhat different place. So, rather than seeing a relatively inflexible structure with a limited and determinable list of structural properties, we have to conceive of a ward, hospital, or any other institution as a structure in process. It therefore has a potential range of properties far greater than the outsider (the researcher) can possibly imagine unless watching the insiders at work. The researcher can be surprised at how the staff, family, or patients can call on diverse properties that he never dreamed existed but that became temporarily or more permanently part of the structural processes of the ward. Structural process, then, relates to the various participants' awareness of which structural properties are operating, or can be brought to operate, during various phases of the (dying) process. The relationships of these awarenesses to structural processes are neither accidental nor unpredictable, and it is up to the researcher to discover those connections. Perhaps, as we wrote in that study, the point that most requires underlining is that structural process has consequences that themselves enter into the emergence of a *new* structural process. For the researcher, this fact implies an important directive: Part of the job is to trace those consequences that significantly affect the unrolling course of events called *structural process*—not for particular cases, but for types of cases. Sociologists, for instance, are not interested in *a* dying person, but in *types* of dying persons and the patterned events relevant to their dying. When focusing on the consequences of structure and process, it is all too easy to settle for lists of consequences for, say, various personnel or for the repetitive functioning of an organization or institution. But the explicit directive given by the concept of structural process is that the researcher cannot rest until he or she has analytically related the interactional consequences to the next phases in interaction—or, in our terms, related present structural processes to later structural processes.

If we now simply insert the word *negotiation* for *dying persons,* the same points hold. Given ideal or at least excellent data, we should be interested in *discovering* relevant structural conditions and analyzing their processual and interactional *linkages.* We would especially be analyzing the emergence of a *new* structural process.

Implications

All of the preceding discussion has implications for the more general question of the limits of negotiation, a question touched on earlier but requiring a more complicated answer than previously given. Structural process considerations suggest quite clearly that what someone takes as limits to negotiation—in any given situation —may not really constitute limits. Given more resources of any kind (Gerson, 1976)—time, money, skill, information, "awareness," boldness, or perhaps desperation—given that, what were previously taken as probably nonnegotiable may in fact be negotiable in some sense, some way, some degree. Whether or not that is so has to be discovered, not merely assumed. I am not claiming, however, that certain things are always negotiable, that the sky is the limit, for at given times and places they may not be. I only say that the limits require exploration. (The researcher's job is to specify exactly the conditions under which people do or do not explore those limits, how, and with what results. If he or she is formulating theory, then an explicit or implicit theory of negotiation will specify those limits; insofar as the theory is incorrect or inaccurate, the predicted limits will be incorrect or inaccurate.)

The most general statement of the argument being presented here, I suppose, is that both the agreements made between respective parties and the situations involving seemingly absolute limits are open to being changed under certain kinds of conditions. The change can be the product of mutual agreement *if* it is not coerced,

manipulated, and so forth but requires working through via negotiation. Both the limits and the agreements are potentially contingent.
In the most general sense, there are no final agreements and no
ultimate limits.

Now this statement represents a general "theory" or theoretical framework about the nature of social reality and also represents, not incidentally, a position on the classic freedom-constraint
issue. Paradoxically, the appreciation of certain aspects of the negotiated order perspective by Robert Day and JoAnne Day allowed
them to summarize quite accurately some of its "broader philo-
sophical assumptions regarding the nature of man and the nature
of social reality" (1977, p. 132). With mutual appreciation and
because of the convenience afforded, I shall quote some of their
summary (p. 132):

> In the case of negotiated order theory, the indi-
> viduals in organizations play an active, self-conscious
> role in the shaping of the social order. Their day-to-day
> interactions, agreements, temporary refusals, and chang-
> ing definitions of the situations at hand are of paramount
> importance. Closely correlated is the perspective's view
> of social reality . . . the negotiated order theory down-
> plays the notions of organizations as fixed, rather rigid
> systems which are highly constrained by strict rules,
> regulations, goals, and hierarchical chains of command.
> Instead, it emphasizes the fluid, continuously emerging
> qualities of the organization, the changing web of inter-
> actions woven among its members, and it suggests that
> order is something at which the members of the orga-
> nization must constantly work. Consequently, conflict
> and change are just as much a part of organizational life
> as consensus and stability. Organizations are thus viewed
> as complex and highly fragile social constructions of
> reality which are subject to the numerous temporal,
> spatial, and situational events occurring both internally
> and externally. The portrayal of the division of labor
> involves the historical development of the organization
> and its occupational and professional groups, as well as
> those relevant changes taking place within the broader
> social, political, and economic spectrum of the organiza-

> tion. Similarly, power is not viewed in an absolute sense
> but rather in its relationship to other factors which
> create coalitions and partnerships varying with time and
> circumstances. . . . Concomitantly, events which take
> place outside the organization may also have a profound
> impact on both . . . informal and formal structures.

The two chief provisos to that summary, since it was drawn from a discussion of social order in mental hospitals, are that "organization" is a unit of any potential scale (including nations) and that, although organizations do vary tremendously in stability and fragility, in a general sense continual social change is assumed in this view of social reality.

Of course, this is only a general "theory," and so no more demonstrably true than anyone else's. The germane question is "What can it do for social research and operational theory?" And, if truth be told, for moral action too, its moral aspect being, as one friendly critic, Berenice Fisher, has remarked, that "if one acts as if the world were that way, then one is more likely to make it that way—you assume."

Finally, some warnings about this approach, which are not unconnected with some of the criticisms directed against it but which are not irrevocably connected with it. Adherents may tend to emphasize the cooperative rather than the coercive side of human activity. They may focus their attention on finding the movable limits while ignoring some of the nastier, even terrifying constraints operating in specific situations, such as an armed robber "negotiating" with a victim. They may cash in on a propensity to show where negotiation is possible when it seemed impossible, but there is danger of their neglecting particular limits and so pragmatically confronting either those realities or probabilities. They may overemphasize the freedom of certain persons or groups to negotiate, while overlooking the fact that others operate under probable constraints and in fact may lose precisely because the former may gain something through the negotiations. There are also consequences, sometimes very harmful, which may be overlooked, for those not included in the negotiations—who may even be quite unaware of those negotiations or who cannot break into the circle of those who are gaining from the negotiation. That list of warnings could be easily extended. My claim, however, is that those are only potential, theoretical, and practical dangers—alas, not only potential, since some work has embodied them—but they are not generic to this approach, which emphasizes negotiation and negotiated order.

Rather than close this book on a negative note, I return now to two of its major themes. First, as a phenomenon negotiation is far too important to be left solely to people who are interested in negotiation: We need to be interested in negotiated orders—varieties of them. Second, quite as important as the study of such orders, if we are to understand the larger issue of social orders, is the correlated study of modes of action that are the alternatives to negotiation. So (perhaps bending the term *social order* a bit uncomfortably), wherever there are social orders there are not only negotiated orders but also coerced orders, manipulated orders, and the like. It is trite to say they are all part of human life; the challenge is to show the connections between them.

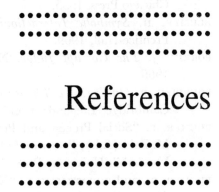

References

ABRAHAMS, R. "Reaching an Agreement over Bridewealth in Labwor, Northern Uganda: A Case Study." In A. Richards and A. Kupe (Eds.), *Councils in Action.* Cambridge, England: Cambridge University Press, 1968.

ALTERMAN, S. "Negotiating the Nuremberg Trial Agreements, 1945." In R. Dennett and J. Johnson (Eds.), *Negotiating with the Russians.* New York: World Peace Foundation, 1951.

BALDWIN, D. "Bargaining with Airline Hijackers." In I. W. Zartman (Ed.), *The Fifty Percent Solution.* Garden City, N.Y.: Doubleday, 1976.

BANFIELD, E. *Political Influence.* New York: Free Press, 1962.

BENSON, J. "Innovation and Crisis in Organizational Analysis." *Sociological Quarterly,* 1977, *18,* 3–16.

BENSON, J., and DAY, R. "On the Limits of Negotiation: A Critique of the Theory of Negotiated Order." Paper presented at the annual meeting of the American Sociological Association, New York, 1976.

BERLE, A., and MEANS, G. *The Modern Corporation and Private Property.* New York: Macmillan, 1940.

263

BLAU, P. *The Dynamics of Bureaucracy.* Chicago: University of Chicago Press, 1955.

BLUMER, H. *Symbolic Interactionism.* Englewood Cliffs, N.J.: Prentice-Hall, 1969.

BORKIN, J. *The Corrupt Judge.* New York: World Publishing, 1966.

BOURDIEU, P. *Outline of a Theory of Practice.* (R. Nice, Trans.) Cambridge, England: Cambridge University Press, 1977.

BUCHER, R. "Social Process and Power in a Medical School." In M. Zald (Ed.), *Power and Organizations.* Nashville, Tenn.: Vanderbilt University Press, 1970.

BUCHER, R., and SCHATZMAN, L. "Negotiating a Division of Labor Among Professionals in the State Mental Hospital." *Psychiatry,* 1964, *27,* 266–277.

BUCHER, R., and STELLING, J. "Characteristics of Professional Organizations." *Journal of Health and Social Behavior,* 1969, *10,* 3–15.

BUCHER, R., and STRAUSS, A. "Professions in Process." *American Journal of Sociology,* 1961, *66,* 325–334.

BUSCH, L. "Structure and Negotiation in the Agricultural Sciences." Unpublished manuscript, Department of Sociology, University of Kentucky, 1977.

CALLOW, A. *The Tweed Ring.* New York: Oxford Press, 1970.

CHAMBERLAIN, N. *Collective Bargaining.* New York: McGraw-Hill, 1951.

CODDINGTON, A. *Theories of the Bargaining Process.* Chicago: Aldine, 1968.

CODDINGTON, A. "On the Theory of Bargaining." In D. Carter and J. Ford (Eds.), *Expectations and Uncertainty in Economics.* Oxford, England: Blackwell, 1972.

COLEMAN, J. "Loss of Power." *American Sociological Review,* 1973, *38,* 1–17.

COLEMAN, J. *Power and the Structure of Society.* New York: Norton, 1974.

CROSS, J. *The Economics of Bargaining.* New York: Basic Books, 1969.

CUMMINGS, L. "The Emergence of the Instrumental Organization." In P. S. Goodman, J. M. Pennings, and Associates, *New Per-*

spectives On Organizational Effectiveness. San Francisco: Jossey-Bass, 1977.

DALTON, M. *Men Who Manage.* New York: Wiley, 1959.

DAY, R., and DAY, J. "A Review of the Current State of Negotiated Order Theory." *Sociological Quarterly,* 1977, *18,* 126–142.

DENZIN, N. "Interaction, Social Orders and Problematics in the American Liquor Industry." In N. Denzin (Ed.), *Studies in Symbolic Interaction,* in press.

ETHRIDGE, M., and BLACK, C. "Negotiating on the Balkans, 1945–1947." In R. Dennett and J. Johnson (Eds.), *Negotiating with the Russians.* New York: World Press Foundation, 1951.

FAGERHAUGH, S., and STRAUSS, A. *The Politics of Pain Management.* Reading, Mass.: Addison-Wesley, 1977.

FARBERMAN, H. "A Criminogenic Market Structure: The Automobile Industry." *Sociological Quarterly,* 1975, *16,* 438–457.

FISHER, B., and STRAUSS, A. "The Chicago Tradition: Thomas, Park and Their Successors." *Symbolic Interaction,* in press.

FISHER, B., and STRAUSS, A. "George Herbert Mead and the Chicago Tradition of Sociology." Unpublished manuscript, A. Strauss, 1373 3rd Avenue, San Francisco, Calif. 94143, 1977.

FREIDSON, E. "Review Essay: Health Factories, the New Industrial Sociology." *Social Problems,* 1967, *14,* 493–500.

GERSON, E. "Commitment Management and Urban Morphology." Paper presented at the annual meeting of the American Sociological Association, Montreal, Canada, 1974.

GERSON, E. "On the Quality of Life." *American Sociological Review,* 1976, *4,* 266–279.

GERSON, E. "Negotiations and Structure: A Comment on Benson and Day." Unpublished manuscript, Pragmatica Systems, Inc., 458–29th Street, San Francisco, Calif. 94131, 1977.

GLASER, B. *The Patsy and the Subcontractor.* New Brunswick, N.J.: Transaction Books, 1976.

GLASER, B., and STRAUSS, A. "Awareness Contexts and Social Interaction." *American Sociological Review,* 1964, *29,* 669–679.

GLASER, B., and STRAUSS, A. *Awareness of Dying.* Chicago: Aldine, 1965.

GLASER, B., and STRAUSS, A. *The Discovery of Grounded Theory.* Chicago: Aldine, 1967.

GOFFMAN, E. "On the Characteristics of Total Institutions." In E. Goffman, *Asylums.* Garden City, N.Y.: Doubleday, 1961a.

GOFFMAN, E. "The Underlife of a Public Institution: A Study of Ways and of Making Out in a Mental Hospital." In E. Goffman, *Asylums.* Garden City, N.Y.: Doubleday, 1961b.

GOFFMAN, E. *Frame Analysis.* New York: Harper & Row, 1974.

GOODMAN, P. S., PENNINGS, J. M., and ASSOCIATES. *New Perspectives on Organizational Effectiveness.* San Francisco: Jossey-Bass, 1977.

GOULDNER, A. *Industrial Bureaucracy.* New York: Free Press, 1954a.

GOULDNER, A. *The Wildcat Strike.* Yellow Springs, Ohio: Antioch Press, 1954b.

HALL, P. "A Symbolic Interactionist Analysis of Politics." *Sociological Inquiry,* 1972, *42,* 35–75.

HARSANYI, J. "Bargaining in Ignorance of the Opponent's Utility Function." *Journal of Conflict Resolution,* 1962, *6,* 29–38.

IKLE, F. *How Nations Negotiate.* New York: Harper & Row, 1964.

KOGAN, E. *The Theory and Practice of Hell.* New York: Berkley, 1975.

MAINES, D. "Social Organization and Social Structure in Symbolic Interactionist Thought." *Annual Review of Sociology,* 1977, *3,* 235–259.

MAINES, D. "Structural Parameters and Negotiated Orders: A Theoretical Clarification." *Sociological Quarterly,* in press.

MAINES, D., and DENZIN, N. *Work and Problematic Situations.* New York: Crowell, in press.

MANNING, P. "Rules in Organizational Context." *Sociological Quarterly,* 1977, *18,* 44–61.

MARKS, R. *Military Lawyers, Civilian Courts and the Organized Bar.* Chicago: American Bar Foundation, 1972.

MARTIN, W. *The Negotiated Order of the School.* Canada: Macmillan of Canada, MacLean-Hunter Press, 1976.

MEAD, G. *Mind, Self and Society.* Chicago: University of Chicago Press, 1934.

MEADE, J. *Negotiations for Benelux.* Princeton Studies in International Finance, No. 6. Princeton, N.J.: Department of Economics and Sociology, Princeton University, 1957.

MEISNER, M. *Li Ta-Chao and the Origins of Chinese Marxism.* Cambridge, Mass.: Harvard University Press, 1967.

MENNEL, S. *Sociological Theory.* New York: Praeger, 1974.

MORGAN, D. "Autonomy and Negotiation in an Industrial Setting." *Sociology of Work and Occupations,* 1975, *2,* 203–226.

MORSE, E. "The Bargaining Structure of NATO: Multi-Issue Negotiations in an Interdependent World." In I. W. Zartman (Ed.), *The Fifty Percent Solution.* Garden City, N.Y.: Doubleday, 1976.

PARK, R. *On Social Control and Collective Behavior.* (R. Turner, Ed.) Chicago: University of Chicago Press, 1967.

RIKER, W. *The Theory of Political Coalitions.* New Haven, Conn.: Yale University Press, 1962.

RIORDAN, W. *Plunkett of Tammany Hall.* New York: Dutton, 1963.

ROSS, H. L. *Settled out of Court.* Chicago: Aldine, 1970.

ROTH, J. *Timetables.* Indianapolis: Bobbs-Merrill, 1963.

ROTH, J., and OTHERS. "Current State of the Sociology of Occupations." *Sociological Quarterly,* 1973, *14,* 309–333.

ROTHSCHILD, D. "Racial Stratification and Bargaining: The Kenya Experience." In I. W. Zartman (Ed.), *The Fifty Percent Solution.* Garden City, N.Y.: Doubleday, 1976.

SCHEFF, T. "Negotiating Reality: Notes on Power in the Assessment of Responsibility." *Social Problems,* 1968, *16,* 3–17.

SCHELLING, T. *The Strategy of Conflict.* Cambridge, Mass.: Harvard University Press, 1960.

SHIBUTANI, T. *Improvised News.* Indianapolis: Bobbs-Merrill, 1966.

STELLING, J., and BUCHER, R. "Autonomy and Monitoring on Hospital Wards." *Sociological Quarterly,* 1972, *13,* 431–446.

STRAUSS, A. "Discovering New Theory from Previous Theory." In T. Shibutani (Ed.), *Human Nature and Collective Behavior.* Englewood Cliffs, N.J.: Prentice-Hall, 1970.

STRAUSS, A., and OTHERS. "The Hospital and Its Negotiated Order." In E. Freidson (Ed.), *The Hospital in Modern Society.* New York: Free Press, 1963.

STRAUSS, A., and OTHERS. *Psychiatric Ideologies and Institutions.* New York: Free Press, 1964.

THOMAS, W. *On Social Organization and Social Personality.* (M. Janowitz, Ed.) Chicago: University of Chicago Press, 1966.

WARREN, R., ROSE, S., and BERGUNDER, A. *The Structure of Urban Reform.* Lexington, Mass.: Heath, 1974.

YOUNG, O. (Ed.). *Bargaining.* Urbana: University of Illinois Press, 1976.

ZARTMAN, I. W. (Ed.). *The Fifty Percent Solution.* Garden City, N.Y.: Doubleday, 1976.

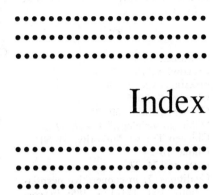

Index

269